This book is about one of the most baffling of all paradoxes – the famous Liar paradox. This paradox is more than an intriguing puzzle, since it turns on our fundamental concepts of truth and falsity. By investigating the Liar, we can hope to deepen our understanding of our basic semantic concepts.

Keith Simmons develops a new account of truth, and a novel 'singularity' solution to the Liar. Most contemporary approaches to the Liar either reject classical semantics or adopt a hierarchical view of truth. In contrast, Simmons's approach is antihierarchical and does not abandon classical semantics. The singularity approach yields a positive resolution of the seemingly intractable problem of semantic universality: Simmons concludes that no semantic concept is beyond the reach of our language.

The book also provides a formal analysis of the method of diagonalization, which lies at the heart of the Liar and the problem of universality. This analysis is utilized in a critical discussion of a wide variety of recent attempts to solve the Liar. Medieval resolutions are also discussed – and one is found to contain the seeds of the singularity proposal.

The book will appeal to logicians and philosophers, as well as linguists and historians of medieval philosophy.

Universality and the Liar

Universality and the Liar

An essay on truth and the diagonal argument

KEITH SIMMONS

UNIVERSITY OF NORTH CAROLINA, CHAPEL HILL

CAMBRIDGE
UNIVERSITY PRESS

Published by the Press Syndicate of the University of Cambridge
The Pitt Building, Trumpington Street, Cambridge CB2 1RP
40 West 20th Street, New York, NY 10011-4211, USA
10 Stamford Road, Oakleigh, Melbourne 3166, Australia

First published 1993

Printed in the United States of America

Library of Congress Cataloging-in-Publication Data
Simmons, Keith.
Universality and the Liar : an essay on truth and the diagonal
argument / Keith Simmons.
p.   cm.
Includes bibliographical references.
ISBN 0-521-43069-0 (hc)
1. Liar paradox.   2. Universals (Philosophy)   I. Title.
BC199.2.S56   1993
165–dc20   92–28986
                                     CIP

A catalog record for this book is available from the British Library.

ISBN 0-521-43069-0 hardback

*To my parents
Amy Simmons and Stanley Simmons
with love and gratitude*

Contents

Preface   *page* ix

Chapter 1   The Liar paradox   1
  1.1   Some versions of the Liar   2
  1.2   Proposals   7
  1.3   Universality and semantic universality   13
  1.4   Diagonalization   16

Chapter 2   The diagonal argument   20
  2.1   Cantor's use of the diagonal argument   20
  2.2   General analysis of the diagonal argument   22
  2.3   Good and bad diagonal arguments   27
  Appendix   Extensions of the diagonal theorem   37

Chapter 3   The diagonal argument and the Liar, I   45
  3.1   A problem for truth gap theories   46
  3.2   Kripke's theory of truth   47
  3.3   Fuzzy logic   55
  3.4   A thesis of expressive incompleteness   58

Chapter 4   The diagonal argument and the Liar, II   62
  4.1   Herzberger and Gupta and stable truth   62
  4.2   Feferman: A type-free theory of partial predicates   70
  4.3   McGee and definite truth   72
  4.4   Inconsistency views   78

Chapter 5   A medieval solution to the Liar   83
  5.1   An outline of the Ockham–Burley–Pseudo-Sherwood
      solution   84
  5.2   An interpretation of the Ockham–Burley–
      Pseudo-Sherwood solution   86

Contents

5.3   Comparisons and contrasts with some modern
approaches   94

Chapter 6   A singularity solution to the Liar   99
   6.1   An informal presentation of the singularity solution   100
   6.2   A glimpse of the formal account   112
   6.3   A suggestion of Gödel's   116

Chapter 7   A formal account of singularities   118
   7.1   Pragmatic and semantic aspects   118
   7.2   The reflective hierarchy and singularities   121
   7.3   English and the reflective hierarchy   139

Chapter 8   Applications and further singularities   142
   8.1   Applications of the formal account   142
   8.2   Further singularities   153

Chapter 9   Semantic universality   159
   9.1   Groundedness (and "singularity" in one sense)   159
   9.2   Truth in a context (and "singularity" in a second sense)   163
   9.3   The object language and the language of the theory   174
   9.4   Universality   181

Notes   183
Bibliography   217
Index   225

Preface

Many ways out of the Liar have been proposed over the past twenty-four centuries. But the Liar is more than a fascinating puzzle of long standing. The paradox turns on our most fundamental semantic concepts, most notably that of truth. By investigating the Liar, we can hope to deepen our understanding of the concept of truth and related semantic notions.

This book is about the Liar. It is also about the problem of universality. The problem is this: is a natural language like English universal in the sense that it can say everything there is to say? Or are there concepts beyond the reach of English, rendering it expressively incomplete? In particular, we can ask whether English is *semantically* universal; whether, that is, it can express every semantic concept. Ever since Tarski, the Liar and the problem of semantic universality have been linked. In my view, they are at root the same.

There is another closely related theme that runs through the book: the method of diagonalization. The diagonal argument is a method of argument that establishes some fundamental theorems of mathematical logic. Yet the diagonal argument also generates certain paradoxes. For example, in 1936 Tarski used the method of diagonalization to prove that classical formal languages are *not* semantically universal: no such language can express its own concept of truth. And yet it is also a diagonal argument that generates versions of the Liar paradox. Diagonalization is at the heart of the Liar and the problem of universality.

In this book, I provide a systematic treatment of the Liar, the problem of universality, and the diagonal argument. In Chapter 1, I present a taxonomy of versions of the Liar and a survey of proposed solutions, drawing on ancient, medieval, and contemporary sources. I go on to introduce the notions of universality and semantic universality, and the method of diagonalization.

In Chapter 2, I present an original analysis of the diagonal argument. Diagonal arguments are found in various areas of mathematical logic and are also associated with semantic and set-theoretic paradoxes. My general analysis makes it clear what these arguments have in common. It also answers a question raised by Russell, among others: why do some diagonal arguments establish theorems, while others generate paradoxes? My answer provides a characterization of *good* diagonal arguments (those leading to theorems, like Tarski's theorem and Gödel's first incompleteness theorem) and *bad* diagonal arguments (those leading to paradoxes, like the heterological paradox and Russell's paradox).

In Chapters 3 and 4, my analysis of the diagonal argument is then brought to bear on a number of leading contemporary solutions to the Liar. I argue that good diagonal arguments demonstrate, in a systematic way, the inadequacy of the disparate approaches taken by Kripke (and truth gap theorists in general), Herzberger, Gupta, Feferman, McGee, and Rescher and Brandom. The good diagonal arguments that tell against these theories yield results of expressive incompleteness. This may suggest that natural languages are *not* universal, that expressive incompleteness is just the lesson that the Liar teaches. I argue that this line, advanced by Herzberger, turns on a bad diagonal argument. One of my major aims in these critical investigations is to uncover criteria of adequacy for any solution to the Liar.

In Chapters 5 through 9, I develop a new proposal, a *singularity* solution to the Liar. One leading idea of the proposal is that 'true' is a context-sensitive expression, shifting its extension according to context. This feature of my approach places it in the category of *contextual* solutions to the Liar, along with the recent influential proposals of Parsons, Burge, Gaifman, and Barwise and Etchemendy. There is, however, a fundamental difference. These other contextual approaches all appeal to a hierarchy, analogous to Tarski's hierarchy of formal languages. I argue (in Chapters 6 and 9) that this kind of Tarskian approach is inappropriate where natural language is concerned. In contrast, the singularity proposal makes no appeal to a hierarchy: there is no splitting of 'true' into a series of increasingly comprehensive predicates, no splitting of English into a hierarchy of languages. According to the singularity proposal, there is in English a single, context-sensitive truth predicate. And a given use of 'true' applies to all the truths, except for certain *singularities* – sentences to which the given use does not apply truly or falsely.

In Chapter 5, I discuss in detail a medieval resolution to the Liar found in the writings of Ockham, Burley, and Pseudo-Sherwood. On my interpretation, this resolution contains a number of suggestive, if undeveloped, ideas. In Chapter 6, I present and defend the main ideas of the singularity proposal. In Chapter 7, I provide a formal account of truth. In Chapter 8, I apply the formal account to a wide variety of Liar-like examples drawn from Chapter 1. I also investigate further the singularities of a given use of 'true'.

Finally, in Chapter 9, I return to the problem of universality. I argue that the singularity proposal satisfies the criteria of adequacy developed earlier. In particular, I argue that my proposal does justice to Tarski's intuition that natural languages are semantically universal, in a way that is not undermined by diagonal arguments. I show that the singularity theory can accommodate not only our ordinary uses of 'true', but also the very semantic notions in which the theory is couched: the notions of *groundedness, truth in a context,* and *singularity.* Moreover, on the singularity account, the language of the theory does not stand to the object language as Tarskian metalanguage to object language. Indeed, an ordinary use of 'true' in the object language includes in its extension the sentences of the theory, since these theoretical sentences are not identified as singularities. I conclude that the singularity theory respects the intuition that a natural language like English is semantically universal.

I have been helped by many people in the course of writing this book, and it's a pleasure to acknowledge them here. My earliest debt is to W. D. Hart, who was my M. Phil. adviser at University College, London. He was an inspiring teacher – and continues to be a valuable critic. I also would like to thank my dissertation advisers at UCLA, especially D. A. Martin, Tyler Burge, Marilyn Adams, and David Kaplan. They were very generous with their help, and I learned a great deal from all of them. I was fortunate to be a graduate student at UCLA.

Versions of nearly every part of the book have been given at various colloquiums and conferences. An early version of Chapter 5 was given at the 1985 International Conference on the Philosophy of William of Ockham, St. Bonaventure University. A condensed version of Chapters 2, 3, 4, and 6 was presented at the Central American Philosophical Association, at the Logic Colloquium, SUNY Buffalo, and at a number of philosophy department colloquiums, including Carnegie Mellon and the University of North Carolina, Chapel Hill. A shortened version of Chapters 6, 7, and 9 was presented at the Pacific American Philosophical Association, at the *Logica 91* International Conference on Logic in Czechoslovakia, and at the University of Rochester. I've benefited from all these occasions – and I've tried to acknowledge individual debts in the text. But Calvin Normore deserves a special mention here.

Thanks also to my colleagues at Chapel Hill. Mike Resnik has read different drafts of various chapters, and his comments have led to significant improvements. And I've had a number of useful exchanges with Bill Lycan. The members of my graduate seminar on the paradoxes suggested

Preface

various improvements to the final draft. And thanks to David Bain for his editorial assistance. I have greatly valued the collegial and supportive atmosphere here at Chapel Hill.

My greatest debt, though, is to Dorit Bar-On, for more than ten years of intellectual and moral support.

I am grateful to Kluwer Academic Publishers and to Taylor and Francis for their permission to use copyrighted material.

Chapel Hill, North Carolina
Fall 1992

Chapter 1

The Liar paradox

Suppose I say,

I am lying now.

Am I telling the truth, or am I lying? Suppose I'm telling the truth. Then what I say is the case – and so I'm lying. On the other hand, suppose I'm lying. But that's what I say. So I'm telling the truth. Either way, we are landed in contradiction: We are caught in the paradox of the Liar.

We get into the same kind of trouble if I say,

This sentence is false.

If what I say is true, then it's false; and if what I say is false, then it's true. We are confronted with the Liar again, under a slightly different guise.

Here is another version of the Liar, sometimes called the *heterological paradox*. Some words are true of themselves: For example, the word 'polysyllabic', itself a polysyllabic word, is true of itself; and so are the words 'significant', 'common', and 'prosaic'. Other words are false of themselves – the word 'new', for example, is not itself a new word, and so is false of itself; and so are the words 'useless', 'ambiguous', and 'long'. Let's call these words that are false of themselves *heterological*. But now take the word 'heterological' and ask whether *it* is true of itself or false of itself. If it is true of itself, then it is heterological, and so not true of itself; and if it is false of itself, then it is heterological, and therefore true of itself. And so we have a paradox.

Now these paradoxes arise out of quite ordinary concepts – in particular, the concepts of truth and falsity. The first two paradoxes arise directly from these concepts; in the case of the heterological paradox, we construct from our ordinary notion of falsity what seems to be a perfectly clear-cut semantic concept. There is nothing technical or recherché about the Liar paradox – it is quickly appreciated by ordinary speakers of English. This points to the significance of the Liar: It suggests that we do

1

not have a proper understanding of our ordinary notions of truth and falsity. An investigation of the Liar promises to correct and deepen our understanding of our basic semantic concepts. Then, and only then, will we be able to develop an adequate theory of truth and a satisfactory account of the relation between language and the world.

1.1. SOME VERSIONS OF THE LIAR

The Liar comes in many forms. The rich variety of Liar paradoxes is of intrinsic interest. But it has a further significance: the different versions of the Liar generate a constraint on any purported solution to the Liar. An adequate solution should deal with the Liar in *all* its manifestations, not just some. In my view, the Liar is as yet unsolved: no proposal has provided a satisfactory treatment of all the versions of the Liar we are about to see. Like any paradox, we should think of the Liar as a kind of argument, leading from apparently unexceptionable premises to an apparent contradiction, by apparently valid reasoning. Associated with distinct versions of the paradox are distinct Liar sentences. It is often convenient to identify a version of the paradox via its associated Liar sentence (or sentences).

Perhaps the simplest kind of Liar sentence involves just falsity and self-reference:

(1) This sentence is false.

Another simple Liar sentence involves truth, negation, and self-reference:

(2) This sentence is not true.

And, given the term 'heterological', we can construct this paradoxical sentence:

(3) 'Heterological' is heterological.

There are Liar sentences that display truth-functional complexity. Consider

(4) $2+2=4$ and this conjunct is not true.

If we suppose that (4) is true, then both conjuncts are true; but if the second conjunct is true, it follows that it is not true. And if the second conjunct is not true, then (4) is not true. On the other hand, if (4) is not true, then the second conjunct is true; and then, since the first conjunct is also true, (4) is true. We obtain a contradiction either way. Contrast (4) with

(5) $2+2 \neq 4$ and this conjunct is not true.

2

Sentence (5) raises a new question: Should we evaluate (5) as false in virtue of its first conjunct, or should we evaluate (5) as paradoxical in virtue of its paradoxical second conjunct?

We may construct "Truth Tellers" as well as Liars. Consider

(6) (6) is true.

Unlike the Liar, we can assume that the Truth Teller is true, or false, without contradiction. (6) is not strictly paradoxical: no contradiction is generated from it. But the assignment of either truth value to the Truth Teller is entirely arbitrary. Even if not paradoxical, (6) is still semantically pathological. If we add a little truth-functional complexity to the Truth Teller, we find ourselves apparently able to prove any claim we like – we are landed in Curry's paradox.[1] Consider the following proof of the existence of God. We start with a version of the Truth Teller:

(7) If (7) is true then God exists.

We argue as follows: Assume

(a) (7) is true.

From (a) and the substitutivity of identicals, we obtain

(b) 'If (7) is true then God exists' is true.

Now truth is disquotational: To say a sentence is true is equivalent to asserting the sentence itself. So, in particular, we have the following biconditional:

(c) 'If (7) is true then God exists' is true iff if (7) is true then God exists.

From (b) and (c), it follows that

(d) If (7) is true then God exists.

From (a) and (d), we infer

(e) God exists.

Thus far, we have inferred (e) on the basis of (a) alone. So we may assert

(f) If (7) is true then God exists.

From (c) and (f), it follows that

(g) 'If (7) is true then God exists' is true.

From (g) and the substitutivity of identicals, we infer

(h) (7) is true.

And now, finally, from (d) and (h), we obtain our desired conclusion:

(i) God exists.

Thus far, we have considered only single sentences that generate semantic pathology. But Liar paradoxes may involve networks of sentences where the semantic status of one sentence depends on that of others. John Buridan's tenth sophism is:

> 10.0 *There are the same number of true and false propositions.*
> Let us posit that there are only four propositions: (1) 'God exists', (2) 'A man is an animal', (3) 'A horse is a goat', and (4) the above sophism. Given that situation, the question is whether the sophism is true or false.[2]

Given the truth of the first two propositions[3] and the falsity of the third, we arrive at a contradiction whether we assume the fourth is true or false.

Looped sentences provide another kind of paradoxical network. Consider this simple loop:

(8) (9) is true.
(9) (8) is false.

It's easily checked that we cannot consistently evaluate either sentence as true or as false. Here is a Truth Teller loop:

(10) (11) is true.
(11) (10) is true.

We can consistently evaluate both sentences as true, or both as false; but as with the Truth Teller, these evaluations are quite arbitrary. Loops can be of arbitrarily finite length:

(ρ_1) ρ_2 is true.
(ρ_2) ρ_3 is true.
$\vdots$
(ρ_k) ρ_{k+1} is true.
(ρ_{k+1}) ρ_1 is not true.

There is no consistent assignment of truth values to the members of this loop. The upper limit on the length of a loop will be a delicate matter, turning on the cardinality of the language in which the sentences of the loop are expressed.

Besides loops, there are chains: infinite sequences of sentences without repetitions, where each sentence refers to the next. For example:

(σ_1) σ_2 is false.

4

(σ_2) σ_3 is true.
$\vdots$

(σ_{2k-1}) σ_{2k} is false.
(σ_{2k}) σ_{2k+1} is true.
$\vdots$

With this chain, there are consistent ways of assigning truth values.[4] Suppose, for example, we assign to σ_1 the value true; then we may assign the next pair of sentences σ_2 and σ_3 the value false, the pair σ_4 and σ_5 the value true, the pair σ_6 and σ_7 the value false, and continue to alternate in this way. Alternatively, we may assign to σ_1 the value false, to σ_2 and σ_3 the value true, to σ_4 and σ_5 the value false, and so on. Any such consistent assignment of truth values to the members of a chain is arbitrary.

Loops and chains may be intertwined. Consider this truth-functionally complex system of sentences:

(τ_1) τ_2 is false.
(τ_2) τ_1 is true and τ_3 is true.
(τ_3) τ_4 is false.
(τ_4) τ_3 is true and τ_5 is true.
$\vdots$

(τ_{2k-1}) τ_{2k} is false.
(τ_{2k}) τ_{2k-1} is true and τ_{2k+1} is true.
$\vdots$

There is no consistent way of assigning truth values to the sentences of this system.

Each version of the Liar we have seen so far has its "empirical" counterparts. For example, suppose you pass by my classroom and see that I've written something false on the board. Intending to expose your fraudulent colleague, you write

(12) The sentence written on the board in room 101 is false.

But you are yourself in room 101, and so the sentence you have written is a Liar sentence, an empirical counterpart of (1). Both (1) and (12) are Liar sentences; but (12) is a Liar sentence because the empirical circumstances so conspire. If the empirical circumstances had been different, if indeed I was in room 101, then your sentence would be straightforwardly true. Your sentence is not semantically ill-formed; it is not intrinsically pathological. Pathologicality here depends on the empirical circumstances. Parallel remarks can be made about the Truth Teller and Curry's paradox. An empirical version of (7) makes the "proof" of the existence of God even more striking.

1 The Liar paradox

Empirical loops are easily constructed. Plato might say,

(13) What Aristotle is saying now is true,

while, at that very moment, Aristotle is saying,

(14) What Plato is saying is false.

Here we have an empirical analogue of the pair (8) and (9). Again, there is nothing intrinsically ill-formed about (13) or (14): on other occasions, Plato or Aristotle may utter tokens of the same type that are straightforwardly true or false. Such empirical loops may be extended indefinitely, by adding participants in the appropriate way. And we can construct empirical chains, too. Suppose that each day someone goes to the Great Rock and says, "The next sentence uttered here will be true." A variant of this case will provide an empirical counterpart of the chain $\sigma_1, \sigma_2, \ldots$; and another variant will yield an empirical analogue of the system $\tau_1, \tau_2, \ldots$.

We can produce more sophisticated empirical cases. Consider a case due to Saul Kripke.[5] Suppose Jones says,

(15) Most of Nixon's assertions about Watergate are false.

In ordinary circumstances, it would be straightforward to evaluate (15): we would list Nixon's utterances about Watergate and assess each for truth and falsity. But suppose that the empirical circumstances are such that Nixon's Watergate-related assertions are equally divided between the true and the false, except for this one:

(16) Everything Jones says about Watergate is true.

And suppose further that (15) is Jones's only utterance about Watergate (or that everything else Jones has said about Watergate is true). Then it is easily seen that, under these empirical circumstances, (15) and (16) are paradoxical.

We turn now to a version of the Liar that is sometimes called the *Strengthened Liar.* This is a version of the Liar that will occupy us quite a bit in later chapters. As we shall see, for some theories of truth the Strengthened Liar presents a stiff challenge; for other theories, it provides a starting point. Consider a simple Liar sentence:

(17) (17) is not true.

We may reason about (17) in the usual way and conclude that (17) is paradoxical. But if (17) is paradoxical, then it cannot be true. That is, we may infer

(18) (17) is not true.

1.2 Proposals

But if we can truly assert (18), then (17) must be true after all, since (17) just says what (18) says.

Finally, we come to a type of Liar that is perhaps the most virulent. We may call it the *Revenge Liar*. There are different strains for different solutions to the Liar. If a solution to the Liar invokes truth-value gaps, so that a Liar sentence is treated as neither true nor false, then the Revenge Liar invokes these gaps too. Consider

(19) (19) is false or neither true nor false.

We are led to a contradiction whether we suppose (19) is true, false, or neither true nor false. In particular, invoking a truth-value gap will not help where (19) is concerned.

Similarly for other solutions: whatever semantic concepts are invoked by the solution, these form the basis for the Revenge Liar. If Liar sentences are diagnosed as semantically unstable, than a Revenge Liar is generated from

(20) (20) is not a semantically stable truth.

If we offer a Tarskian approach, according to which we split natural language into a hierarchy of object languages and metalanguages, each with its own distinct truth predicate, then we must deal with sentences like

(21) (21) is not true at any level of the hierarchy.

And a contextual theory, which avoids semantic paradox by the identification of shifts in the context of utterance, faces its own Revenge Liar:

(22) (22) is not true in any context of utterance.

Needless to say, some version of the Revenge Liar threatens to infect any attempt to produce a consistent theory of truth.

1.2. PROPOSALS

This wide range of cases should make us wary of taking too quick a way with the Liar. For example, it has been claimed that Liar sentences do not express propositions: Since Liar sentences do not really say anything, no paradox is forthcoming.[6] But more needs to be said. Empirical versions of the Liar create difficulties for undeveloped claims of this sort. Paul of Venice puts the point vividly: It is a consequence of the present claim that "some statement is not a proposition and becomes a proposition merely through a change in something else a thousand miles away."[7] Adapting Paul's example, suppose that someone says, "A false statement exists," and nothing else is said. Under these conditions, the statement is paradoxical. Now suppose that someone (a thousand miles away) makes a false statement. Then the original statement is no longer paradoxical, but true. It follows from the present claim that whether or not the original statement expresses a proposition depends on the empirical circumstances. But that shows that there is no intrinsic feature of the original sentence that determines whether or not it expresses a proposition. We lack an independent principle for distinguishing utterances that express propositions and those that don't. One cannot say that a sentence fails to express a proposition if it leads to semantic paradox, once all the empirical facts are determined. That would be plainly circular.

Some have suggested that Liar utterances fail to express a proposition because they are not syntactically well-formed.[8] In the face of empirical versions of the Liar, the proposal seems quite implausible. On such a view, (12) is not a syntactically well-formed sentence. However, under different empirical circumstances, a token of the same type as (12) is a perfectly well-formed sentence and does express a proposition. But how can syntactic well-formedness vary with the empirical circumstances?

Others have proposed that we ban self-reference: Liar sentences cannot express propositions because they are self-referential.[9] If we focus on simple Liar sentences, like (1) and (2), then the proposal seems natural enough: self-reference is a prominent feature of these sentences. But when we move on to loops and chains, then a simple ban on self-reference will no longer do. And the heterological paradox, generated by (3), does not involve any self-referential sentence.[10]

In this century, there have been two main kinds of response to the Liar (the two need not be mutually exclusive). One response is to reject classical logic and semantics. The other is a hierarchical response, associated with Russell and Tarski. These responses will be sketched now. In subsequent chapters, I shall argue against both responses and develop my own alternative.

1.2.1. Nonstandard logic and semantics

Nearly all who take this route abandon the *principle of bivalence,* according to which every sentence is true or false. Sometimes, a third truth value is introduced.[11] More usually in the literature, truth-value gaps are admitted.[12] According to the truth-value gap approach, paradoxical sentences are simply neither true nor false and have no other semantic value. Recall the version of the Liar generated by

(1) This sentence is false.

1.2 Proposals

The Liar reasoning depended on the assumption that (1) is either true or false. If we say that (1) is neither true nor false, but gappy, then the reasoning is blocked.

Proponents of this approach typically offer motivation for truth gaps independently of the Liar; invoking gaps just to get around the Liar would be unsatisfyingly ad hoc. Van Fraassen motivates truth-value gaps by appeal to Strawson's theory of presuppositions: The failure of a presupposition gives rise to truth-value gaps.[13] The notion of presupposition is characterized by

A presupposes B iff A is neither true nor false unless B is true.

For example, the sentence 'The present King of France is bald' presupposes the sentence 'The present King of France exists'. Since the later sentence is not true, the former is neither true nor false. According to van Fraassen, a Liar sentence like 'What I now say is false' "presupposes a contradiction, and hence cannot have a truth-value."[14]

Robert L. Martin's approach to the liar is motivated by category considerations: objects may fail to belong to the range of applicability of a predicate, so that certain predications yield "category-mistake sentences," sentences that are "semantically incorrect." Such sentences lack truth value. As examples, Martin cites "Virtue is triangular" and "The number 2 is green."[15] If we suppose that "heterological" does not belong to its own range of applicability, the contradiction of the heterological paradox is no longer derivable: The sentences '"Heterological" is heterological' and '"Heterological" is not heterological' are without truth value.[16]

Others have appealed to nonstandard semantics to give an account of vagueness.[17] The application of a vague predicate like 'bald' leads to sentences that are neither definitely true nor definitely untrue. It may be unsettled whether or not Harry is bald. But then it is likewise unsettled whether or not "Harry is bald" is true. According to Vann McGee, "The notion of truth inherits the vagueness of vague non-semantical terms."[18] This leads, according to McGee, to a tripartite division of sentences: those that are definitely true, those that are definitely untrue, and those that are unsettled. Liar sentences are unsettled.

There is another, more radical way of denying the principle of bivalence. We might allow sentences to be *both* true and false: there are truth-value "gluts," as opposed to gaps. A sentence like (1) is paradoxical, that is, both true and false. On such a *paraconsistent* approach, we embrace the contradiction generated by Liar sentences. This kind of approach has been taken by Nicholas Rescher and Robert Brandom, Graham Priest, and many others. We shall discuss paraconsistent accounts in Chapter 4.

9

1 The Liar paradox

1.2.2. Hierarchical views: Russell and Tarski

According to Russell, there is something that all the paradoxes have in common: Each involves an assertion that refers to an illegitimate totality. Consider the case of the Liar: "The liar says, 'everything that I assert is false'. This is, in fact, an assertion which he makes, but it refers to the totality of his assertions and it is only by including it in that totality that a paradox results."[19] Russell concludes:

> Whatever we suppose to be the totality of propositions, statements about this totality generate new propositions which, on pain of contradiction, must lie outside the totality. It is useless to enlarge the totality, for that equally enlarges the scope of statements about the totality. Hence there must be no totality of propositions, and "all propositions" must be a meaningless phrase.[20]

Similarly with the other paradoxes:

> All our contradictions have in common the assumption of a totality such that, if it were legitimate, it would at once be enlarged by new members defined in terms of itself.
> This leads us to the rule: "Whatever involves *all* of a collection must not be one of the collection," or, conversely, "If provided a certain collection had a total, it would have members only definable in terms of that total, then the said collection has no total."[21]

These are two formulations of Russell's vicious circle principle.[22]

As Russell goes on to say, this principle is negative in scope: "It suffices to show that many theories are wrong, but it does not show how the errors are to be rectified."[23] The theory of types is Russell's positive account of the paradoxes. Now Russell's ramified theory of types is notoriously complicated. For present purposes, we shall simplify considerably and restrict our attention to the hierarchy of orders of propositions.

Some propositions are themselves about propositions (e.g., the proposition 'Every proposition is true or false'); other propositions are not (e.g., the proposition 'Snow is white'). By the vicious circle principle, "Those that refer to some totality of propositions can never be members of that totality."[24] A hierarchy of orders of propositions is generated. "We may define first-order propositions as those referring to no totality of propositions; second-order propositions, as those referring to totalities of first-order propositions; and so on, *ad infinitum*."[25] And now the Liar is resolved:

10

1.2 Proposals

Thus our liar will now have to say, 'I am asserting a proposition of the first order which is false'. But this is itself a proposition of the second order. He is thus not asserting any proposition of the first order. What he says is, thus, simply false, and the argument that it is also true collapses.[26]

Tarski's seminal work, "The Concept of Truth in Formalized Languages," is devoted to the problem of defining truth.[27] Tarski seeks a definition of truth that does justice to the classical Aristotelian conception of truth: "To say of what is that it is not, or of what is not that it is, is false, while to say of what is that it is, or of what is not that it is not, is true."[28] Tarski writes:

Let us start with a concrete example. Consider the sentence "snow is white." We ask the question under what conditions this sentence is true or false. It seems clear that if we base ourselves on the classical conception of truth, we shall say that the sentence is true if snow is white, and that it is false if snow is not white. Thus, if the definition of truth is to conform to our conception, it must imply the following equivalence:

The sentence "snow is white" is true if, and only if, snow is white.[29]

The account is easily generalized:

Let us consider an arbitrary sentence; we shall replace it by the letter 'p'. We form the name of this sentence and we replace it by another letter, say 'X'. We ask now what is the logical relation between the two sentences "X is true" and 'p'. It is clear that from the point of view of our basic conception of truth these sentences are equivalent. In other words, the following equivalence holds:

(T)   X is true if, and only if, p.[30]

Now, says Tarski,

We are able to put into a precise form the conditions under which we will consider the usage and the definition of the term "true" as adequate from the material point of view: we wish to use the term "true" in such a way that all equivalences of the form (T) can be asserted, and *we shall call a definition of truth "adequate" if all these equivalences follow from it.*[31]

Tarski's schema (T) plays a critical role in the Liar paradox, as he presents it. Tarski considers an empirical version of the Liar, rather like (12). I follow closely Tarski's presentation.[32] Consider the following sentence:

The sentence printed in this chapter on p. 11, l. 35, is not true.

Let the letter 's' be an abbreviation of this sentence. Now, we may assert the following instance of schema (T):

11

'‘s' is true iff the sentence printed in this chapter on p. 11, l. 35, is not
true.

We can establish empirically that

'‘s' is identical to the sentence printed in this chapter on p. 11, l. 35.

By the logic of identity, we obtain

'‘s' is true iff '‘s' is not true.

And we arrive at an obvious contradiction.

Tarski identifies two assumptions that are essential to the construction
of the Liar. The first assumption is this:

> (I) We have implicitly assumed that the language in which the antinomy is
> constructed contains, in addition to its expressions, also the names of these
> expressions, as well as semantic terms such as the term "true" referring to
> sentences of this language; we have also assumed that all sentences which
> determine the adequate usage of this term can be asserted in the language.[33]

Tarski calls a language with these properties "semantically universal"[34]
or "semantically closed."[35] The second assumption is this:

> (II) We have assumed that in this language the ordinary laws of logic hold.[36]

As we have seen, a possible response is to give up assumption (II), to reject classical logic. But for Tarski, the rejection of (II) is not an option.[37]
And so Tarski concludes that we should seek a definition of truth for languages that are not semantically universal.

This leads to a distinction between *object language* and *metalanguage*:

> The first of these languages is the language which is "talked about" and
> which is the subject-matter of the whole discussion; the definition of truth
> which we are seeking applies to the sentences of this language. The second
> is the language in which we "talk about" the first language, and in terms of
> which we wish, in particular, to construct the definition of truth for the
> first language.[38]

Tarski points out that the terms "object language" and "metalanguage"
apply only in a relative way:

> If, for instance, we become interested in the notion of truth applying to
> sentences, not of our original object language, but of its metalanguage, the
> latter becomes automatically the object language of our discussion; and in
> order to define truth for this language, we have to go to a new metalan-
> guage – so to speak, to a metalanguage of a higher level. In this way we
> arrive at a whole hierarchy of languages.[39]

1.3 Universality and semantic universality

Those who take a "Tarskian" approach to the Liar attribute such a hierarchical structure to a natural language like English. English can be divided into a series of object languages and metalanguages, none of which is semantically universal. According to the standard Tarskian approach, these languages are not semantically universal because they do not contain their own truth predicates. Given a language O at some level of the hierarchy, the predicate 'true-in-O', referring to exactly the true sentences of O, is contained not in O, but in the metalanguage M at the next higher level.

On the Tarskian approach, there is no absolute predicate 'true' in English: 'true' is always to be understood as 'true in some language of the hierarchy' and never as 'true' *simpliciter*. Similarly, the schema (T) is always relativized to some language of the hierarchy; for example,

X is true-in-O iff p.

For the Tarskian, there are restrictions on what we may substitute for 'X' and for 'p' within this schema, since the application of 'true-in-O' is limited to sentences of O.

We can now turn to the Tarskian resolution of the Liar. Recall Tarski's empirical Liar sentence, abbreviated by the letter 's'. The Tarskian analysis of 's' is along the following lines:

The sentence printed in this chapter on p. 11, l. 35, is not true-in-O.

This is not a sentence of O, since 's' contains the predicate 'true-in-O'. So 's' may not be substituted for 'X' in the schema

X is true-in-O iff p.

And this blocks the Liar reasoning: we do not obtain an instance of the schema (T) that generates a contradiction.

The Tarskian resolution of the Liar invites a comparison with that of Russell. Just as on the Tarskian analysis, 's' is not a sentence of O but of the metalanguage M, so, on Russell's account, what the Liar says is not a first-order proposition but a second-order proposition. Russell remarks that his hierarchical theory and the doctrine of a hierarchy of languages belong to "the same order of ideas."[40] According to Church, "Russell's resolution of the semantical antinomies is not a different one than Tarski's but is a special case of it."[41]

1.3. UNIVERSALITY AND SEMANTIC UNIVERSALITY

Natural languages are remarkably flexible and open-ended. If there is something that can be said, it might seem that a natural language like

1 The Liar paradox

English has at least the potential to say it. Natural languages evolve; they always admit of extension, of increased expressive power. According to Tarski, natural languages are *universal*:

> A characteristic feature of colloquial language (in contrast to various scientific languages) is its universality. It would not be in harmony with the spirit of this language if in some other language a word occurred which could not be translated into it; it could be claimed that 'if we can speak meaningfully about anything at all, we can also speak about it in colloquial language'.[42]

In the same vein, Tarski remarks on the "all-comprehensive, universal character" of natural language and continues:

> The common language is universal and is intended to be so. It is supposed to provide adequate facilities for expressing everything that can be expressed at all, in any language whatsoever; it is continually expanding to satisfy this requirement.[43]

According to Tarski, it is the universality of natural languages "which is the primary source of all semantical antinomies."[44] For if a language can say everything there is to say, then in particular, it can everything that there is to say about its own semantics. Such a language will be semantically universal. But a semantically universal language, together with the usual laws of logic, leads to semantic paradox.[45] Tarski concludes:

> *The very possibility of a consistent use of the expression 'true sentence' which is in harmony with the laws of logic and the spirit of everyday language seems to be very questionable, and consequently the same doubt attaches to the possibility of constructing a correct definition of this expression.*[46]

In his search for a definition of truth, then, Tarski turns away from natural languages and considers only formal languages. Tarski doubts that we can define truth in natural language: The attempt will lead us to abandon either the laws of logic or the spirit of natural language. In particular, Tarski does *not* endorse the "Tarskian" solution, for that seems to abandon the spirit of natural language. It is doubtful that natural language, once regimented into a series of object languages and metalanguages, "would still preserve its naturalness and whether it would not rather take on the characteristic features of the formalized languages."[47]

We should avoid misunderstandings about Tarski's notion of universality. To claim that natural languages are universal in Tarski's sense is not to claim that all concepts are expressible in natural language. This latter claim would be highly controversial, or perhaps just plain false.

14

1.3 Universality and semantic universality

Consider, for example, the sets in the ZF hierarchy. For each set, there is a distinct concept – say, *being a member of that particular set*. Given certain assumptions about natural languages (in particular, about upper limits on the size of vocabularies and on the length of sentences), these concepts would outrun the expressive capacity of any natural language. But Tarski does not make the claim that natural languages can express all concepts. Rather, he claims that *if* a concept is expressible in *some* language, then it is expressible in any natural language. This claim is perfectly compatible with the existence of concepts that are inexpressible (in every language).

We should also be careful to distinguish Tarski's notions of *universality* and *semantic universality*. We might doubt Tarski's claim that natural languages are universal while accepting that they are semantically universal. For example, one can take issue with Tarski's claim that any word of a language can be translated into any natural language. Good translations, even adequate ones, are often hard to come by.[48] Is this chapter translatable into a language spoken by a semantically undeveloped culture?[49] Would the language survive the morphological expansion required for such a translation, or would it have been superseded by another language?

But the claim that natural languages are semantically universal seems far less controversial. A language like English, for example, does contain names for its own expressions, does contain its own semantic predicates, like 'true', 'false', and 'refers', and does seem to have the resources for describing the proper use of these expressions. Perhaps English cannot express every concept that is expressible in some language; but it seems that it can express all of its own semantic concepts. And as Tarski makes quite clear, this presents a seemingly impossible challenge: provide a way out of the Liar paradox but do not sacrifice semantic universality. A solution to the Liar for a natural language, say English, might be couched in terms of some semantic concept that applies to the sentences of English (truth gaps, or groundedness, or stable truth, or true at a level, or true in a context, etc.). In the language in which the solution is presented, this semantic concept is expressible; and so, if English is semantically universal, this semantic concept is expressible in English too. But now paradox will be present for this semantic concept, too, and we may ask whether the proposed account provides a way out of this new paradox. If it cannot, we may ask what progress has been made if one paradox has been resolved only for another to take its place? These issues will be discussed in Chapters 3 and 4.

Of course, the claim that natural languages are semantically universal may be rejected; such a rejection itself constitutes an approach to the Liar. Russell writes that, in the face of the paradoxes, "it appeared that, given any language, it must have a certain incompleteness, in the sense that there are things to be said *about* the language which cannot be said *in* the language."[50] Perhaps there are semantic concepts of English that English itself *cannot* express. Such an approach will be discussed in Chapter 3.

1.4. DIAGONALIZATION

Cantor first used the diagonal argument to prove that the real numbers are not denumerable. In Chapter 2, we discuss Cantor's proof and diagonal arguments in general. For now, we present an intuitive sketch of the proof. Our aim is to uncover the close relation between the diagonal argument, the Liar, and semantic universality.

Let $\{r_1, r_2, r_3, \dots\}$ be any denumerable set of reals. Under a binary representation, a real number may be uniquely represented as an infinite sequence of 0s and 1s. Without loss of generality, let the representation of $r_1, r_2, r_3, \dots$ be given by the following array:

	1	2	3	4 ...
r_1	0	1	1	0 ...
r_2	1	1	0	0 ...
r_3	0	0	0	1 ...
r_4	0	1	0	1 ...
⋮	⋮	⋮	⋮	⋮ ⋱

Within the box are rows (and columns) composed of denumerable sequences of 0s and 1s. The first row of 0s and 1s represents the real number r_1, the second row represents r_2, and so on. The natural numbers heading each column indicate position in a row.

Cantor showed that we can always find a real number that is not among $r_1, r_2, r_3, \dots$. Consider the *diagonal sequence* of 0s and 1s, from top left to bottom right:

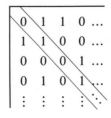

16

1.4 Diagonalization

Given the present array, the diagonal sequence is 0101 ... . Notice that this diagonal sequence may also occur as a row. (In our illustration, we may suppose it is the fourth row.) Now form the *antidiagonal sequence,* by changing each 0 to 1, and each 1 to a 0, in the diagonal sequence. We obtain the sequence 1010... . Now this sequence *cannot* occur as a row. It differs from the first row in at least the first place, from the second row in at least the second place, and in general, from the nth row in at least the nth place. So the real number represented by the antidiagonal sequence is not among $r_1, r_2, r_3, \ldots$. But the set $\{r_1, r_2, r_3, \ldots\}$ was an arbitrary denumerable set of reals. So, given any denumerable set of reals, we can always find a real that is not in that set. No denumerable set of reals is the set of all the reals: the real numbers are not denumerable.

We can present the heterological paradox in the form of a diagonal argument. Consider the following array:

	'mono-syllabic'	'poly-syllabic'	'long'	'new'	...
'monosyllabic'	f	f	t	t	...
'polysyllabic'	t	t	f	f	...
'long'	t	t	f	f	...
'new'	f	f	f	f	...
⋮	⋮	⋮	⋮	⋮	⋱

Down the side, and along the top, taken in the same order, are the one-place predicates of English. We write 't' if the predicate at the side is true of the predicate at the top; and we write 'f' if the predicate at the side is false of the predicate at the top. We obtain rows of t's and f's. For example, the row associated with the predicate 'monosyllabic' is fftt... . Each t in this row belongs to a column headed by a predicate in the extension of 'monosyllabic'. For example, 'long' and 'new' are in the extension of 'monosyllabic'. Consider now the diagonal sequence of t's and f's, the sequence ftff... . Each t in this sequence corresponds to a predicate true of itself (e.g., the second member of the sequence is a t, corresponding to the predicate 'polysyllabic', which is true of itself); and each f in this sequence corresponds to a predicate false of itself (the first member of the sequence is an f, corresponding to the predicate 'monosyllabic', which is false of itself). Now form the antidiagonal sequence tftt... . This antidiagonal sequence cannot occur as a row. Now suppose there were a predicate of English that was true of exactly those predicates false of themselves. The row associated with this predicate would be exactly our antidiagonal sequence. So, by the diagonal argument, there is no such predicate. But in English there *is* such a predicate, namely 'heterological'. And we have a paradox.

When the paradox is put in this way, it can be seen as a violation of Russell's vicious circle principle. The term 'heterological' is defined in terms of the totality of one-place predicates of English. If we include 'heterological' in this totality and count it among the predicates of English, then paradox results. Russell writes that, in each paradox he considers, "something is said about *all* cases of some kind, and from what is said a new case seems to be generated, which both is and is not of the same kind as the cases of which *all* were concerned in what was said."[51] In the present case, it is a diagonal argument that produces a problematic "new case": the term 'heterological' is a predicate of English, and yet, by the diagonal argument, it is not in the totality of all English predicates. We will see in Chapter 2 that a number of other paradoxes are generated by diagonal arguments, and they too may be seen as violations of the vicious circle principle.

Suppose we now consider the one-place predicates not of natural languages like English, but of certain exactly specified formal languages. Then the corresponding diagonal argument yields not a paradox, but a positive result. Roughly speaking, Tarski used such a diagonal argument to prove his celebrated theorem about truth. Given a suitable formal language L,[52] we assume, toward a contradiction, that L contains its own truth predicate; that is, L contains a predicate true of exactly the true sentences of L. We then show that L must contain a predicate true of exactly those predicates false of themselves. But by the diagonal argument, L cannot contain such a predicate, and we have our contradiction. This establishes Tarski's theorem for L: the truth predicate for L cannot be contained in L. (We will return to Tarski's theorem in Chapter 2.) Here the diagonal argument establishes that L is not semantically universal: the formal language L does not have the resources to talk about its own semantics. To talk about truth in L, an essentially richer metalanguage is required. And if this metalanguage is itself a classical formal language, then a diagonal argument will establish Tarski's theorem for it too. Tarski's hierarchy of formal languages is generated by diagonal arguments.

By Tarski's theorem, we diagonalize out of language L and into a metalanguage. But what will serve as a metalanguage for English? We cannot, it seems, diagonalize out of English: when we try, paradox results.

1.4 Diagonalization

Where English, or any natural language, is concerned, we are pulled in opposite directions. Diagonal arguments pull us in the direction of expressive incompleteness: There are certain semantic concepts that English cannot express. But the apparent universal character of English, in particular its apparent semantic universality, pushes us back: English can say everything there is to say about its own semantics. Caught between these two opposing forces, we find ouselves landed in semantic paradox.

These themes of semantic paradox, diagonalization, and semantic universality will be with us for the rest of this book. In Chapter 2, we focus on diagonal arguments. We see what makes an argument a diagonal argument, and why it is that some diagonal arguments lead to theorems (like Cantor's theorem that the reals are nondenumerable, or Tarski's theorem), while others lead to paradox (like the heterological paradox). In Chapters 3 and 4, we examine a number of contemporary theories of truth; we find that diagonal arguments present difficulties for them all. In the rest of the book, Chapters 5 to 9, we turn to a new proposal, a singularity solution to the Liar. In Chapter 5, a medieval solution to the Liar is examined and is found to contain a number of suggestive ideas. In Chapter 6, the main ideas of the singularity proposal are presented in an informal way. A formal account is presented in Chapter 7. In Chapter 8, the account is applied to a wide variety of Liar cases, drawn in part from our foregoing list. Finally, in Chapter 9, we return to the problem of semantic universality. I argue that the singularity proposal does justice to the intuition that natural languages are semantically universal, in a way that is not undermined by diagonal arguments.

Chapter 2

The diagonal argument

There are arguments found in various areas of mathematical logic that are taken to form a family: the family of *diagonal* arguments. Much of recursion theory may be described as a theory of diagonalization; diagonal arguments establish basic results of set theory; and they play a central role in the proofs of the limitative theorems of Gödel and Tarski. Diagonal arguments also give rise to set-theoretic and semantic paradoxes. What do these arguments have in common: What makes an argument a diagonal argument? And to ask a question first raised by Russell, why do some diagonal arguments establish theorems, while others generate paradoxes?

In this chapter, I attempt to answer these questions. In Section 2.1, Cantor's original diagonal arguments are described. A general analysis of the diagonal argument is present in Section 2.2. This analysis is then brought to bear on the second question. In Section 2.3, I give an account of the difference between *good* diagonal arguments (those leading to theorems) and *bad* diagonal arguments (those leading to paradox). In an appendix, I discuss various extensions of our analysis of the diagonal argument.

2.1. CANTOR'S USE OF THE DIAGONAL ARGUMENT

In 1891, Cantor presented a striking argument that has come to be known as Cantor's diagonal argument.[1] One of Cantor's purposes was to replace his earlier, controversial proof that the reals are nondenumerable.[2] But there was also another purpose: to extend this result to the general theorem that any set can be replaced by another of greater power. To these ends, Cantor gave two proofs. The first established the existence of a nondenumerable set that may be associated with the set of reals; the second provided an example of the replacement of a set by one of greater power. Each proof used the method of diagonalization.

20

2.1 Cantor's use of the diagonal argument

The first proof runs as follows. Consider the two elements m and w. Let M be the set whose elements E are sequences

$$\langle x_1, x_2, \ldots, x_\nu, \ldots \rangle,$$

where each of $x_1, x_2, \ldots, x_\nu, \ldots$ is either m or w. Cantor gave three examples of elements of M:

$$E^I = \langle m, m, m, m, \ldots \rangle, \quad E^{II} = \langle w, w, w, w, \ldots \rangle, \quad E^{III} = \langle m, w, m, w, \ldots \rangle.$$

He asserted that M is nondenumerable and proceeded to establish this by a proof of the following theorem:

If $E_1, E_2, \ldots, E_\nu, \ldots$ is any simply infinite[3] sequence of elements of the set M, then there is always an element E_0 of M which corresponds to no E_ν.[4]

To prove this theorem, Cantor arranged a denumerable list of elements in an array:

$$E_1 = \langle a_{1,1}, a_{1,2}, \ldots, a_{1,\nu}, \ldots \rangle,$$
$$E_2 = \langle a_{2,1}, a_{2,2}, \ldots, a_{2,\nu}, \ldots \rangle,$$
$$\vdots$$
$$E_\mu = \langle a_{\mu,1}, a_{\mu,2}, \ldots, a_{\mu,\nu}, \ldots \rangle,$$
$$\vdots$$

Each $a_{\mu,\nu}$ is either m or w. Cantor next defined a sequence $b_1, b_2, b_3, \ldots$, where each of $b_1, b_2, b_3, \ldots$ is either m or w, and further, if $a_{\nu,\nu} = m$, then $b_\nu = w$, and if $a_{\nu,\nu} = w$, then $b_\nu = m$. Let $E_0 = \langle b_1, b_2\, b_3, \ldots \rangle$. Then no E_ν corresponds to E_0. For suppose that $E_0 = E_\nu$, for some ν; then the νth coordinate of E is identical with the νth coordinate of E_ν, which contradicts the definition of the sequence $b_1, b_2, b_3, \ldots$.

Of his first proof, Cantor wrote:

This proof seems remarkable not only because of its great simplicity, but also because the principle which it follows can be extended directly to the general theorem, that the powers of well-defined sets have no maximum, or, what is the same, that in place of any given set L another set M can be placed which is of greater power than L.[5]

However, Cantor did not go on to prove the general theorem, but instead proved an instance of it. Cantor took L to be the linear continuum [0, 1],[6] M to be the set of single-valued functions $f(x)$ that yield only the values 0 or 1 for any value of $x \in [0, 1]$, and proved that M is of greater power than L.

2 The diagonal argument

This second proof proceeded in two stages. First, Cantor established that M is at least as large as L, by showing that there is a subset of M that can be put into 1-1 correspondence with L. Consider the following subset of M: the set of those functions on [0, 1] that have value 0 except for one argument x_0. There are as many of these functions as there are reals on [0, 1]. Second, Cantor proved that there is no 1-1 correspondence between M and L. Suppose, toward a contradiction, that there is a 1-1 correspondence φ between M and L: for each z in L, there is a function $f(x)$ in M such that $\varphi(x, z) = f(x)$, and for each $f(x)$ in M, there is exactly one z in L such that $\varphi(x, z) = f(x)$. Now Cantor defined the function $g(x)$ in M, where, for any x, $g(x)$ is either 0 or 1, and if $\varphi(x, x) = 0$ or 1, then $g(x) = 1$ or 0, respectively. Since $g(x)$ is a single-valued function that yields only the values 0 or 1 for any value of x in [0, 1], $g(x)$ is an element of M. Given the 1-1 correspondence φ, there is a z_0 in L such that $\varphi(x, z_0) = g(x)$. Putting $x = z_0$, we obtain $\varphi(z_0, z_0) = g(z_0)$; but this contradicts the definition of the function $g(x)$. This completes the second proof.[7]

2.2. GENERAL ANALYSIS OF THE DIAGONAL ARGUMENT

As we have seen, Cantor's first diagonal argument involves an array, which we may illustrate as follows:

	1	2	3	...
E_1	m	w	m	...
E_2	w	m	m	...
E_3	m	w	w	...
⋮	⋮	⋮	⋮	⋱

We can think of this array as composed of two collections – the "side" $\{E_1, E_2, E_3, \ldots\}$ and the "top" $\{1, 2, 3, \ldots\}$ – and the "values" m and w. There is a unique value for any pair of elements taken from the side and the top. Any diagonal argument involves such an array.

Definition. Let R be a 3-place relation, and D_1 (the side) and D_2 (the top) be sets.[8] Then,

R is an *array* on D_1 and $D_2 \leftrightarrow_{df} \forall x \, \forall y (x \in D_1 \, \& \, y \in D_2 \rightarrow \exists ! z R xyz)$.

In Cantor's first proof, the array R is given by

2.2 *General analysis of the diagonal argument*

$$R(x, y) = \begin{cases} m, & \text{if element } x \text{ has m in its } y\text{th place,} \\ w, & \text{if element } x \text{ has w in its } y\text{th place.} \end{cases}$$

Now consider an array with finite top and side, for example:

D$_2$

0	1	0	1
1	1	0	1
0	0	0	1
1	1	1	0

(to the left of the array: D$_1$)

Think of the values (here, 0 and 1) as occupying *cells,* given by coordinates $\langle x, y \rangle$, where $x \in$ D$_1$ and $y \in$ D$_2$. We will take diagonals to be composed of cells. The leading diagonal, from top left to bottom right, corresponds to our intuitive notion of a diagonal:

However, other configurations of cells serve just as well in diagonal arguments. What is essential is the pairing of each member of D$_1$ with some unique member of D$_2$, and this is equally well supplied by another "diagonal," say

In Cantor's presentation of his first proof, for example, the diagonal considered is the leading diagonal, the cells of which are given by $\langle E_1, 1 \rangle$, $\langle E_2, 2 \rangle$, $\langle E_3, 3 \rangle$, ... But the leading diagonal is just one diagonal among many. An alternative is suggested by the coordinates $\langle E_1, 2 \rangle$, $\langle E_2, 1 \rangle$, $\langle E_3, 4 \rangle$, $\langle E_4, 3 \rangle$, ... The notion of a leading diagonal does not apply unless top and side are ordered, and there is a correlation corresponding to

2 The diagonal argument

this ordering. But in diagonal arguments, ordering plays no essential role: it is the pairing of elements from the side with elements from the top that is crucial.[9]

This pairing need not exhaust every member of the top. According to our analysis, diagonals must pass through every row, but need not pass through every column:

So we are led to the following definition of a diagonal:

Definition. F is *a diagonal on* D_1 *and* D_2 $\leftrightarrow_{df}$ F is a 1-1 function from D_1 into D_2.

The notion of a diagonal has to do only with *position*. As yet there is no link between the cells that constitute the diagonal and the value associated with each cell.

Definition. Let R be an array on D_1 and D_2, and let F be a diagonal on D_1 and D_2. Then,

G is *the value of the diagonal* F *in* R

$$\leftrightarrow_{df} \forall x\, \forall y\, \forall z (Gxyz \leftrightarrow Fxy\, \&\, Rxyz).$$

In Cantor's first proof, the value in each cell of the leading diagonal is changed. The procedure is illustrated by the replacement of

	1	2	3	...		by		1	2	3	...
E_1	m						E_1	w			
E_2		m					E_2		w		
E_3			w				E_3			m	
⋮				⋱			⋮				⋱

We introduce the notion of a countervalue in order to generalize this procedure.

Definition. Let R be an array, and F a diagonal, on D_1 and D_2. H is a countervalue of F in R $\leftrightarrow_{df}$

24

2.2 General analysis of the diagonal argument

(i) $\forall x \forall y (\exists z Hxyz \leftrightarrow Fxy)$
(ii) $\forall x \forall y \forall z \forall z'(Hxyz \,\&\, Hxyz' \rightarrow z = z')$
(iii) $\forall x \forall y \forall z(Hxyz \rightarrow z \in \mathrm{range}R)$
(iv) $\forall x \forall y \forall z(Hxyz \rightarrow \neg Rxyz)$.

The countervalue corresponding to our illustration of Cantor's first proof may be given as this set of ordered triples:

$$\{\langle E_1, 1, w\rangle, \langle E_2, 2, w\rangle, \langle E_3, 3, m\rangle, \ldots\}.$$

Note that, if R yields $n+1$ values ($n \geq 1$), there are $n^{\mathrm{card(domainF)}}$ countervalues. Later we will make use of this feature of our analysis: that if R yields more than two values, there is more than one countervalue. Previous attempts in the literature to provide a general characterization of the diagonal argument have pointed to this theorem of quantificational logic:

(Ru) $\qquad\qquad \neg \exists x \forall y (J(x, y) \leftrightarrow \neg J(y, y))$.

The idea is that diagonal theorems are interpretations of (Ru) or some variant of (Ru).[10] Call this the "Russell analysis." On the Russell analysis, the analogue of our countervalue is the set of those elements of the domain of discourse that do not bear J to themselves. There is just one such set. The Russell analysis is captured by a special case of our general analysis, the case where R yields two values, and there is just one countervalue.

In final preparation for the diagonal theorem, we define the notion of a value or a countervalue occurring as a row. A value or countervalue occurs as a row if its associated values form a row of the array.

Definition. Let R be an array on D_1 and D_2, and let K be a value or countervalue of a diagonal F of R. Then,

K *occurs as a row of* R $\leftrightarrow_{\mathrm{df}} \exists d \in D_1 \forall x \forall y \forall z(Hxyz \rightarrow Rdyz)$.

Theorem 2.1 (The basic diagonal theorem). *Let R be an array on D_1 and D_2, and let F be a diagonal on D_1 and D_2. Let H be a countervalue of F. Then, H does not occur as a row of R.*

Proof.[11]

(1) Show $\neg \exists w \in D_1 \forall x \forall y \forall z(Hxyz \rightarrow Rwyz)$
(2) $\exists w \in D_1 \forall x \forall y \forall z(Hxyz \rightarrow Rwyz)$
                                          Assumption (H occurs as a row)
(3) $\forall x \forall y \forall z(Hxyz \rightarrow Rdyz)$ 2, EI
(4) $\forall x \forall y (\exists z Hxyz \leftrightarrow Fxy)$ Premise (H is a countervalue)

25

(5)	$\forall y(\exists z Hdyz \leftrightarrow Fdy)$	4, UI
(6)	$\forall x \in D_1 \exists y \in D_2 Fxy$	Premise (F is a diagonal)
(7)	$\exists y \in D_2 Fdy$	6, UI
(8)	Fde	7, EI
(9)	$Fde \to \exists z Hdez$	5, UI, SL
(10)	$\exists z Hdez$	8, 9, SL
(11)	$Hdef$	10, EI
(12)	$Hdef \to Rdef$	3, UI
(13)	$Rdef$	11, 12, SL
(14)	$\forall x \forall y \forall z(Hxyz \to \neg Rxyz)$	Premise (H is a countervalue)
(15)	$Hdef \to \neg Rdef$	14, UI
(16)	$\neg Rdef$	11, 15, SL

We may distinguish two kinds of diagonal argument: *direct* and *indirect*. In an indirect diagonal argument, the diagonal theorem is embedded in a proof by reductio; in a direct diagonal argument, it is not.

A *direct diagonal argument* specifies in set-theoretic terms a side, a top, an array, and a diagonal, each of which exists. The diagonal result is an interpretation of our diagonal theorem. Cantor's first proof is a direct diagonal argument. The element d appearing in the proof corresponds to Cantor's E_0. By the diagonal theorem, d does not belong to D_1; in Cantor's words, "there is always an element E_0 of M which corresponds to no E_ν."

An *indirect diagonal argument* also provides a set-theoretic specification of a side, a top, an array, and a diagonal, but it assumes the existence of at least one of these *toward a contradiction*. Here, the diagonal argument generates the contradiction via a proof of the diagonal theorem under the appropriate interpretation. Cantor's second proof is an indirect diagonal argument. Cantor assumed the existence of an array on a side (the set M) and a top (the set L), where the values of the array are 0 and 1. (Given a function from the side and a real number between 0 and 1 from the top, the value coincides with the output the function yields with that real number as input). Now Cantor further assumed, *toward a contradiction,* the existence of a diagonal, the 1–1 correspondence φ. Cantor went on to define the function $g(x)$ in terms of φ. But here the diagonal theorem tells us that there is no function in M that satisfies the definition of the function $g(x)$, and we have a contradiction.

Direct and indirect diagonal arguments are the two kinds of diagonal arguments that establish theorems (these are the good diagonal arguments). In the next section we shall also characterize bad diagonal arguments, which are neither direct nor indirect diagonal arguments.

2.3. GOOD AND BAD DIAGONAL ARGUMENTS

In *The Principles of Mathematics,* Russell remarks that Cantor's diagonal argument "appears to contain no dubitable assumption. Yet there are certain cases in which the conclusion seems plainly false."[12] Russell reviews a number of such cases,[13] including his own paradox, and concludes, "The application of Cantor's argument to the doubtful cases yields contradictions, though I have been unable to find any point in which the argument appears faulty."[14] As well as those considered by Russell, there are other "doubtful cases," including Richard's paradox, the heterological paradox, and the cycling paradoxes in set theory and in semantics. In each of these cases, the diagonal argument leads to paradox. And yet in other cases, the diagonal argument leads to a theorem: for example, to the nondenumerability of the reals, the power set theorem, Gödel's first incompleteness theorem, Tarski's undefinability theorem, and many theorems of recursion theory. Why is it that some diagonal arguments are good, and yet others are bad? In this section, I shall suggest an answer to this question. At the same time, the adequacy of the foregoing general analysis will be put to the test: We'll apply the analysis to a number of particular cases.

One example of a diagonal argument that leads to a contradiction is the paradox discovered in 1905 by Jules Richard.[15] Richard presents his paradox as follows. A certain set of numbers, the set E, is defined through the following considerations: Write in alphabetical order all permutations of pairs of letters of the alphabet, followed by all permutations of triples of letters of the alphabet taken in alphabetical order, and so on for quadruples, quintuples, and so on. Cross out all permutations of letters that do not define numbers. E is the set whose members are u_1, the first number defined by a permutation, u_2, the second number defined by a permutation, and so on: that is, E is the set of all numbers that can be defined by finitely many words. Now consider the following collection G of letters between the quotation marks: "Let p be the digit in the nth decimal place of the nth number of the set E; let us form a number having 0 for its integral part and, in its nth decimal place, $p+1$ if p is not 8 or 9, and 1 otherwise." Call the number so defined N. Then N cannot belong to the set E. Suppose it were the nth member in E; then the digit in its nth place would be the same as the digit in the nth decimal place of the nth number, which is not the case. Yet N is defined by finitely many words, hence it should belong to the set E. So we have a contradiction.

We should note in passing two easily corrected flaws in Richard's presentation. Though he refers to E as a set, Richard treats it as a sequence.

And he overlooks the fact that different permutations of letters may define the same number.

We can capture Richard's paradox in our terms as follows. Let the side D_1 be the set of real numbers definable by an expression of English, and let the top D_2 be the set of natural numbers. Let $R(x, y) = p$, where p is the digit in the yth decimal place of x; here the array is many-valued. Let F be a 1–1 function from D_1 onto D_2. A countervalue H of F is given by

$$H(x, y) = \begin{cases} p+1, & \text{if p is the digit in the } y\text{th place of the decimal} \\ & \text{expansion of } x, \text{ and } p \neq 8 \text{ or } 9, \\ 1, & \text{if p is the digit in the } y\text{th place of the decimal} \\ & \text{expansion of } x, \text{ and } p = 8 \text{ or } 9. \end{cases}$$

The diagonal argument leads to the conclusion that there is no number, definable by an English expression, *that has in its yth decimal place either the number* $p+1$ *or the number* 1, *according to whether the number correlated with y has in its yth decimal place the number* p, *where* $p \neq 8$ *or* 9, *or the number* 8 *or* 9. But if we now append the italicized expression in the previous sentence to the expression "The number that has 0 for its integral part and," we obtain an English expression defining a number that, we just concluded, was not definable by an English expression.

Richard offers a way out of his paradox that does not work.[16] But a leading idea of Richard's solution is suggestive. According to Richard, the contradiction is only apparent, because the set that we have labeled D_1 is not "totally defined."[17] And it is plausible that the problem lies with D_1. Notice that if we had taken D_1 to be some well-determined set of numbers, the diagonal argument would yield unproblematically an English expression that defines a number outside D_1. According to Richard, trouble arises when we take D_1 to be the set of *all* numbers defined by English expressions. Richard's diagnosis is very much in the spirit of Russell's vicious circle principle.[18]

Of course, Richard's diagnosis falls short of a solution to the paradox. We lack an account of the notion of *definability* that explains why it is that the side is not well-determined, why it is that the predicate 'real number definable by an English expression' does not determine a set. This is supplied, for example, by the positive side of a Russellian approach, where the illegitimate totality of definitions is divided into a hierarchy of types, or by a Tarskian approach, according to which the predicate 'defines' is split into infinitely many distinct predicates arranged in a hierarchy.

Still, Richard does give us a diagnosis of what is wrong with the diagonal argument. One of the components of the diagonal argument, the side, is not a well-determined set. This in turn suggests a more general characterization of bad diagonal arguments, one that is independent of Richard's particular diagnosis. Any diagonal argument assumes the existence of a number of components: a side, a top, an array, a diagonal, a value, and a countervalue. In a bad diagonal argument, one or more of these sets is not well-determined. This places bad diagonal arguments in a no-man's-land between the two types of good diagonal arguments, the direct and indirect diagonal arguments. Direct diagonal arguments assume the existence of only well-determined sets; bad diagonal arguments do not. In an indirect diagonal argument, any component that is not a well-determined set is assumed to exist *toward a contradiction*. But in a bad diagonal argument, we assume the existence of a component that is not well-determined, but we do *not* make this an assumption for reductio.[19]

This characterization of a bad diagonal argument requires the notion of a well-determined set. This is supplied if we suppose we are working with some standard set theory, say ZF. Relative to ZF set theory, then, we can say that a bad diagonal argument, like any diagonal argument, specifies a top, a side, an array, a diagonal, and a countervalue in set-theoretic terms. But at least one of these components is not a well-determined set. There is nothing wrong with the *reasoning* of a bad diagonal argument – rather, what is at fault is the assumption that all of the diagonal components exist. Since the reasoning is valid, a bad diagonal argument may be converted to a direct diagonal argument – just replace any problematic component by a suitable well-determined set. Or we may be able to convert a bad diagonal argument into an indirect diagonal argument; if we can identify the problematic component, we can make the assumption that it exists an assumption for reductio.

For example, there are good direct analogues of the bad diagonal argument associated with Richard's paradox. If we let D_1 be any well-determined denumerable set of reals, and keep the rest of the interpretation fixed, we obtain a direct diagonal argument that constitutes a proof of the nondenumerability of the reals, quite analogous to Cantor's first proof.

Or consider Gödel's first incompleteness theorem. Gödel begins his 1931 paper with an outline of the proof,[20] and then comments, "The analogy of this argument with the Richard antinomy leaps to the eye."[21] Gödel works with PM, the system of Russell and Whitehead's *Principia Mathematica*. We consider the formulas of PM with exactly one free variable, where the variable ranges over the natural numbers. Gödel calls such a formula a *class sign*. Now,

We assume that the class signs have been arranged in a sequence in some way, we denote the nth one by R(n), and we observe that the notion "class sign," as well as the ordering relation R, can be defined in the system PM.[22]

2 The diagonal argument

So associated with each class sign is a unique natural number. Now Gödel goes on to show, in effect, that we can construct a class sign of PM that is true of exactly the Gödel numbers of wffs not provable of their own Gödel numbers.[23] Gödel sketches the construction as follows:

> Let a be any class sign; by [c; n] we denote the formula that results from the class sign c when the free variable is replaced by the sign denoting the natural number n. The ternary relation $x = [y; z]$, too, is seen to be definable in PM. We now define a class K of natural numbers in the following way:
>
> $$n \in K \equiv \overline{Bew}[R(n); n]$$
>
> (where *Bew x* means: x is a provable formula).[24] Since the notions that occur in the *definiens* can all be defined in PM, so can the notion K formed from them; that is, there is a class sign S such that the formula [S; n], interpreted according to the meaning of the terms of PM, states that the natural number n belongs to K.[25]

Notice that the number n belongs to K iff the nth class sign is not provable of n. So the class sign S is true of exactly those numbers associated with class signs not provable of their associated numbers.

But now a diagonal argument shows that S is not *provable of* exactly these numbers. Let the side D_1 be the set of class signs of PM. D_2 is the set of natural numbers. The array R is given by

$$R(x, y) = \begin{cases} 1, & \text{if } x \text{ is provable of } y, \\ 0, & \text{if } x \text{ is not provable of } y. \end{cases}$$

The diagonal F carries each class term in D_1 to its associated number. For all x and y such that Fxy, the countervalue H of F is given by

$$H(x, y) = \begin{cases} 1, & \text{if } x \text{ is not provable of } y, \\ 0, & \text{if } x \text{ is provable of } y. \end{cases}$$

The diagonal theorem tells us that H does not occur as a row of R. That is, no class sign of PM is provable of exactly those numbers associated with class signs not provable of their own associated numbers.

In particular, the class sign S is not provable of exactly these numbers. Yet S *is true of* exactly these numbers. So there must be some number m such that either

(1) [S; m] is provable, but not true, or
(2) [S; m] is true, but not provable.

If we assume that PM is sound, then we must conclude that (2) is the case; that is, there is an unprovable truth. Since the negation of [S; m] is false, and so not provable, we may also conclude that there exists an undecidable sentence, a sentence such that neither it nor its negation are provable.

2.3 Good and bad diagonal arguments

We can be more specific, if we attend to the details of the diagonal argument. We suppose, toward a contradiction, that S is provable of exactly the numbers of which it is true; in our terms, we suppose that the countervalue occurs as a row. Given that the diagonal F associates with each member of the side some member of the top, let F associate with S the number q. We now take as argument for the countervalue H the cell ⟨S, q⟩ of the diagonal. Now a contradiction is forthcoming. For since H is a countervalue,

$$H(S, q) = 1 \text{ iff } R(S, q) = 0.$$

But since H is a row,

$$H(S, q) = 1 \text{ iff } R(S, q) = 1.$$

Now consider the sentence [S; q]. Suppose [S; q] were provable; then it is true.[26] So q is a number associated with a class term that is not provable of its associated number; that is, [S; q] is not provable, which contradicts our assumption. Suppose on the other hand that ¬[S; q] is provable; then [S; q] does not hold. Then q is a number associated with a class sign that is provable of its associated number; that is, [S; q] is provable, which is impossible. So ¬[S; q] is not provable. So neither [S; q] nor ¬[S; q] is provable in PM: [S; q] is our undecidable sentence. Under the intended interpretation, [S; q] says that q is a number associated with a class term not provable of its associated number; that is, [S; q] says about itself that it is not provable. And so [S; q] is also our unprovable truth.

The shared diagonal structure of Gödel's proof and the Richard paradox draws out Gödel's analogy. In each case, the diagonal serves to index or code the elements of the side. The key difference lies in the collections forming the side. As we have seen, the side associated with Richard's paradox is problematic; in Gödel's proof, the side is the unproblematic set of class signs of PM.

Other good analogues of the Richard diagonal argument are to be found in recursion theory. The diagonal argument raises a prima facie difficulty for any attempt to capture formally the notion of algorithmic function. Given a variety of formally characterized classes of algorithmic functions, the diagonal argument produces an algorithmic function falling outside the class. As Hartley Rogers puts it, the diagonal method "suggests the possibility that no single formally characterizable class of algorithmic functions can correspond exactly to the informal notion of algorithmic function."[27] Consider, for example, the primitive recursive functions. A function f is primitive recursive iff there is a finite sequence of functions $f_1, f_2, ..., f_n$ such that $f_n = f$, and for each $j \leq n$, either f_j is a constant function, successor function, or identity function, or f_j is

31

obtainable from some of the f_i, $i \leq j$, by substitution or by primitive recursion.[28] A *derivation* for f is a description of such a sequence of functions for f, with a specification of how each f_j is obtained for $j \leq n$. Consider all possible primitive recursive derivations. Each derivation may be represented as a finite string of symbols. These strings can be ordered alphabetically and according to length. Further there is an effective test for determining whether a given string is a primitive recursive derivation. So we are able to devise an algorithmic procedure that lists all primitive recursive derivations. From this list, we can effectively obtain a list of the derivations for primitive recursive functions of one variable. Now let Q_x be the $(x+1)$st derivation in the list. Let g_x be the function determined by Q_x. Define h by

$$h(x) = g_x(x) + 1.$$

We clearly have an algorithm for computing h. But h cannot be primitive recursive. If h were primitive recursive, we would have $h = g_{x_0}$ for some x_0. But then we would obtain

$$g_x(x_0) = h(x_0) = g_x(x_0) + 1,$$

which is a contradiction.[29]

In our terms, the side D_1 is a set of derivations for all primitive recursive functions of one variable. The top D_2 is the set of all natural numbers. The many-valued array R is given by

$R(x, y) =$ the result of applying the primitive recursive function determined by x to argument y.

F is any 1-1 function from D_1 onto D_2. For all x and y such that Fxy, a countervalue H of F is given by

$H(x, y) =$ the result of applying the primitive recursive function determined by x to argument y, and adding 1.

The diagonal theorem tells us that H cannot occur as a row: that is, there is no derivation in D_1 for the function h. But D_1 is a set of derivations for all primitive recursive functions – and so h is an algorithmic function that is not primitive recursive.[30]

Here the side is well-defined, and the diagonal argument gives rise to a set of instructions for an algorithmic function that is not a member of the side. But in the Richard case, the side is not well-defined, and the diagonal argument gives rise to an English definition of a real that both is and is not a member of the side.

We have now considered three direct diagonal arguments: the nondenumerability of the reals, Gödel's theorem, and a proof that there are

32

algorithmic functions that are not primitive recursive. In each case, the top, side, array, and diagonal are all well-defined sets. This is not so with the bad diagonal argument that constitutes Richard's paradox. Here, *unlike direct diagonal arguments,* not all of the top, side, array, and diagonal are well-defined sets. And *unlike indirect diagonal arguments,* the assumption that they are all well-defined sets is not made toward a contradiction. If we are convinced that the problem lies with the side, there is an obvious way to rehabilitate the bad diagonal argument: make the assumption that the side exists an assumption for reductio, and thereby obtain a good indirect diagonal argument.

A similar diagnosis can be made for other bad diagonal arguments. Consider Russell's paradox. Suppose that the predicate 'is a non-self-membered set' does determine a set, that there is a set M of exactly those sets that are not members of themselves. The side and the top are each the proper class of all sets, where the side and top are taken to include the set M. The array R is given by

$$R(x, y) = \begin{cases} 1, & \text{if } y \in x, \\ 0, & \text{if } y \notin x. \end{cases}$$

The diagonal F is identity. The countervalue H of F is given by

$$H(x, x) = \begin{cases} 1, & \text{if } x \notin x, \\ 0, & \text{if } x \in x. \end{cases}$$

By the diagonal theorem, there is no set of exactly those sets that do not belong to themselves, contradicting our assumption. According to the standard response to Russell's paradox, it is the assumption that the predicate 'is a non-self-member' determines a set that generates the paradox. If we make this assumption for reductio and assume that all other components of the diagonal argument are unproblematic, we obtain an indirect diagonal argument that establishes that there is no set M.[31]

There are good analogues of this bad diagonal argument. Consider, for example, the argument from recursion theory that establishes the recursive unsolvability of the halting problem. Given the theorem that a set A is recursively enumerable (r.e.) iff A is the domain of a partial recursive function, we let $W_x = \text{domain} \varphi_x$, where x is a Gödel number for the r.e. set W_x. Let $K = \{x \mid \varphi_x(x) \text{ convergent}\} = \{x \mid x \in W_x\}$. So $\bar{K} = \{x \mid x \notin W_x\}$. One way of expressing the recursive unsolvability of the halting problem is to say that K is not recursive. Since, in general, A is recursive iff A and $\bar{A}$ are both r.e., and since K is r.e., we can prove that K is not recursive by showing that $\bar{K}$ is not r.e. The proof that $\bar{K}$ is not r.e. is a diagonal argument. The side D_1 and the top D_2 are a set of Gödel numbers of all r.e. sets. The array R is given by

33

$$R(x, y) = \begin{cases} 1, & \text{if } y \text{ is a member of the r.e. set with Gödel no. } x, \\ 0, & \text{if } y \text{ is not a member of the r.e. set with Gödel no. } x. \end{cases}$$

The diagonal F is identity. The countervalue H of F is given by

$$H(x, x) = \begin{cases} 1, & \text{if } x \text{ is not a member of the r.e. set with Gödel no. } x, \\ 0, & \text{if } x \text{ is a member of the r.e. set with Gödel no. } x. \end{cases}$$

By the diagonal theorem, H cannot occur as a row. So the set $\bar{K} = \{x \mid x \notin W_x\}$ is not r.e. Clearly, this diagonal argument is analogous to that associated with the Russell paradox. But here the diagonal argument is good. Unlike M, the set $\bar{K}$ exists.[32]

Russell's paradox is one of an infinite number of set-theoretic paradoxes. If we call a set that is a member of itself a 1-*cyclic set,* then Russell's paradox involves the set of 1-acyclic sets. Call a set s k-*cyclic,* where $k \in N$, if $\exists s_1, s_2, \ldots, s_k$ such that $s_0 \in s_1 \in s_2 \in \cdots \in s_k$, and $s_0 = s_k = s$. For each natural number k, there is a paradox associated with the set of k-acyclic sets. Each of these paradoxes is generated by a diagonal argument.

Some terminology: Given an $\in$-chain, we call the first element of the chain (the leftmost element) the *left-extreme,* and the last element of the chain (the rightmost element) the *right-extreme.* We say that an $\in$-chain has length k if it has $k + 1$ elements. Let the side D_1 and the top D_2 be the collection of all sets, and let the array R be given by

$$R(x, y) = \begin{cases} 1, & \text{if } x \text{ and } y \text{ are respectively the right and left extremes} \\ & \text{of an } \in\text{-chain of length k,} \\ 0, & \text{otherwise.} \end{cases}$$

The diagonal F is identity. The countervalue H is given by

$$H(x, x) = \begin{cases} 1, & \text{if } x \text{ is k-acyclic,} \\ 0, & \text{if } x \text{ is k-cyclic.} \end{cases}$$

Let h be a set associated with the countervalue. Then if we take all $\in$-chains of length k of which h is the right-extreme, the left-extremes are all and only the k-acyclic sets. By the diagonal theorem, the set h is not in D_1; but h is in D_1, since D_1 is the collection of all sets, and we have a contradiction.

Here is the connection between our bad diagonal argument and the paradox of the set of k-acyclic sets. Suppose there is a set h' of the k-acyclic sets. Then we are led to a contradiction, since we can form the set

$$h = \{\{\ldots\{h'\}\ldots\}\}, \\ \underbrace{\qquad}_{k-1}$$

which is a set associated with the countervalue of our bad diagonal argument. If we assume the existence of h toward a contradiction and thereby convert the bad diagonal argument into a good indirect one, we may conclude that there is no such set h and, hence, no set h′ of k-acyclic sets.

As noted previously (see note 19), a bad diagonal argument may take the form of a direct or indirect argument. So far, our examples have been of the former kind. For an example of the latter, consider Cantor's paradox. Let the top D_2 be the set of all sets, and let the side D_1 be the power set of D_2. The array R is given by

$$R(x, y) = \begin{cases} 1, & \text{if } y \in x, \\ 0, & \text{if } y \notin x. \end{cases}$$

We suppose toward a contradiction that there is a diagonal F on D_1 and D_2. We can now define a certain member of D_1 in terms of F: the set of those elements of D_2 that do not belong to the subset of D_1 with which they are correlated by F. But by the diagonal theorem, there is no such subset in D_1. We have a contradiction, and so there is no diagonal F. And now we have a paradox: D_1 is neither smaller nor equal in size to D_2, yet D_2 is the set of all sets. Paradox is generated from the assumption that the side, top, array, and countervalue exist. The standard response is to deny that the top exists – the argument is bad because it assumes the existence of a universal set. There is a good analogue of this bad diagonal argument: Let the top be any set, and we obtain an indirect diagonal argument that establishes Cantor's power set theorem.

Finally, let us turn to a bad diagonal argument related to the Liar. In Chapter 1, we presented the heterological paradox in the form of a diagonal argument. In our present terms, let the side and the top be the set of 1-place predicates of English, where the side and top are taken to include the predicate 'heterological'. The array R is given by

$$R(x, y) = \begin{cases} 1, & \text{if } y \text{ has the property denoted by } x, \\ 0, & \text{if } y \text{ does not have the property denoted by } x. \end{cases}$$

The diagonal F on R is identity. The countervalue H of F is given by

$$H(x, x) = \begin{cases} 1, & \text{if } x \text{ does not have the property denoted by } x, \\ 0, & \text{if } x \text{ does have the property denoted by } x. \end{cases}$$

By the diagonal theorem, there is no predicate of English that denotes the property had by exactly those predicates of English that do not have the property they denote. Yet 'heterological' is just such a predicate, and we have a paradox.

Again, according to our analysis, this diagonal argument is bad because it assumes that all of the side, top, and so on exist, where none of these assumptions are made for reductio. The principled conversion of this bad diagonal argument to an indirect one constitutes an attempt to solve the paradox. We might deny that the array exists. For example, a Tarskian would say that the expression 'has the property denoted by' is ill-formed and must be divided up between languages that form a hierarchy. Alternatively, we might deny that the array exists on the grounds that it cannot be bivalent – allowing truth-value gaps is one approach along these lines. Or we might deny that the top and side exist – though there is a concept of *heterologicality,* there is no predicate of the language that expresses it, contra our assumption about the top and side. These responses, and others, will be discussed in subsequent chapters.

There are good direct analogues of this bad diagonal argument. Tarski is quite explicit about the close analogy between the proof of his undefinability theorem and the argument that generates the Liar.[33] In particular, Tarski points to the analogy with the heterological version of the Liar. Just before sketching the proof of his undefinability theorem, Tarski remarks:

> If we analyze the sketch of the proof given below we easily note that an analogous reconstruction could be carried out even on the basis of colloquial language, and that in consequence of this reconstruction the antinomy of the liar actually approximates to the antinomy of the expression 'heterological'.[34]

We capture Tarski's theorem as follows. Let S be a usual first-order theory with identity that is based on Peano's postulates and is adequate for the proofs of all the basic results of number theory. The side D_1 is the set of 1-place wffs of S, and D_2 is the set of natural numbers. The array R is given by

$$R(x, y) = \begin{cases} 1, & \text{if } x \text{ is true (in the standard model) of } y, \\ 0, & \text{if } x \text{ is not true of } y. \end{cases}$$

The diagonal F carries each wff in D_1 to its Gödel number.[35] The counter-value H of F is

$$H(x, y) = \begin{cases} 1, & \text{if } x \text{ is not true of its Gödel number } y, \\ 0, & \text{if } x \text{ is true of its Gödel number } y. \end{cases}$$

By the diagonal theorem, no wff of S is true of exactly the Gödel number of wffs not true of their own Gödel numbers. But there is such a wff of S on the assumption that the set of Gödel numbers of wffs of S that are true in the standard model is arithmetical. We conclude that this set is not arithmetical.[36]

The diagonal argument here closely resembles that of the heterological case. But the set of wffs of S not true of their own Gödel numbers exists; and so too does a wff with this set as its extension, *in a suitable metalanguage.* There is nothing problematic about the wff or the set; this is in contrast with the predicate 'heterological' and the concept of hetero-logicality.

Like Russell's paradox, the heterological paradox is the simplest of an infinite series of cycling paradoxes. If we call a term that is true of itself a 1-*cyclic term,* then the heterological paradox involves the term true of the 1-acyclic terms. The definition of a k-cyclic term is just like the definition of a cyclic set with '∈' now interpreted as 'satisfies' (where satisfaction is the converse of the 'true of' relation). For each natural number k, there is a paradox associated with the term 'is a k-acyclic term'. These semantic paradoxes are generated by diagonal arguments in exactly the same way that the set-theoretic paradoxes are generated.

To sum up, bad diagonal arguments specify a top, a side, an array, a diagonal, and a countervalue in set-theoretic terms. As with indirect diagonal arguments, the specification of this set-theoretic apparatus involves somewhere the assumption of a set that is not well-determined. And so, like indirect diagonal arguments, bad diagonal arguments generate a con-tradiction, via valid reasoning that incorporates the proof of the diagonal theorem. But unlike indirect diagonal arguments, this contradiction is not part of a proof by reductio.

As we've seen, there are two ways to rehabilitate a bad diagonal argu-ment. One way is to replace any problematic diagonal component by a suitable well-determined set: We convert the bad argument to a direct di-agonal argument. The other way is to convert it to an indirect diagonal argument. A principled conversion may not be an easy matter: Such a conversion may amount to a solution to paradox.

APPENDIX: EXTENSIONS OF THE DIAGONAL THEOREM

In Section 2.2, we analyzed the diagonal argument in its most basic form. The analysis may be extended in various directions. We shall look at two of them in this appendix. In Section 2.2, we considered two-dimensional arrays constructed from a side and a top. Intuitively, we might think of the array as a square grid containing values. It is possible to extend the array to three dimensions, to a cube. And we can go further, to four-dimensional arrays, five-dimensional arrays, and so on. In general, we can take the relation R to be an $(n+1)$-place relation, associated with an n-dimensional array. This leads to generalized formulations of our definitions.

Definition. Let R be an $(n+1)$-place relation, and $D_1, \ldots, D_n$ be sets. Then,

2 The diagonal argument

R is an *array* on $D_1, \ldots, D_n$

$$\leftrightarrow_{df} \forall x_1, \ldots, x_n(x_1 \in D_1 \& \ldots x_n \in D_n \to \exists!z R x_1 \ldots x_n z).$$

Definition. If for all k, $1 \le k \le n$, F_k is a 1-1 function from D_k into D_{k+1} and range(F_k) = domain(F_{k+1}), then

F is *a diagonal on* $D_1 \ldots D_n$

$\leftrightarrow_{df}$ F is a set of ordered n-tuples such that

$$\langle w_1, w_2, \ldots, w_n \rangle \in F \text{ iff } w_k \in \text{domain} F_k \text{ and } F_k(w_k) = w_{k+1}.$$

Definition. Let R be an array, and F a diagonal, on $D_1, \ldots, D_n$. Then,

G is *the value of the diagonal* F *in* R

$$\leftrightarrow_{df} \forall x_1, \ldots, x_n, z(G x_1 \ldots x_n z \leftrightarrow F x_1 \ldots x_n \& R x_1 \ldots x_n z).$$

Definition. Let R be an array, and F a diagonal, on $D_1, \ldots, D_n$. H is *a countervalue of* F *in* R $\leftrightarrow_{df}$

(i) $\forall x_1, \ldots, x_n(\exists z H x_1 \ldots x_n z \leftrightarrow F x_1 \ldots x_n).$
(ii) $\forall x_1, \ldots, x_n, z, z'(H x_1 \ldots x_n z \& H x_1 \ldots x_n z' \to z = z').$
(iii) $\forall x_1, \ldots, x_n, z(H x_1 \ldots x_n z \to z \in \text{range} R).$
(iv) $\forall x_1, \ldots, x_n, z(H x_1 \ldots x_n z \to \neg R x_1 \ldots x_n z).$

Definition. Let R be an array on D_1 and D_2, and let K be a value or countervalue of a diagonal F of R. Then,

K *occurs as a row of* R

$$\leftrightarrow_{df} \exists d \in D_1 \forall x_1, \ldots, x_n, z(H x_1 \ldots x_n z \to R d x_2 \ldots x_n z).$$

We can now prove a generalized version of the diagonal theorem:

Theorem 2.2. *Let* R *be an array, and* F *a diagonal, on* $D_1, \ldots, D_n$. *Let* H *be a countervalue of* F. *Then,* H *does not occur as a row of* R.

Proof.

(1) Show $\neg \exists w \in D_1 \forall x_1, \ldots, x_n, z(H x_1 \ldots x_n z \to R w x_2 \ldots x_n z)$
(2) $\exists w \in D_1 \forall x_1, \ldots, x_n, z(H x_1 \ldots x_n z \to R w x_2 \ldots x_n z)$
                          Assumption (H occurs as a row)
(3) $\forall x_1, \ldots, x_n, z(H x_1 \ldots x_n z \to R w x_2 \ldots x_n z)$
                          2, EI
(4) $\forall x_1, \ldots, x_n(\exists z H x_1 \ldots x_n z \leftrightarrow F x_1 \ldots x_n)$
                          Premise (H is a countervalue)

(5) $\forall x_2 \ldots x_n (\exists z H d x_2 \ldots x_n z \leftrightarrow F d y)$
                                      4, UI

(6) $\forall x \in D_1 \, \exists x_2 \in D_2 \ldots \exists x_n \in D_n \, F x x_2 \ldots x_n$
                                        Premise (F is a diagonal)

(7) $\exists x_2 \in D_2 \ldots \exists x_n \in D_n \, F d x_2 \ldots x_n$
                                        6, UI

(8) $F d e_1 \ldots e_{n-1}$ 7, EI

(9) $F d e_1 \ldots e_{n-1} \rightarrow \exists z H d e_1 \ldots e_{n-1} z$
                                        5, UI, SL

(10) $\exists z H d e_1 \ldots e_{n-1} z$ 8, 9, SL

(11) $H d e_1 \ldots e_{n-1} f$ 10, EI

(12) $H d e_1 \ldots e_{n-1} f \rightarrow R d e_1 \ldots e_{n-1} f$
                                           3, UI

(13) $R d e_1 \ldots e_{n-1} f$ 11, 12, SL

(14) $\forall x_1, \ldots, x_n, z (H x_1 \ldots x_n z \rightarrow \neg R x_1 \ldots x_n z)$
                                       Premise (H is a countervalue)

(15) $H d e_1 \ldots e_{n-1} f \rightarrow \neg R d e_1 \ldots e_{n-1} f$
                                           14, UI

(16) $\neg R d e_1 \ldots e_{n-1} f$ 11, 15, SL

In Section 2.3, we presented a number of diagonal results that were interpretations of the diagonal theorem for the case $n = 2$. In fact, *any* of these results may be presented as diagonal results for *any* value of n. It is just a matter of finding suitable adjustments of the array and the diagonal. Consider, for example, a three-dimensional diagonal argument that establishes Cantor's power set theorem. Given any set X, let D_1 be the power set of X, let D_2 be X, and let D_3 be the proper class of all sets. Let the array R be given by

$$R(x_1, x_2, x_3) = \begin{cases} 1, & \text{if } x_2 \in x_1 \ \& \ x_2 \in x_3, \\ 0, & \text{otherwise.} \end{cases}$$

We suppose, for reductio, that there is a diagonal F, a set of ordered triples, where the associated functions F_1 and F_2 are as follows: F_1 is a 1–1 function from D_1 into D_2, and $F_2 = F_1^{-1}$, the inverse of F_1. A countervalue H of F is given by

$$H(x_1, x_2, x_1) = \begin{cases} 1, & \text{if } x_2 \notin x_1, \\ 0, & \text{otherwise.} \end{cases}$$

We may go on to obtain Cantor's theorem in the obvious way. The argument is easily expanded to still higher dimensions – one could, for example, add a fourth dimension by letting $D_4 = D_3$, replacing '$x_2 \in x_1 \ \&$ $x_2 \in x_3$' by '$x_2 \in x_1 \ \& \ x_2 \in x_3 \ \& \ x_2 \in x_4$' in the characterization of R, and letting F_3 be the identity function. Such mutual adjustments of the array and the diagonal are easily found for the other diagonal arguments of Section 2.3.

The generalization to diagonal arguments of higher dimensions prompts a search for new paradoxes and new diagonal results. We are familiar with paradoxes constructed from two-place predicates, like 'is true of' or 'is a member of'. Are there further paradoxes constructible from three-place, and perhaps higher-place predicates?

Consider the two-place predicates of English. Take any three, say 'is longer than', 'loves', and 'hits'. Suppose we construct a sentence by flanking the first of these predicates by the quotations of the other two. We obtain

'Loves' is longer than 'hits'.

We can ask whether these three predicates are related so as to produce a true sentence. In the present case, the predicates are so related.

Now take any one two-place predicate, say 'is longer than'. We can form a sentence by flanking this predicate by quotations of itself:

(1) 'Is longer than' is longer than 'is longer than'.

Here we obtain a false sentence. Other predicates generate true sentences; for example,

(2) 'Is an expression of the same language as' is an expression of the same language as 'is an expression of the same language as'.

So we may divide the two-place predicates into two groups: those that yield true sentences when flanked by their own quotations, and those that yield false sentences when flanked by their own quotations.

Let us introduce the two-place predicates 'truly joins quotations of' and 'falsely joins quotations of'. In general, where F and G are two-place predicates,

F truly (falsely) joins quotations of G iff the result of flanking F by quotations of G is a true (false) sentence.

So, for example, 'is an expression of the same language as' truly joins 'loves', and truly joins 'is an expression of the same language as' (since sentence (2) is true). On the other hand, 'is longer than' falsely joins quotations of 'loves' and also falsely joins 'is longer than' (since sentence (1) is false).

Now consider the sentence

(3) 'Falsely joins quotations of' falsely joins quotations of 'falsely joins quotations of'.

Appendix: Extensions of the diagonal theorem

Suppose (3) is true. Then what (3) says is the case, and so when the predicate 'falsely joins quotations of' is flanked by quotations of itself, a false sentence is produced. But the sentence produced is (3), and so (3) is false. Suppose, on the other hand, that (3) is false. Then the predicate 'falsely joins quotations of' *does* falsely join quotations of itself, and since that is what (3) says, (3) is true. We have a contradiction either way, and we are landed in paradox.

We can represent our paradox as a three-dimensional diagonal argument. Let $D_1 = D_2 = D_3 = $ the set of two-place predicates of English. The three-dimensional array R is given by

$$R(x, y, z) = \begin{cases} 1, & \text{if the result of flanking } x \text{ to the left by the quotation of } y \\ & \text{and to the right by the quotation of } z \text{ is a true sentence,} \\ 0, & \text{if the result of flanking } x \text{ to the left by the quotation of } y \\ & \text{and to the right by the quotation of } z \text{ is a false sentence.} \end{cases}$$

The diagonal F on D_1, D_2, and D_3 is the set of identity triples of two-place predicates of English: F_1 and F_2 are each the identity function. The countervalue of F in R is given by

$$H(x, x, x) = \begin{cases} 1, & \text{if the result of flanking } x \text{ to the left and to the right} \\ & \text{by the quotation of } x \text{ is a false sentence,} \\ 0, & \text{if the result of flanking } x \text{ to the left and to the right} \\ & \text{by the quotation of } x \text{ is a true sentence.} \end{cases}$$

Now the countervalue cannot occur as a row. That is, there is no two-place predicate d of English such that

R(d, x, x) iff the result of flanking x to the left by the quotation of x and to the right by the quotation of x is a false sentence.

But consider the predicate 'falsely joins quotations of'. If we flank this predicate by quotations of a predicate x, we obtain a true sentence iff the result of flanking x to the left and to the right by the quotation of x is a false sentence. So we obtain a contradiction. Our diagonal argument generates a paradox.

We might think of our paradox as a three-dimensional analogue of the two-dimensional heterological paradox. The heterological paradox is constructed from the two-place relation that holds between one-place predicates x and y iff appending x to the quotation of y yields a true sentence. Our present paradox is constructed from the three-place relation that holds between two-place predicates x, y, and z iff flanking x by the quotations of y and of z yields a true sentence. This suggests a pattern that extends to higher dimensions.

2 The diagonal argument

In general, we can construct an "n-dimensional" analogue of the heterological paradox. Let $p_1, p_2, ..., p_{n+1}$ be n-place predicates of English, and consider the $(n+1)$-place relation that holds between them iff the result of filling the gaps in p_1 in order by quotations of $p_2, ..., p_{n+1}$ is a true sentence. We can go on to consider those n-place predicates that yield a false sentence when each of their gaps is filled by their own quotations. Consider now the n-place predicate d: 'x_1 falsely joins quotations of x_2 and ... and x_n'. If all the gaps of d are filled by the quotation of an n-place predicate that yields a false sentence when each of its gaps is filled by its own quotation, we obtain a true sentence; and if the gaps of d are filled by the quotation of an n-place predicate that yields a true sentence when each of its gaps is filled by its own quotation, we obtain a false sentence. The appropriate n-dimensional diagonal argument establishes that there is no such n-place predicate d, and we have a paradox. Notice that we obtain a Liar sentence analogous to (3) if we fill each gap in d by the quotation of d.

Let us turn now to a second kind of extension of the diagonal theorem. The intuition behind this extension runs as follows. Suppose we have a (two-dimensional) array and a diagonal, as suggested by

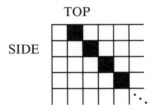

Recall that a diagonal need not cross every column; in our present illustration, the diagonal does not cross the first column. Suppose we were to move each cell of this diagonal to another row and/or another column, in such a way that no other cell is moved to this row or column, and every row contains a cell. One systematic way to do this in the present case is to shift each cell one column to the left, so as to obtain

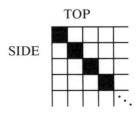

Appendix: Extensions of the diagonal theorem

We produce a new diagonal (one that happens to cross every column). There are countless ways to produce new diagonals (e.g., moving each cell one column to the right, two columns to the right, etc.). The present idea is that the diagonal theorem will hold for any of these new diagonals. In general we can state a version of the diagonal theorem that holds not only for the original diagonal, but for any diagonal obtainable from it.

Theorem 2.3. *Let* R *be an array, and* F *a diagonal on* D_1 *and* D_2. *Let* j *be a* 1-1 *function from* D_1 *(the domain of* F*) onto* D_1, *and let* k *be a* 1-1 *function from the range of* F *into* D_2. *Then* H *does not occur as a row, where*

    (i) $\forall x \, \forall y (\exists z \mathrm{H} \mathrm{j}(x) \mathrm{k}(y) z \leftrightarrow \mathrm{F} xy)$,
    (ii) $\forall x \, \forall y \, \forall z \, \forall z' (\mathrm{H} xyz \,\&\, \mathrm{H} xyz' \leftrightarrow z = z')$,
    (iii) $\forall x \, \forall y \, \forall z (\mathrm{H} xyz \rightarrow z \in \mathrm{range} \mathrm{R})$, *and*
    (iv) $\forall x \, \forall y \, \forall z (\mathrm{H} xyz \rightarrow \neg \mathrm{R} xyz)$.

Proof. Let $F = \{\langle x_1, y_1 \rangle, \langle x_2, y_2 \rangle, \langle x_3, y_3 \rangle, \dots\}$ and let

$$F' = \{\langle \mathrm{j}(x_1), \mathrm{k}(y_1) \rangle, \langle \mathrm{j}(x_2), \mathrm{k}(y_2) \rangle, \langle \mathrm{j}(x_3), \mathrm{k}(y_3) \rangle, \dots\}.$$

It is straightforward to show that F is a diagonal iff F' is a diagonal. So H is the countervalue of the diagonal F', and so, by the basic diagonal theorem, H cannot occur as a row.

For an application of this generalized diagonal theorem, consider Kleene's proof that there is no effective procedure for deciding, given any x, whether or not φ_x is a total function. Kleene's result can be stated as follows: There is no recursive function f such that

$$f(x) = \begin{cases} 1, & \text{if } \varphi_x \text{ is total,} \\ 0, & \text{if } \varphi_x \text{ is not total.} \end{cases}$$

Suppose, toward a contradiction, that there is such a recursive f. We will assume that we have fixed an algorithmic procedure that lists all sets of instructions for recursive functions. This procedure associates with each integer x the set of instructions at the $(x+1)$st place in the list. Integer x is the Gödel number of the associated set of instructions and a Gödel number of the function that those instructions determine. The side D_1 is the set of sets of instructions for total recursive functions; the top D_2 is the set of natural numbers. The many-valued array R is given by

    $R(x, y) =$ the result of applying the function determined by x
                to argument y.

The diagonal F is a 1-1 function from D_1 into D_2 that carries each set of instructions to its Gödel number. Notice that this diagonal does not pass through every column, since not all recursive functions are total. Our strategy is to obtain from this diagonal another that *does* cross every column. Define g by

$g(0) = \mu y[f(y) = 1]$ (where 'μy' is read as 'the least y such that'),

$g(x+1) = \mu y[y > g(x)$ and $f(y) = 1]$.

Function g is a 1-1 function from N onto the set G of Gödel numbers of total functions, and its inverse g^{-1} is a 1-1 function from G onto N. Via the function g^{-1}, we can obtain a new diagonal from the original: if $\langle x, y \rangle$ is a cell of the original diagonal, then $\langle x, g^{-1}(y) \rangle$ is the corresponding cell of the new diagonal. This new diagonal crosses every column.

Let a countervalue H be given by

$H(x, y) =$ the result of applying the function determined by x to argument y, and adding 1,

where $\forall x \, \forall y (\exists z H x g^{-1}(y) z \leftrightarrow F x y)$. The countervalue is associated with the following set of instructions: "Given any natural number y, compute $g(y)$, apply $\varphi_{g(y)}$ to y, and then add 1"; let the function determined by this set of instructions be h. By our generalized diagonal theorem, the countervalue does not occur as a row; that is to say, the set of instructions that determine h is not a member of D_1. But now we can obtain a contradiction, since we can now show that h *is* total and recursive, and so the set of instructions that determine h *is* a member of D_1. Since there are denumerably many total recursive functions, $f(y) = 1$ for denumerably many y, and so g is a total function. Since g is total, and $\varphi_{g(y)}$ is total, h is total. *The point of constructing a new diagonal that passes through every column emerges here.* Since we have an algorithm for g, by Church's thesis, g is recursive. And since we have an algorithm for h, in terms of recursive g, h is recursive, by Church's thesis. And so h is total and recursive.[37]

No doubt more can be done by way of extending and generalizing our basic diagonal theorem.[38] And certainly we have not exhausted the applications of those generalizations that we have described.[39] But I hope to have identified two central ways in which we can build on our basic diagonal theorem.

Chapter 3

The diagonal argument and the Liar, I

In this chapter and the next, our analysis of good and bad diagonal arguments is applied to a variety of leading solutions to the Liar. I shall argue that good diagonal arguments show the inadequacy of several current proposals. These proposals, though quite different in nature, are shown to fail for the same reason: They fail to capture our ordinary semantic concepts. I shall also argue that another proposal, according to which natural languages are not universal but rather expressively incomplete, gives rise to a bad diagonal argument, and so leads us back to paradox. The critical examination of these proposals provides criteria of adequacy for any solution to the Liar.

In Chapter 1, we saw that diagonalization and semantic universality tend in opposite directions. We spoke of "diagonalizing out of a language": Given any language, a diagonal construction apparently produces semantic concepts beyond the expressive capacity of the language. And yet, it seems, natural languages are semantically universal: Any natural language can express its own semantic concepts. It would appear that we must either find fault with the diagonal construction or else give up semantic universality.

Some truth-value gap theorists are motivated by the intuition that natural languages are universal.[1] According to R. L. Martin, gap solutions of the kind he endorses "retain the intuitive view of language as universal and give up intuitions about what we thought there was to be said."[2] Faced with semantic paradox, we may be pulled in two different directions. Unwilling to give up the idea that natural languages are semantically universal, we might be drawn to a gap approach like Martin's. According to such a view, sentences like ' "Heterological" is heterological' are without truth value, and the associated diagonal reasoning is blocked. On the other hand, we might convert the heterological paradox into a diagonal proof that *heterologicality* is an inexpressible concept, since the assumption that there is a term that expresses this concept leads to contradiction. This is an instance of the more general claim that natural languages are expressively incomplete. These opposed ways out of the Liar – the "truth gap" proposal and the "incompleteness" proposal – are the subjects of the present chapter.

3.1. A PROBLEM FOR TRUTH GAP THEORIES

The admission of truth gaps may raise hopes that we can maintain the intuition that natural languages are universal, or at least semantically universal. Martin claims that if we allow truth-value gaps, we may deny that there is any concept of heterologicality *to be* expressed. The gap at the level of language is matched by a gap at the level of ontology. Martin speaks of another gap, between the situations before and after analysis: Before analysis we thought there was more to be said than what analysis reveals there is to be said.[3] There is no unrestricted concept of heterologicality, but instead a *restricted* concept of heterologicality, which *is* expressible. We might think of it as a Fregean concept that yields neither truth nor falsity as value for certain arguments.

If we accept Martin's argument thus far, hopes of universality are not yet dashed. However, there is a difficulty for any truth gap account.[4] Paul of Venice challenges the proponent of truth gaps this way:

> Socrates says "I do not say what is true" and nothing else that is not part of it. [I] ask whether Socrates says what is true or what is not true. If [he says] one of these, then I have my intended [conclusion]. If neither, it follows that there is a mean between contradictories – which is impossible.[5]

Paul's argument is in terms of nontruth rather than falsity. Paul's example "closes the gap" – there is nothing between truth and nontruth. But then, how can such examples be resolved in terms of truth gaps?[6]

We can carry over Paul's challenge to the case of the heterological paradox. There too we can "close the gap": Given truth gaps, we can legitimately form the concept *is an expression which is false or neither true nor false of itself* (or *superheterologicality,* for short). The assumption that *this* concept is expressible leads to a contradiction. For suppose that the term 'superheterological' denotes this concept. Then, whether we assume 'superheterological' is true of itself, false of itself, or neither true nor false of itself, we obtain a contradiction. Adopting gaps and assuming universality leads to contradiction: The gaps allow the construction of a concept that, if assumed to be expressible, generates a paradox. But the point is not just that an appeal to truth gaps fails to preserve intuitions about universality. This new paradox arises out of the appeal to gaps and must be resolved in some other way. The truth-value gap theorist fails to provide a general, unified account of semantic paradox.

3.2. KRIPKE'S THEORY OF TRUTH

Kripke's theory of truth has been perhaps the most influential work on the Liar since that of Tarski.[7] Unlike previous proponents of truth gap approaches, Kripke provided a fully developed *theory* of truth. I shall argue that Kripke's theory is subject to the problem just rehearsed. Since Kripke supplies a formally rigorous account, we will be able to articulate the problem in a correspondingly precise way.

Kripke investigates languages allowing truth-value gaps. One intuition about truth that Kripke wants to capture is the following. Suppose you are explaining the word 'true' to someone who does not understand it. You might start with sentences not themselves containing the word 'true', say

(1) Snow is white,

and explain that we are entitled to assert that such a sentence is true under precisely those circumstances in which we can assert the sentence itself. Now what of sentences themselves containing the word 'true'? Our subject can begin to deal with these. Consider the sentence

(2) Some sentence printed on p. 15 of Tarski's "The Semantic Conception of Truth" is true.

If our subject has learnt her lesson concerning sentence (1), and is willing to assert that snow is white, she will also be willing to assert '(1) is true'. Since (1) appears on p. 15 of Tarski's "The Semantic Conception of Truth", our subject can deduce (2) by existential generalization. She will then be able to assert (2), and hence to assert (3):

(3) (2) is true.

In this way, our subject will be able to attribute truth (or falsity) to more and more sentences themselves containing the notion of truth (or falsity). The notion of level has a clear, intuitive role to play here. Those sentences not containing any semantic predicate are of level 0; those sentences that say of sentences of level 0 that they are true or false are of level 1; those sentences that say of sentences of level 1 that they are true or false are of level 2; and so on. The sentences that receive a truth value in this process are the *grounded* sentences. Pathological, though nonpara-doxical sentences, like

(4) (4) is true,

and paradoxical sentences, like

(5) (5) is false,

never receive a truth value in this process and are ungrounded. These sen-tences, then, suffer from truth-value gaps.

To formalize these ideas, Kripke develops a semantic scheme that can deal with predicates that are only partially defined. Given a nonempty domain D, a one-place predicate $P(x)$ is interpreted by the pair $\langle S_1, S_2 \rangle$ of disjoint subsets of D. Kripke calls S_1 the *extension* of $P(x)$, and S_2 the *anti-extension* of $P(x)$; $P(x)$ is true of the objects in S_1, false of the ob-jects in S_2, and undefined otherwise.

Connectives are handled using Kleene's strong three-valued logic.[8] Negation, disjunction, conjunction, and the conditional are character-ized by the following tables:

P	¬P
t	f
f	t
u	u

PvQ P\Q	t	f	u
t	t	t	t
f	t	f	u
u	t	u	u

P&Q P\Q	t	f	u
t	t	f	u
f	f	f	f
u	u	f	u

P→Q P\Q	t	f	u
t	t	f	u
f	t	t	t
u	t	u	u

Turning to the quantifiers, $\exists x A(x)$ is true if $A(x)$ is true for some assign-ment of an element of D to x, false if $A(x)$ is false for all assignments to x, and undefined otherwise. $\forall x A(x)$ is true if $A(x)$ is true for all assign-ments to x, false if $A(x)$ is false for at least one such assignment, and undefined otherwise.

Kripke proceeds by letting L be an interpreted, classical first-order language, with a finite or denumerable list of primitive predicates. The variables range over some nonempty domain D, and the primitive n-ary predicates are interpreted by (totally defined) n-ary relations on D. The language L is rich enough to express its own syntax and, for some coding scheme, to code finite sequences of elements of D into elements of D. Now, L is extended to a language $\mathcal{L}$ by adding the one-place truth predi-cate $T(x)$, which is partially defined. Let a partial interpretation of $T(x)$ be given by $\langle S_1, S_2 \rangle$; $\mathcal{L}(S_1, S_2)$ is the interpretation of $\mathcal{L}$ with $T(x)$ thus interpreted. Let S_1' be the set of codes of true sentences of $\mathcal{L}(S_1, S_2)$, and S_2' be the set of all elements of D that are either not codes of sentences of

$\mathcal{L}$ or are codes of false sentences of $\mathcal{L}(S_1, S_2)$. Let the unary function φ be given by $\varphi(\langle S_1, S_2 \rangle) = \langle S_1', S_2' \rangle$. We can show that φ is *monotonic* – any sentence true or false in $\mathcal{L}(S_1, S_2)$ retains its truth value in $\mathcal{L}(S_1', S_2')$. Some terminology: $\langle X, Y \rangle \leqslant \langle Z, U \rangle$ iff $X \subseteq Z$ & $Y \subseteq U$. If $\langle X, Y \rangle \leqslant \langle Z, U \rangle$, we say that $\langle Z, U \rangle$ *extends* $\langle X, Y \rangle$.

Theorem 3.1. φ *is monotonic. That is, if* $\langle S_1, S_2 \rangle \leqslant \langle S_1^*, S_2^* \rangle$, *then* $\varphi(\langle S_1, S_2 \rangle) \leqslant \varphi(\langle S_1^*, S_2^* \rangle)$. *That is, if* $\langle S_1, S_2 \rangle \leqslant \langle S_1^*, S_2^* \rangle$, *then* $\langle S_1', S_2' \rangle \leqslant \langle S_1^{*\prime}, S_2^{*\prime} \rangle$.

Proof. The proof is by induction on the complexity of sentences.

Consider first the case in which σ is an atomic sentence. There are two subcases to consider:

(1) 'T' is not the predicate symbol of σ.

If $\sigma \in S_1'$, then σ is a true sentence of L, so $\sigma \in S_1^{*\prime}$. If $\sigma \in S_2'$, then σ is a false sentence of L, so $\sigma \in S_2^{*\prime}$.

(2) σ is T([τ]), for τ a sentence.

Suppose $\sigma \in S_1'$. Then $\tau \in S_1$. Given $S_1 \subset S_1^*$, $\tau \in S_1^*$. So T([τ]) $\in S_1^{*\prime}$, i.e., $\sigma \in S_1^{*\prime}$. Similarly, we can show that, if $\sigma \in S_2'$, then $\sigma \in S_2^{*\prime}$.

Consider next molecular cases.

(3) σ is $\tau_1 \vee \tau_2$.

Suppose $\sigma \in S_1'$. Then $\tau_1 \in S_1'$ or $\tau_2 \in S_1'$. Then, by the inductive hypothesis, $\tau_1 \in S_1^{*\prime}$ or $\tau_2 \in S_1^{*\prime}$. So $\sigma \in S_1^{*\prime}$. Suppose $\sigma \in S_2'$. Then $\tau_1 \in S_2'$ and $\tau_2 \in S_2'$. Then, by the inductive hypothesis, $\tau_1 \in S_2^{*\prime}$ and $\tau_2 \in S_2^{*\prime}$. So $\sigma \in S_2^{*\prime}$.

(4) σ is $\neg \tau$.

Suppose $\sigma \in S_1'$. Then $\tau \in S_2'$. Then, by the inductive hypothesis, $\tau \in S_2^{*\prime}$. So $\sigma \in S_1^{*\prime}$. Suppose $\sigma \in S_2'$. Then $\tau \in S_1'$. Then, by the inductive hypothesis, $\tau \in S_1^{*\prime}$. So $\sigma \in S_2^{*\prime}$.

(5) σ is $\exists x A(x)$.

Suppose $\sigma \in S_1'$. Then $A(x)$ is true for some assignment, say d, of an element of D to x. So $A(d) \in S_1'$. Then, by the inductive hypothesis, $A(d) \in S_1^{*\prime}$. So $\sigma \in S_1^{*\prime}$. Suppose $\sigma \in S_2'$. Then $A(x)$ is false for every assignment d of an element of D to x. So, for any d, $A(d) \in S_2'$. Then, by the inductive hypothesis, for any d, $A(d) \in S_2^{*\prime}$. So $\sigma \in S_2^{*\prime}$.

This completes the proof of Theorem 3.1

Kripke goes on to construct the *minimal fixed point*. Let $\mathcal{L}_0 = \mathcal{L}(\emptyset, \emptyset)$, where $\emptyset$ is the empty set. If α is a successor ordinal ($\alpha = \beta + 1$), $\mathcal{L}_\alpha =$

$\mathcal{L}(S_{1,\alpha}, S_{2,\alpha})$, where $S_{1,\alpha}$ is the set of codes of true sentences of $\mathcal{L}_\beta$, and $S_{2,\alpha}$ is the set of all elements of D that are either codes of false sentences of $\mathcal{L}_\beta$ or are not codes of sentences of $\mathcal{L}_\beta$. If λ is a limit ordinal, $\mathcal{L}_\lambda = \mathcal{L}(\bigcup_{\beta<\lambda} S_{1,\beta}, \bigcup_{\beta<\lambda} S_{2,\beta})$.

The following lemma is a consequence of the monotonicity of φ:

Lemma. *For each* α, $\langle S_{1,\alpha}, S_{2,\alpha} \rangle \leqslant \langle S_{1,\alpha+1}, S_{2,\alpha+1} \rangle$.

Proof. The proof is by transfinite induction.

Suppose first that $\alpha = 0$. Since in $\mathcal{L}_0$, $T(x)$ is undefined for all x, any interpretation of $T(x)$ extends the extension and anti-extension of $T(x)$. In particular, $\langle S_{1,0}, S_{2,0} \rangle \leqslant \langle S_{1,1}, S_{2,1} \rangle$.

Suppose second that $\alpha = \beta + 1$ (i.e., α is a successor ordinal). By the inductive hypothesis,

$$\langle S_{1,\beta}, S_{2,\beta} \rangle \leqslant \langle S_{1,\beta+1}, S_{2,\beta+1} \rangle.$$

By the monotonicity of φ,

$$\varphi(\langle S_{1,\beta}, S_{2,\beta} \rangle) \leqslant \varphi(\langle S_{1,\beta+1}, S_{2,\beta+1} \rangle),$$

that is, $\langle S_{1,\beta+1}, S_{2,\beta+1} \rangle \leqslant \langle S_{1,\beta+2}, S_{2,\beta+2} \rangle$. That is, $\langle S_{1,\alpha}, S_{2,\alpha} \rangle \leqslant \langle S_{1,\alpha+1}, S_{2,\alpha+1} \rangle$, as required.

Suppose third that α is a limit ordinal. By the definition of $\mathcal{L}_\alpha$ for α a limit ordinal, we have for each $\beta < \alpha$

$$\langle S_{1,\beta}, S_{2,\beta} \rangle \leqslant \langle S_{1,\alpha}, S_{2,\alpha} \rangle.$$

By the monotonicity of φ, for each $\beta < \alpha$

$$\varphi(\langle S_{1,\beta}, S_{2,\beta} \rangle) \leqslant \varphi(\langle S_{1,\alpha}, S_{2,\alpha} \rangle),$$

that is, $\langle S_{1,\beta+1}, S_{2,\beta+1} \rangle \leqslant \langle S_{1,\alpha+1}, S_{2,\alpha+1} \rangle$. By the inductive hypothesis, for each $\beta < \alpha$

$$\langle S_{1,\beta}, S_{2,\beta} \rangle \leqslant \langle S_{1,\beta+1}, S_{2,\beta+1} \rangle.$$

So $\langle S_{1,\beta}, S_{2,\beta} \rangle \leqslant \langle S_{1,\alpha+1}, S_{2,\alpha+1} \rangle$. Given the definition of $\mathcal{L}_\alpha$, it follows that $\langle S_{1,\alpha}, S_{2,\alpha} \rangle \leqslant \langle S_{1,\alpha+1}, S_{2,\alpha+1} \rangle$, as required.

This completes the proof of the lemma.

It is now straightforward to show that the extension and the anti-extension of the truth predicate $T(x)$ increase as the ordinal levels increase.

Theorem 3.2. *The extension and anti-extension of* $T(x)$ *increase with increasing* α.[9] *That is,*

$$\forall \alpha \, \forall \beta (\beta < \alpha \rightarrow \langle S_{1,\beta}, S_{2,\beta} \rangle \leqslant \langle S_{1,\alpha}, S_{2,\alpha} \rangle).$$

Proof. We prove $\forall \beta (\beta < \alpha \rightarrow \langle S_{1,\beta}, S_{2,\beta} \rangle \leqslant \langle S_{1,\alpha}, S_{2,\alpha} \rangle)$ by transfinite induction on α. The case $\alpha = 0$ is vacuous.

Suppose that $\alpha = \beta + 1$. Assume, as inductive hypothesis, that

$$\forall \gamma (\gamma < \beta \rightarrow \langle S_{1,\gamma}, S_{2,\gamma} \rangle \leqslant \langle S_{1,\beta}, S_{2,\beta} \rangle).$$

Now assume $\delta < \alpha$. We want to show $\langle S_{1,\delta}, S_{2,\delta} \rangle \leqslant \langle S_{1,\alpha}, S_{2,\alpha} \rangle$. Either $\delta = \beta$ or $\delta < \beta$. Suppose $\delta = \beta$. By the lemma, $\langle S_{1,\beta}, S_{2,\beta} \rangle \leqslant \langle S_{1,\beta+1}, S_{2,\beta+1} \rangle$, that is, $\langle S_{1,\delta}, S_{2,\delta} \rangle \leqslant \langle S_{1,\alpha}, S_{2,\alpha} \rangle$. Suppose $\delta < \beta$. Then by the inductive hypothesis, $\langle S_{1,\gamma}, S_{2,\gamma} \rangle \leqslant \langle S_{1,\beta}, S_{2,\beta} \rangle$. So, given the lemma, $\langle S_{1,\gamma}, S_{2,\gamma} \rangle \leqslant \langle S_{1,\alpha}, S_{2,\alpha} \rangle$. Either way, we have $\langle S_{1,\gamma}, S_{2,\gamma} \rangle \leqslant \langle S_{1,\alpha}, S_{2,\alpha} \rangle$ as required.

Suppose that α is a limit ordinal. Since at the limit level we take the union of sentences declared true or false at previous levels, we have $\langle S_{1,\beta}, S_{2,\beta} \rangle \leqslant \langle S_{1,\alpha}, S_{2,\alpha} \rangle$ for all $\beta < \alpha$.

This completes the proof of Theorem 3.2.

We can show that the process just described stops: there is an ordinal level at which all statements that *are* true (false) are *declared* true (false). That is, there is an ordinal ρ such that $\langle S_{1,\rho}, S_{2,\rho} \rangle = \langle S_{1,\rho+1}, S_{2,\rho+1} \rangle$, so that $\varphi(\langle S_{1,\rho}, S_{2,\rho} \rangle) = \langle S_{1,\rho}, S_{2,\rho} \rangle$, and $\langle S_{1,\rho}, S_{2,\rho} \rangle$ is a fixed point of φ.

Theorem 3.3. *There is a fixed point of φ.*

Proof. Suppose, toward a contradiction, that φ does not have a fixed point. Then for any ordinal β, there is a sentence of $\mathcal{L}$ that is first declared true at level $\beta + 1$.[10] The sentences of $\mathcal{L}$ form a set.[11] Consider the following function f: f carries each sentence of $\mathcal{L}$ to the ordinal number that corresponds to the level at which the sentence is declared true. Then the domain of f is the set of sentences of $\mathcal{L}$, while the range of f is a proper class of ordinals. But such a function violates the axiom of Replacement.

This completes the proof of Theorem 3.3.

Given that we started with the empty interpretation of $T(x)$, we have constructed a "smallest" fixed point, one that is extended by all other fixed points.[12]

Theorem 3.4. *The minimal fixed point is minimal.*

Proof. We will show that any fixed point extends the minimal fixed point. Let $\langle S_1, S_2 \rangle$ be any fixed point. We show by transfinite induction that $\langle S_{1,\alpha}, S_{2,\alpha} \rangle \leqslant \langle S_1, S_2 \rangle$, for all α. Suppose first $\alpha = 0$. Obviously, $\langle \emptyset, \emptyset \rangle \leqslant \langle S_1, S_2 \rangle$. Suppose second $\alpha = \beta + 1$. By the inductive hypothesis, $\langle S_{1,\beta}, S_{2,\beta} \rangle \leqslant \langle S_1, S_2 \rangle$. By monotonicity,

$$\varphi(\langle S_{1,\beta}, S_{2,\beta} \rangle) \leqslant \varphi(\langle S_1, S_2 \rangle).$$

So $\langle S_{1,\alpha}, S_{2,\alpha} \rangle \leqslant \langle S_1, S_2 \rangle$.

Suppose third that α is a limit ordinal. By the inductive hypothesis, $\langle S_{1,\beta}, S_{2,\beta} \rangle \preccurlyeq \langle S_1, S_2 \rangle$ for all $\beta < \alpha$. Then $\langle S_{1,\alpha}, S_{2,\alpha} \rangle \preccurlyeq \langle S_1, S_2 \rangle$, since at the limit level, we take the union of sentences declared true or false at previous levels.

This completes the proof of Theorem 3.4.

At the minimal fixed point, only the ungrounded and the paradoxical sentences are without truth value. $\mathcal{L}_\rho$ is a language that contains its own truth (falsity) predicate: There is a predicate of $\mathcal{L}_\rho$ which is true of exactly the codes of true (false) sentences of $\mathcal{L}_\rho$.

The language $\mathcal{L}_\rho$ is semantically universal to a remarkable degree. Kripke has shown that, by admitting truth gaps, we are able to construct formal languages that contain their own truth predicates.[13] The question naturally arises: Is $\mathcal{L}_\rho$ fully closed semantically? Can $\mathcal{L}_\rho$ express all of its own semantic concepts? The answer is in the negative. It can be shown that the complement of truth is *not* expressible in $\mathcal{L}_\rho$.[14]

The argument that yields this result is a good diagonal argument. Let the side D_1 be the set of one-place wffs of $\mathcal{L}$, and let the top D_2 be the set of natural numbers. The array R is given by

$$R(x, y) = \begin{cases} 1, & \text{if } x \text{ is true of } y, \\ 0, & \text{if } x \text{ is not true (i.e., is false or undefined) of } y. \end{cases}$$

The diagonal F is a 1–1 function that carries each wff in D_1 to its code. The countervalue H of F is given by

$$H(x, y) = \begin{cases} 1, & \text{if } x \text{ is not true (is false or undefined) of } y, \\ 0, & \text{if } x \text{ is true of } y. \end{cases}$$

The diagonal theorem tells us that no wff of $\mathcal{L}$ is true of exactly the codes of those wffs false or undefined of their own codes. This is an exact analogue of Tarski's theorem, with 'not true' now understood as 'false or undefined' since we are admitting truth gaps. Just as Tarski's good diagonal argument is associated with the heterological paradox, so our good diagonal argument is associated with the superheterological paradox. Both arguments establish that the respective object languages are not semantically universal.

Our theorem indicates that Kripke's truth-value gap approach cannot dispense with a Tarskian hierarchy.[15] The theorem forces the first step up such a hierarchy, to a metalanguage for $\mathcal{L}$, in which we can talk about the complement of T. One such metalanguage (call it $\mathfrak{M}$) is the language of Kripke's paper. $\mathfrak{M}$ can be regarded as containing no truth gaps, since a sentence either does or does not have a truth value in a given fixed point.[16] But now Tarski's theorem applies to $\mathfrak{M}$: 'True-in-$\mathfrak{M}$' is not contained in $\mathfrak{M}$, but in some further metalanguage. And so a Tarskian hierarchy is generated. Alternatively, one could add to $\mathfrak{M}$ a predicate T′, and by Kripke's construction obtain a fixed point interpretation of $\mathfrak{M} + T'$, so that T′ is the truth predicate of $\mathfrak{M} + T'$. Then we will need a further metalanguage to express the complement of T′ – and again, a Tarskian hierarchy is generated.

It is not just the goal of a universal language that Kripke must give up. We are forced up the hierarchy in order to avoid semantic paradoxes with which truth gaps cannot deal. And this shows that Kripke's gap theory does not provide a *general* solution to the Liar: ultimately, it is a Tarskian hierarchy of languages that allows us to escape semantic paradox.[17]

I think Kripke must (and in fact does) accept this objection. And I think Kripke would respond by arguing that the limitations forced on his theory do not diminish its significance. According to Kripke, though the minimal fixed point does not model a universal language, *it is a model of a significant stage of development of natural language.* Kripke writes:

> Such semantical notions as "grounded," "paradoxical," etc. belong to the metalanguage. This situation seems to me to be intuitively acceptable; in contrast to the notion of truth, none of these notions is to be found in natural language in its pristine purity, before philosophers reflect on its semantics (in particular, the semantic paradoxes). If we give up the goal of a universal language, models of the type presented in this paper are plausible as models of natural language at a stage before we reflect on the generation process associated with the concept of truth, the stage which continues in the daily life of nonphilosophical speakers.[18]

Kripke is claiming that, *for this stage of natural language,* his theory provides an adequate account of truth.[19]

Let us return to the proof of our diagonal theorem. Informally, we construct the sentence

"Is not true of itself" is not true of itself,

and go on to derive a contradiction; the theorem requires only the notions of truth and negation. The relevant notion of negation here is *exclusion negation.* If we interpret '¬' as exclusion negation, ¬A is true iff A is false or undefined, and ¬A is false iff A is true. Exclusion negation is contrasted with *choice negation.* If '¬' is interpreted as choice negation, ¬A is true iff A is false, ¬A is false iff A is true, and ¬A is undefined iff A is undefined. Now Kripke's construction of the minimal fixed point uses choice negation: Our theorem shows that the construction cannot be carried out if negation is taken to be exclusion negation. So Kripke has to relegate exclusion negation to a metalanguage.[20] Others too have sought to defend truth-value gap approaches this way. Terence Parsons writes,

"When we 'exclude exclusion negation' from our language we are not in fact excluding anything at all. For there is no such thing as exclusion negation in any formal language which accurately reflects our own native speech."[21]

This claim seems to me wrong as a matter of empirical fact. The notion of a meaningless sentence (in its ordinary, nontechnical sense) surely is in the repertoire of nonphilosophical speakers, and it is natural enough to infer 'A is not true' from 'A is meaningless'. This is a use of 'not' that is most plausibly analyzed as exclusion negation – here, 'not true' is not equivalent to 'false'. Further, if we accept that ordinary speakers have available to them the notion of a sentence being neither true nor false, then the inference from 'A is neither true nor false' to 'A is not true' is an intuitive one, and a use of exclusion negation appears in the conclusion.

But I think that this focus on negation is misguided anyway. It is not *negation* that is the real source of the gap theorist's troubles. Let us construct the superheterological paradox according to our analysis of the diagonal argument. The side D_1 and the top D_2 are the one-place predicates of English; the nonbivalent array R is given by

$$R(x, y) = \begin{cases} t, & \text{if } x \text{ is true of } y, \\ f, & \text{if } x \text{ is false of } y, \\ u, & \text{if } x \text{ is neither true nor false of } y, \end{cases}$$

and the diagonal F is identity. There are 2^ω ways of forming a countervalue. And just one of these countervalues, call it H_N, is associated with exclusion negation:

$$H_N(x, x) = \begin{cases} f, & \text{if } x \text{ is true of } x, \\ t, & \text{if } x \text{ is false of } x, \\ t, & \text{if } x \text{ is neither true nor false of } x. \end{cases}$$

This countervalue builds the concept *false of itself or neither true nor false of itself,* which can be alternatively expressed as *not true of itself,* where "not" is exclusion negation. But exclusion negation is not required to express this concept: We have just constructed it from the notions of *false* and *neither true nor false.* And the concepts associated with the other countervalues are each expressible in terms of the notions of *true, false,* and *neither true nor false.*[22] It is, in general, a mistake to see the emergence of paradox as having anything essentially to do with exclusion negation: What is essential, rather, is the *construction of a countervalue.*

In the present case, each countervalue is constructed from notions that *are* to be found in "nonphilosophical" language. In particular, the notion of a sentence being neither true nor false surely is in the repertoire of the ordinary speaker. This notion is composed of the everyday notions of truth and falsity, and the 'neither–nor' construction. And the notion has clear, intuitive application – for example, to meaningless or nonsensical sentences. Indeed, gap theorists themselves motivate truth gaps by appeal to our semantic intuitions, in ways independent of semantic paradox. As we have seen, Martin appeals to category considerations, while van Fraassen starts out from the Frege–Strawson theory of presupposition. Kripke himself is motivated by Strawson's doctrine. Of course, defending the introduction of truth gaps in these ways will involve *some* semantic reflection on language. But such reflection is couched in quite ordinary language; to use Kripkean terminology, it is expressed in language at a stage *prior to* reflection on the generation process associated with the concept of truth. Such intuitive motivation does not involve philosophical reflection on the Liar, on pain of circularity.

These are points missed by those who would defend truth-value gap theories by excluding exclusion negation. Parsons argues that though the noncreative definition

$$\psi =_{df} \text{the function that maps t to f and both f and u to t}$$

defines a function, the existence of exclusion negation is not thereby guaranteed. For according to Parsons, it must also be the case that "the truth-function in question can be assigned as the denotation of a unary connective that consistently forms falsehoods from truths and truths from sentences that are either false or neuter."[23] But even if there is no such unary connective in ordinary English, there are other means available *within ordinary English* for the construction of the associated countervalue, and the other countervalues too. Each of these countervalues is associated with a version of the Liar that may be expressed in ordinary language but may not be resolved by an appeal to truth gaps.[24]

Let me recapitulate my objection to Kripke's theory. There are two stages. First, our diagonal theorem demonstrates the need to ascend to a metalanguage: Hence, Kripke's truth gap approach is not a general or unified solution to semantic paradox. Second, Kripke cannot retreat to the claim that his approach provides a solution to the Liar for a certain significant stage of natural language: Diagonal arguments show that this stage of natural language has the resources to formulate paradoxes that Kripke's theory cannot solve.[25]

3.3. FUZZY LOGIC

The limitations of truth gap approaches to the Liar might suggest that we should make a more radical break with classical logic and semantics.

3 The diagonal argument and the Liar, I

Some have drawn this moral in connection with the formal treatment of vagueness. The application of a vague predicate like 'bald' yields sentences that are neither definitely true nor definitely false, and this encourages the introduction of truth gaps to provide a semantics for vague predicates. But now we are in danger of just pushing the problem back: we must avoid sharp lines between applications that are borderline and those that are not. And so we may turn to fuzzy logic.

The term 'fuzzy logic' is sometimes applied to systems that admit *nondenumerably many* truth values. One such system is obtained by a generalization of Łukasiewicz's three-valued logic. His three-valued tables for the sentential connectives are as follows:

P	¬P			$P \lor Q$				$P \& Q$				$P \to Q$	
			Q	t	f	u	Q	t	f	u	Q	t	f	u
		P					P				P			
t	f	t		t	t	t	t	t	f	u	t	t	f	u
f	t	f		t	f	u	f	f	f	f	f	t	t	t
u	u	u		t	u	u	u	u	f	u	u	t	u	t

Let the values t, f, u be represented by the numerical values $1, 0, 0.5$ respectively. Then, if $v(P)$ denotes the truth value of the proposition P, we have

$$v(\neg P) = 1 - v(P),$$
$$v(P \lor Q) = \max(v(P), v(Q)),$$
$$v(P \& Q) = \min(v(P), v(Q)),$$
$$v(P \to Q) = \min(1, 1 - v(P) + v(Q)).$$

These rules hold for the extended system in which the truth values are the real numbers in the interval $[0, 1]$.

Our corresponding array will have nondenumerably many values, as shown in the diagram on the facing page. And now it is clear that this kind of fuzzy logic fails to solve semantic paradox, and fails to ground the intuition that natural languages are universal, in an especially dramatic way. *We can form nondenumerably many countervalues.* (Again, negation plays no essential role here.) So there are uncountably many versions of the Liar with which fuzzy logic cannot deal. And there are more inexpressible semantic concepts than there are expressions in the language.

According to one influential writer, the extended Łukasiewicz system is a *non*fuzzy multivalued system and should be regarded only as a base

D_2 (predicates of English)

		P_1	P_2	P_3	...
	P_1	real in $[0, 1]$	real in $[0, 1]$	real in $[0, 1]$	...
D_1 (predicates of English)	P_2	real in $[0, 1]$	real in $[0, 1]$	real in $[0, 1]$	...
	P_3	real in $[0, 1]$	real in $[0, 1]$	real in $[0, 1]$	...
	⋮	⋮	⋮	⋮	⋱

logic for a genuinely fuzzy system. L. A. Zadeh starts with the nondenumerable set – call it L_1 – of truth values and, on the basis of L_1, constructs *fuzzy truth values*.[26] Central to Zadeh's construction is the notion of a *fuzzy set*. A fuzzy set has members to a certain degree. A fuzzy subset S of L_1 is associated with a *compatibility function,* which associates with each member of L_1 a real from $[0, 1]$ that indicates the grade of membership in S. The number 0 indicates no membership to any degree; 1 indicates full membership. We now specify a fuzzy subset of L_1 to be the fuzzy truth value *true*. Other fuzzy truth values are then defined derivatively. For example, as Zadeh characterizes it, the modifier 'very' "has the effect of squaring the compatibility function of its operand."[27] So if the value 0.6 belongs to *true* to degree 0.8, then it belongs to the fuzzy truth value *very true* to degree 0.64. The fuzzy truth values of Zadeh's logic, then, are *fuzzy subsets* of L_1. Zadeh distinguishes denumerably many fuzzy truth values, each with a linguistic label, "e.g., *true, very true, more or less true, rather true, not true, false, not very true and not very false,* etc."[28]

An example may bring out the intuitive content of Zadeh's fuzzy logic FL. Consider the sentence

(S) 'Heterological' is long.

Now 'long' is a vague predicate. The extension of 'long' is a fuzzy set: things belong to its extension to a greater or lesser degree. Suppose the word 'heterological' belongs to this fuzzy set to degree 0.9. The base logic, then, assigns the truth value 0.9 to (S). But according to Zadeh, 'true' itself is a vague predicate, and so no precise truth value is to be assigned to (S). Instead, (S) receives a fuzzy truth value, perhaps 'very true' (since 0.9 is a high degree of truth in the base logic, and 'very true' will correspond roughly to high degrees of truth in L_1). Zadeh argues that if we are trying to provide an account of fuzzy propositions like (S), it is clear that "the fuzzy truth-values of FL are more commensurate with the fuzziness of such propositions than the numerical truth-values of L_1."[29]

But the treatment of the notion of truth as itself fuzzy will not prevent the formation of countervalues. Our array now has denumerably many values: Each is a fuzzy subset of L_1. An array will look like this:

	P_1	P_2	P_3	...
P_1	true	not very true	not false	...
P_2	not very true and not very false	not true	very true	...
P_3	more or less true	false	not true and not false	...
⋮	⋮	⋮	⋮	⋱

We can form infinitely many countervalues. For one example, consider

$$H(x, x) = \begin{cases} \text{true,} & \text{if the result of predicating } x \text{ of itself receives} \\ & \text{a value other than true,} \\ \text{false,} & \text{if the result of predicating } x \text{ of itself is true.} \end{cases}$$

The associated good diagonal argument yields a semantic concept that is not expressible in Zadeh's fuzzy logic. There are infinitely many of these inexpressible semantic concepts, one for each countervalue. Each inexpressible semantic concept is associated with a version of the Liar that Zadeh's fuzzy logic cannot accommodate. And since Zadeh's fuzzy truth values are expressed in ordinary linguistic terms, these are versions of the Liar expressible in ordinary language.

3.4. A THESIS OF EXPRESSIVE INCOMPLETENESS

The introduction of truth gaps does not make possible semantic universality, on pain of the Liar. And fuzzy logic fares no better. In both cases, good diagonal arguments establish the expressive incompleteness of the object language. Perhaps then, *this is just the lesson that the Liar teaches:* There are (semantic) concepts that natural language cannot express. Such a line is taken by Herzberger.[30]

3.4 A thesis of expressive incompleteness

Herzberger's inexpressibility claims take the following form: A concept is inexpressible in some conceptual system if the semantic rules assign its extension to no term of that system.[31] Herzberger writes:

> Let a word or phrase be called *heterological* in case it is not true of itself. Grelling's paradox arises from the natural assumption that the word 'heterological', so defined, is true-of exactly those words or phrases which are not true-of themselves. A natural enough assumption; and yet it contradicts a theorem of elementary logic. *No* word can be true-of exactly those words or phrases which are not true-of themselves. Relative to a very simple view of concepts and the way they relate to words, we have our first negative expressibility result:

> No word of any unambiguous language can express the concept of heterologicality for that language.[32]

I think that we should reject this inexpressibility claim, even relative to the simple extensional view of concepts assumed here.[33]

Consider an extensional version of the heterological array from 2.3:

$$R(x, y) = \begin{cases} 1, & \text{if } x \text{ is true of } y, \\ 0, & \text{if } x \text{ is not true of } y. \end{cases}$$

If we follow Herzberger's line, we have no Liar-related reason to suppose that we are unable to fill in all the values of the bivalent array. Notice that though the English expression 'heterological' (or, 'is not true of itself') is in the side and top, there is no particular problem about its extension, since, according to Herzberger's claim, whatever its extension is, it is not such as to produce semantic paradox.[34] And we do not need to concern ourselves about gaps or fuzzy truth values: The thesis of expressive incompleteness is offered as an alternative to these ways out of the Liar. So it is a consequence of Herzberger's claim that the array can be completed, in a form like this:

	P_1	P_2	P_3	P_4	...
P_1	1	0	1	0	...
P_2	1	0	0	0	...
P_3	0	0	0	1	...
P_4	0	0	0	1	...
⋮	⋮	⋮	⋮	⋮	⋮	⋱

3 The diagonal argument and the Liar, I

Now we can produce a countervalue in the usual way. In our example, the countervalue looks like this:

$$
\begin{array}{c|ccccc}
 & P_1 & P_2 & P_3 & P_4 & \cdots \\
\hline
P_1 & 0 & & & & \\
P_2 & & 1 & & & \\
P_3 & & & 1 & & \\
P_4 & & & & 0 & \\
\vdots & & & & & \ddots
\end{array}
$$

And associated with this countervalue is a certain set (*the set of heterological terms of English,* we might be tempted to say, but of course these italicized words won't do the job). Our analysis provides a precise way of specifying the countervalue, given the fully determinate array, and so a precise way of specifying the associated set of English predicates.

But since our analysis may be expressed in English, the set associated with the countervalue may be specified in English. To deny this is to deny that we can talk about what we clearly *can* talk about: We surely can talk about the array and the various functions and sets associated with it. The countervalue is a determinate set of ordered triples, and the associated set of predicates of English is a determinate set of English predicates definable in terms of the countervalue. We can say that an English predicate P_i is a member of this set iff $\langle P_i, P_i, 1 \rangle$ is a member of the countervalue. And we can talk about all this in English – indeed, that is just what we are doing. Herzberger's inexpressibility claim has itself provided conditions that allow the specification of the countervalue and the associated set, *in English*. But if we can specify this set in English, then the set is the extension of a predicate of English.

Let 'Het' stand for this predicate. Is Het a member of the top and side of our array? If it isn't, then neither the side nor the top is the set of *all* one-place English predicates, contra Herzberger's assumption. Pursuing this line, one might conclude that a natural language like English is indefinitely extendable, continually expanding to cover more concepts. But this is not the thesis that Herzberger is proposing.

Suppose, then, that Het *is* a member of the top and side. Now we are landed in contradiction. In assuming that Het is a member of the top and side, we assume that we can fill in the values of its row and column; that is, we assume it has a definite extension. But supposing that we can fill in the value for the cell $\langle \text{Het}, \text{Het} \rangle$ leads to a contradiction. Herzberger does not prevent the formation of an array associated with a bad diagonal argument. The thesis of expressive incompleteness does not escape paradox. Of course, there are various ways to rehabilitate this bad diagonal argument. But Herzberger's way is no longer available: We have fixed the extension of Het on the basis of Herzberger's own assumptions. One way that *is* available is to deny the well-formedness of the set associated with the countervalue. But if we take this way, then we have given up Herzberger's thesis of expressive incompleteness.

A good diagonal argument has shown that Kripke's theory of truth ultimately cannot dispense with a Tarskian hierarchy. This limits the scope of Kripke's truth gap theory. Further, since the diagonal arguments utilize ordinary semantic concepts, the significance of Kripke's theory, qua solution to the Liar, is questionable. We can extract here a simple criterion of adequacy for a solution to the Liar: The formal theory must represent our semantic terms and concepts. I have argued that Kripke's theory fails to meet this criterion. Parallel remarks can be made about fuzzy logic.

We may identify another related criterion. A solution to the Liar must do justice to the expressive capacity of natural language. Tarski's intuition that natural languages are semantically universal is not easily dismissed. We should beware of claims that natural language is not semantically universal, that certain semantic concepts are inexpressible. As we have seen, at least one claim of this sort gives rise only to a bad diagonal argument and paradox.

Chapter 4

The diagonal argument and the Liar, II

Recall our objection to Kripke's truth gap theory. A good diagonal argument shows that there are semantic concepts beyond the reach of Kripke's object language: These concepts are expressible only in a metalanguage. So although Kripke's object language can be said to contain its own truth predicate, it is not semantically universal. Further, Kripke's theory does not provide a model of "ordinary" English, or of some "significant stage" of natural language. For the semantic concepts that are inexpressible in Kripke's object language are available to the ordinary speaker of English.

This two-part objection to Kripke's theory may be generalized. *In its general form, it presents a challenge to any purportedly non-Tarskian approach to the Liar,* not just those, like Kripke's, that appeal to truth gaps. We can express the challenge in the form of two questions. First, does the theory give rise to semantic concepts that can be expressed only in a metalanguage, on pain of paradox? If the answer to this question is affirmative, then the scope of the proposed non-Tarskian theory is limited. And an affirmative answer to the first question prompts this second question: Are these semantic concepts available to the ordinary speaker, independently of philosophical reflection on the Liar? If the answer to this second question is also in the affirmative, then not only is the scope of the proposed solution put into question, but so is its significance. For the Liar is constructed out of our ordinary semantic concepts, concepts expressed by our ordinary semantic terms. A proposed solution that fails to give an account of *our* semantic concepts fails to come to grips with the Liar. In this chapter, I shall argue that a wide range of current approaches to the Liar are vulnerable to this general form of objection.

4.1. HERZBERGER AND GUPTA AND STABLE TRUTH

The theories of Herzberger and Gupta are technically very similar.[1] As Herzberger notes, both theories "spring from a common concern: to

62

4.1 Herzberger and Gupta and stable truth

modify Kripke's theory of truth so as to admit the classical valuation scheme."[2] As with Kripke's theory, we start with an interpreted, first-order language L of the classical type and extend it to $\mathcal{L}$ by adding the truth predicate T. Now for Kripke, the interpretation of T is only partially defined. But for Herzberger and Gupta, the interpretation of T is classical: the "anti-extension" of T complements its extension. This means that certain sentences, like the Liar, will have inconsistent valuations at different levels: for example, 'This sentence is false' will be declared true at one stage, then false at the next, and so on. This is in sharp contrast with Kripke's construction: for Kripke, once a sentence is declared true or false, it retains its truth value at higher levels. Kripke's rejection of the classical valuation scheme makes possible a monotonic construction; Herzberger and Gupta adopt the classical scheme and give up monotonicity.

Let us fix some terminology. M is a model for L, and U is a set of sentences of $\mathcal{L}$. $\mathfrak{M} = \langle M, U \rangle$ is a classical model for $\mathcal{L}$ such that

$$T(k) \leftrightarrow A \in U,$$

where 'k' abbreviates a name of the sentence A. Intuitively, U is the extension of T in the model (M, U) – in Herzberger's phrase, U is the set of sentences "declared true" in $\mathfrak{M}$. Let U′ be the set of sentences of $\mathcal{L}$ that "are true" in $\mathfrak{M}$. Then the "jump operator" G is defined by

$$G(\langle M, U \rangle) = \langle M, U' \rangle.$$

As with Kripke's construction, the interpretation of T is built up through a transfinite ordinal process. Successor stages can be treated in Kripke's way. But limit stages cannot. Kripke's limit rule forms the union of all previous stages; and so, at stage ω, a Liar sentence like 'This sentence is false' would be placed in both the extension *and* the anti-extension of T, since its truth value alternates from one finite level to the next. So a critical difference between Kripke's construction, on the one hand, and the constructions of Herzberger and Gupta, on the other, lies in the choice of limit rules.

Suppose U is some subset of all sentences of $\mathcal{L}$. We now define $\mathfrak{M}_\alpha = \langle M, U_\alpha \rangle$ for all ordinals α. Let $U_0 = U$. $U_{\alpha+1}$ is the set of sentences true in $\mathfrak{M}_\alpha$. That is, the successor rule can be stated as $\mathfrak{M}_{\alpha+1} = G(\mathfrak{M}_\alpha)$. Herzberger's limit rule, for any (positive) limit ordinal λ, is given by

$$U_\lambda = \liminf_{\beta < \lambda} U_\beta = \{\sigma : \exists \beta < \lambda \ \forall \gamma (\beta \leqslant \gamma < \lambda \rightarrow \sigma \in U_\gamma)\}.$$

The intuition behind Herzberger's rule is that "at any transfinite limit stage what will be declared true will be exactly those statements which have been declared true at all sufficiently advanced previous stages."[3]

4 The diagonal argument and the Liar, II

Gupta proposes a different limit rule:

$$U_\lambda = \liminf_{\beta < \lambda} U_\beta \cup (U \cap \{\sigma : \neg\sigma \notin \liminf_{\beta < \lambda} U_\beta\}).$$

According to Gupta's limit rule, we subtract from our initial set U all the sentences that are, in Gupta's terminology, "locally stably false" at λ (these are the sentences declared false at all sufficiently advanced previous stages) and add to U all the sentences that are "locally stably true" at λ (i.e., the sentences declared true at all sufficiently advanced stages).[4] Gupta suggests that underlying our use of 'true' is a *revision procedure:* "When we learn the meaning of 'true' what we learn is a rule that enables us to *improve* on a proposed candidate for the extension of truth."[5] This rule is a *rule of revision*. Gupta's treatment of limit stages captures this idea: "We sum up the effects of all the earlier improvements."[6] Notice that, on Gupta's treatment, sentences in U that turn out to be *un*stable are retained in U_λ – we have no reason to revise them. Such sentences are excluded from U_λ on Herzberger's treatment – Herzberger prefers to make true no more sentences than he needs to.[7]

Both Herzberger's and Gupta's limit rules are concerned with sentences that are at least locally stable. But sentences that are locally stably true (false) at a limit λ may not remain true (false) beyond λ. Of special interest to both Herzberger and Gupta are the sentences that settle down forever, the *stably true* sentences and the *stably false* sentences. Let V be the set of stably true sentences; that is, $V = \{\sigma : (\exists\delta)(\forall\rho > \delta)\sigma \in U_\rho\}$. The following theorem holds for both Herzberger's and Gupta's presentations:

Theorem 4.1. *For all α, there is a limit ordinal $\rho > \alpha$ such that*

$$\liminf_{\alpha < \rho} U_\rho = V.$$

Proof. Let α be given. If $\sigma \in V$, $\exists\beta_\sigma$ such that

$$\rho > \beta_\sigma \to \sigma \in U_\rho.$$

Let $\beta_0 > \alpha$ and $\beta_0 > \beta_\sigma$ for all $\sigma \in V$. (Note that there is only a set of these ordinals β_σ.) Now,

$$\rho > \beta_0 \to V \subseteq U_\rho.$$

Thus, we have established a set U_ρ that contains all the stably true sentences. Having established this, we want to eliminate from U_ρ all the sentences that are not stably true.

$$\sigma \notin V \to \exists\beta'_\sigma \text{ such that } \beta'_\sigma > \beta_0 \ \& \ \sigma \notin U_{\beta'_\sigma}.$$

Let $\beta_1 > \beta'_\sigma$ for all $\sigma \notin V$.

$$\sigma \notin V \to \exists \beta_\sigma'' \text{ such that } \beta_\sigma'' > \beta_1 \,\&\, \sigma \notin U_{\beta_\sigma''}.$$

Let $\beta_2 > \beta_\sigma''$ for all $\sigma \notin V$, and so on, through $\beta_3, \ldots, \beta_i, \ldots$. Each $\sigma \notin V$ is (declared) false somewhere between any two β_i's. Let $\delta = \sup_i \beta_i$. And now,

$$V = \liminf_{\alpha < \delta} U_\delta.$$

For suppose, toward a contradiction, that $\sigma \in \liminf_{\alpha < \delta} U_\delta$ and $\sigma \notin V$. Since $\sigma \in \liminf_{\alpha < \delta} U_\delta$,

$$(\exists \eta < \delta)(\forall \gamma)(\eta \leqslant \gamma < \delta \to \sigma \in U_\gamma).$$

By EI,

(A) $$(\forall \gamma)(\eta_0 \leqslant \gamma < \delta \to \sigma \in U_\gamma).$$

Since $\sigma \notin V$,

$$(\exists \rho > \eta_0)\sigma \notin U_\rho.$$

By EI, $\sigma \notin U_{\rho_0}$. By our choice of δ, $\delta > \rho_0$. By UI on (A),

$$\eta_0 \leqslant \rho_0 < \delta \to \sigma \in U_{\rho_0}.$$

So $\sigma \in U_{\rho_0}$, and we have a contradiction. This completes the proof of Theorem 4.1.

Theorem 4.1 leads directly to another.

Theorem 4.2. *For all* M, U, *there are ordinals* η, β *such that, if* $\alpha \geqslant \eta$, *then* $U_\alpha = U_{\alpha+\beta}$ *and* $\liminf_{\gamma < \alpha} U_\gamma = \liminf_{\gamma < \alpha+\beta} U_\gamma$.

Proof. Let $\eta =$ the least ordinal such that $\liminf_{\gamma < \eta} U_\gamma = V$. Let β be the least ordinal such that

$$\liminf_{\gamma < \eta + \beta} U_\gamma = V.$$

And we now note that

$$U_\alpha = U_{\alpha'} \to U_{\alpha+1} = U_{\alpha'+1},$$

since the jump operator G, applied to identicals, yields identicals.
This completes the proof of Theorem 4.2.

Theorems 4.1 and 4.2 together show that from η, the least (limit) ordinal such that $\liminf_{\gamma < \eta} U_\gamma = V$, the construction cycles endlessly through a loop of length β, which Herzberger calls the "Grand Loop" (see figure at top of next page). On Herzberger's theory (but not Gupta's, because of the difference between their limit rules), we have

65

loop of length β

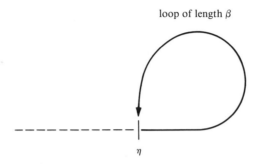

η

$$U\eta = \liminf_{\gamma < \eta} U_\gamma = V,$$ the set of *stably true* sentences.

At stage η, the true sentences are exactly those that will be true forever. Herzberger calls such a stage an *alignment point* – alignment points are continually reached as the construction cycles endlessly.

The alignment points of Herzberger's semi-inductive construction are the analogues of the fixed points of Kripke's inductive construction. And the stable truths of Herzberger's and Gupta's theories correspond to Kripke's grounded truths. Just as any attempt to connect Kripke's formal theory to natural language leads to consideration of the fixed points and the grounded truths, so, with the semi-inductive construction, we are led to Herzberger's alignment points and the stable truths.

But the notion of stable truth gives rise to paradoxes. Consider the sentence

(S) 'Is not stably true of itself' is not stably true of itself.

If (S) is stably true, then the predicate 'is not stably true of itself' is not self-applicable, and so (S) will never settle into the extension of truth – so (S) is not stably true. If (S) is not stably true, then the predicate 'is not stably true of itself' *is* self-applicable, and so (S) will settle into the extension of truth – so (S) is stably true.

A good diagonal argument provides a way out of paradox. Let the side D_1 be the set of one-place predicates of $\mathcal{L}$, and the top D_2 be the set of codes of predicates in D_1. The array R is given by

$$R(x, y) = \begin{cases} 1, & \text{if the result of predicating } x \text{ of } y \text{ is a stable truth,} \\ 0, & \text{otherwise.} \end{cases}$$

The diagonal F is the 1–1 function from predicates in D_1 to their codes. Under this interpretation, the diagonal theorem says that no predicate of $\mathcal{L}$ is stably true of the codes of predicates not stably true of their own codes. This is an analogue of Tarski's theorem. Just as we established the expressive incompleteness of Kripke's object language, so we now establish the expressive incompleteness of the object language of Herzberger and Gupta. Our good diagonal argument shows that $\mathcal{L}$ does not have the resources to express its own concept of stable truth – the predicate 'stably true in $\mathcal{L}$' must belong to a metalanguage for $\mathcal{L}$.

Herzberger accepts this, at least implicitly. He does not discuss the paradox of stable truths, but stable truth is a notion in the metalanguage in which he presents his theory of truth. Gupta is quite explicit about this matter: He says of the notion of stable truth that

> we have used it in the metalanguage to give an account of the concept of truth in the object language [$\mathcal{L}$]. This, it seems to me, does not in any way vitiate our account of the concept of truth. Further, when the notion is viewed this way the paradox does not arise.[8]

The first of our pair of questions was this: Does the theory give rise to semantic concepts that can be expressed only in a metalanguage, on pain of paradox? For the theories of Herzberger and Gupta, the answer is in the affirmative.

Now we can ask our second question, with respect to stable truth: Is the concept of stable truth available to the ordinary speaker, independently of philosophical reflection on the Liar? Herzberger and Gupta themselves suggest that the answer is yes. According to Herzberger and Gupta, the stable sentences of the formal object language $\mathcal{L}$ capture our intuitive notion of *semantically unproblematic sentences.* Gupta remarks, "It is reasonable to believe that [the stable sentences] include all the unproblematic sentences,"[9] and "The problematic sentences – such as the Liar and the truth teller ("This very sentence is true") – are, by our account, unstable."[10] But the ordinary speaker of English surely has the conceptual resources to distinguish semantically unproblematic and semantically problematic sentences: The problematic nature of Liar sentences is perfectly evident to one who has not yet reflected on ways out of semantic paradox.

And so the paradox of stable truths may be expressed in intuitive terms. We can form the concept associated with the relevant countervalue; the concept *does not yield a semantically unproblematic truth when appended to its own quotation.* Paradox issues in the usual diagonal fashion. This is a version of the Liar expressible in ordinary terms but beyond the reach of Herzberger's and Gupta's theories, as presented: The paradox forces an ascent through a Tarskian hierarchy of languages.

Now Gupta does go on to suggest, without elaboration, that it would be possible to view the notion of stable truth as belonging to the object language $\mathcal{L}$. We add the predicate 'stably true in $\mathcal{L}$' to the language $\mathcal{L}$. Then

> the paradox is present for the concept "stably true in $\mathcal{L}$." But we must ask how is the concept "stably true in $\mathcal{L}$" added to $\mathcal{L}$? It must be added, it would appear, by a rule of revision. But then can we not give an account of the new paradox parallel to that we gave of the old? [11]

This suggestion holds out the promise that we *can* dispense with the Tarskian hierarchy, that we can capture our intuitive notion of a semantically unproblematic sentence *within* the object language. But the suggestion will not work.

If the predicate 'stably true in $\mathcal{L}$' is a predicate of $\mathcal{L}$, then the following sentence is a sentence of $\mathcal{L}$:

(S*) (S*) is not stably true in $\mathcal{L}$.

Since (S*) is paradoxical, (S*) is not a stable truth of $\mathcal{L}$. That is, we may assert

(S′) (S*) is not stably true in $\mathcal{L}$.

So, while (S*) is paradoxical, (S′) is a true assertion. To account for this, we need to distinguish two stable truth predicates, one internal to $\mathcal{L}$, and one external to $\mathcal{L}$. The internal stable truth predicate is in the object language and expresses the concept for which the paradox is present. The second is in a metalanguage for $\mathcal{L}$, and (S*) is never in its extension. The need for the essentially richer language may be demonstrated by a good diagonal argument.

We might yet attempt to follow Gupta's general line by enriching the object language with this external stable truth predicate, expressing a further concept added by a rule of revision. But still this enriched object language will not express *its* external notion of stable truth. There is no end to this series of increasingly rich object languages. No language in the series will express its external notion of stable truth: A good diagonal argument guarantees this. This series of languages is quite analogous to a Tarskian hierarchy in which each language includes its predecessor as a proper part. Gupta cannot dispense with a Tarskian hierarchy.

It might be suggested that while we must accept a Tarskian account of the notion of stable truth, we can still accept a Gupta/Herzberger-style account of truth: We should accept a "mixed" theory of our semantic concepts.[12] However, this would mean an asymmetric treatment of our notions of *truth* and *semantically unproblematic truth*. Now it is a version of the Strengthened Liar that has forced a Tarskian treatment of the notion of a semantically unproblematic truth. Given the sentence

4.1 Herzberger and Gupta and stable truth

(1) (1) is not a semantically unproblematic truth,

we reason that (1) is semantically pathological and conclude that

(2) (1) is not a semantically unproblematic truth.

To account for the fact that (2) is true and (1) is paradoxical, we took the first step up a Tarskian hierarchy. But an exactly parallel version of the Strengthened Liar is present for the notion of truth, as we saw in Chapter 1. Given the sentence

(3) (3) is not true,

we reason that (3) is semantically pathological and conclude that

(4) (3) is not true.

Again, (4) is true, while (3) is paradoxical, and this calls for explanation. If we resolve the first version of the Strengthened Liar in the Tarskian way, then, symmetrically, we should treat this second version in the Tarskian way too. These ordinary stretches of reasoning are too similar to be treated differently.[13]

Moreover, once Tarskian hierarchies are admitted for even some of our ordinary semantic concepts, then Herzberger and Gupta face the problems that any Tarskian resolution faces. We can argue that in natural language there is just one predicate 'semantically unproblematic sentence' and just one predicate 'semantically unproblematic truth', and it is artificial to split these predicates into infinitely many distinct predicates, each defined with respect to a distinct language. And we can bring Gupta's own worries about the Tarskian approach to bear.[14] How, for example, are we to assign levels to ordinary occurrences of 'semantically unproblematic sentence' or 'semantically unproblematic truth'? What principles should be used for such assignments of levels? What is the level of the semantic predicates in, say, 'Nothing is both a semantically unproblematic truth and a semantically unproblematic falsehood'?[15]

To sum up, the theories of Herzberger and Gupta give rise to semantic concepts that can be expressed only in a metalanguage. These semantic concepts are available to the ordinary speaker, and so Herzberger and Gupta do not provide a model of our ordinary semantic concepts. A tandem theory that treats some of our semantic concepts via the semi-inductive construction and others via a Tarskian hierarchy fails to capture similarities in our ordinary semantic reasoning. And such a theory inherits the problems of the Tarskian approach.[16]

4 The diagonal argument and the Liar, II

4.2. FEFERMAN: A TYPE-FREE THEORY
OF PARTIAL PREDICATES

Kripke's construction is nonclassical and monotonic; the constructions of Herzberger and Gupta are classical and nonmonotonic. Feferman presents a modification of Kripke's construction that is classical and monotonic.[17] Unlike Kripke's model-theoretic approach, Feferman's approach is *proof theoretic* – the fixed point constructions are characterized axiomatically.

In Kripke's theory, we have the extension and anti-extension of the truth predicate T, where the anti-extension does not complement the extension; in Herzberger's and Gupta's theories, we have the extension of T and its full complement. Feferman's theory provides the extensions of two distinct predicates T and F (truth and falsity). These disjoint extensions are not complementary – but the extensions of T and ¬T, and of F and ¬F, are complementary, negation being classical.

Again, let L be a classical, first-order language. We obtain $\mathcal{L}_{T,F}$ by adding to L the truth predicate T and the falsity predicate F. Feferman's construction evaluates only *positive* formulas, and this is what guarantees monotonicity. A formula of $\mathcal{L}_{T,F}$ is *positive* if it is equivalent to one built up without negation from atomic formulas of $\mathcal{L}_{T,F}$ and negations of atomic formulas of L. Any formula φ of $\mathcal{L}_{T,F}$ has associated with it a formula φ^+ that is positive and approximates φ. Feferman notes that one way to obtain φ^+ is to put φ in prenex disjunctive normal form and replace each occurrence of ¬T or ¬F by F or T, respectively. Feferman calls φ^+ the *positive approximant* of φ; $\varphi^- = (\neg\varphi)^+$ is the positive approximant of the negation of φ. Feferman defines φ^+ and φ^- inductively as follows:

(i) $\varphi^+ = \varphi$ for all atomic φ of $\mathcal{L}_{T,F}$.

(ii) If φ is an atomic formula of $\mathcal{L}_{T,F}$, $\varphi^- = \neg\varphi$; if $\varphi = T([\psi])$, then $\varphi^- = F([\psi])$, and if $\varphi = F([\psi])$, then $\varphi^- = T([\psi])$.

(iii) $(\neg\varphi)^+ = \varphi^-$, and $(\neg\varphi)^- = \varphi^+$.

(iv) $(\varphi\,\&\,\psi)^+ = \varphi^+\,\&\,\psi^+$; $(\varphi\,\&\,\psi)^- = \varphi^-\vee\psi^-$.

(v) $(\varphi\vee\psi)^+ = \varphi^+\vee\psi^+$; $(\varphi\vee\psi)^- = \varphi^-\,\&\,\psi^-$.

(vi) $(\forall x\varphi)^+ = \forall x\varphi^+$; $(\forall x\varphi)^- = \exists x\varphi^-$.

(vii) $(\exists x\varphi)^+ = \exists x\varphi^+$; $(\exists x\varphi)^- = \forall x\varphi^-$.

At a fixed point, the following analogues of the Tarski truth schema hold, where 'k' is an abbreviation of a name for any sentence A of $\mathcal{L}_{T,F}$:

$$T(k) \leftrightarrow A^+,$$

$$F(k) \leftrightarrow A^-.$$

70

4.2 Feferman: A type-free theory of partial predicates

The extension of T consists of all sentences of $\mathcal{L}_{T,F}$ that are equivalent to true positive sentences; the extension of F consists of all sentences of $\mathcal{L}_{T,F}$ that are equivalent to false positive sentences. Liar sentences are neither in the extension of T nor in the extension of F. Consider, for example, the Liar sentence $A = \neg T(k)$. Suppose A is in the extension of T, that is, $T(k)$. Since $T(k) \leftrightarrow A^+$, and $A^+ = F(k)$, we obtain a contradiction. Suppose, on the other hand, A is in the extension of F, that is, $F(k)$. Since $F(k) \leftrightarrow A^-$, and $A^- = (\neg T(k))^- = (T(k))^+ = T(k)$, we obtain a contradiction. In particular, then, A is not in the extension of T – that is, A is not T. But we cannot truly say this in the object language, but only in a metalanguage.

It is straightforward to establish the need to ascend to a metalanguage formally by a good diagonal argument. Let FFP be a fixed point generated by Feferman's construction.[18] We take $\mathcal{L}_{T,F}$ as interpreted by FFP. Let the side D_1 be the set of one-place wffs of $\mathcal{L}_{T,F}$, and let the top D_2 be the set of natural numbers. The array R is given by

$$R(x, y) = \begin{cases} 1, & \text{if } x \text{ is T of } y, \\ 0, & \text{if } x \text{ is not T of } y. \end{cases}$$

The diagonal F carries wffs in D_1 to their codes. The countervalue H of F is given by

$$H(x, y) = \begin{cases} 1, & \text{if } x \text{ is not T of its code } y, \\ 0, & \text{if } x \text{ is T of its code } y. \end{cases}$$

The diagonal theorem says that no predicate of $\mathcal{L}_{T,F}$ under the interpretation FFP is T of exactly those predicates not T of their own codes. Such a predicate may be constructed if it is assumed that the complement of T is a predicate of $\mathcal{L}_{T,F}$.

So the answer to the first of our questions is affirmative: Feferman's theory does give rise to semantic concepts that can be expressed only in a metalanguage. At first glance, this may seem less of a problem for Feferman than it is for Herzberger and Gupta. In their theories, Herzberger and Gupta employ a semantic notion – stable truth – that cannot be expressed in the object language. But Feferman's account does not proceed model-theoretically; instead, Feferman describes the notion of truth axiomatically. And so, while Herzberger and Gupta are forced to a metalanguage in order to express a semantic concept that they themselves utilize, Feferman is not. So it might be argued that the fact that the language of FFP is not universal is not a defect of Feferman's theory.

But this argument misses the point. As we turn to our second question, we want to know whether Feferman provides an account of *our* semantic concepts. If so, then (at least) one of the models of Feferman's axioms is

71

a plausible model of natural language. Suppose it is claimed that, in this model, 'T' represents 'true' in English. Our theorem makes it clear that, on this supposition, Feferman cannot deal with quite 'ordinary' versions of the Liar, like 'This sentence is not true'. Feferman does not discuss this matter but would presumably respond that 'not true' in ordinary English is represented by 'F'. But this is, in essence, Kripke's way out, and as we have seen, it does not work. Again, we need not focus our attention on negation. Countervalues that produce paradoxes beyond the reach of Feferman's theory are constructible from the semantic predicates 'true', 'false', and 'neither true nor false'. So the semantic concepts that Feferman must relegate to a metalanguage are available to the ordinary speaker. The answer to our second question is also affirmative.

It is, then, hard to make out a connection between natural language and the language modeled by FFP. There is some irony in this. According to Feferman, the Strengthened Liar presents a problem for truth gap approaches: It shows that "the formal model-theoretic constructions don't match up with informal usage."[19]

4.3. MCGEE AND DEFINITE TRUTH

Like Feferman, and unlike Herzberger and Gupta, Vann McGee bases his formal theory on Kripke's monotonic constructions.[20] But McGee suggests a different way of thinking about Kripke's fixed point models. Rather than thinking of them as models in which sentences are true, false, or without truth value, we should think of them as "models in which sentences are definitely true, definitely not true, or unsettled, where 'unsettled' means, not 'neither true nor false' but 'either true or false but it is not settled which'."[21] So questions of truth may be left unsettled: McGee treats 'true' as a vague predicate.

He argues:

> That 'true' is a vague predicate should come as no surprise. Intuitively, when we assert or deny that 'Harry is bald' is true, we are saying the same thing as when we assert or deny that Harry is bald. If that is so, then, if the linguistic conventions that govern the use of the vague term 'bald' leave it unsettled whether or not Harry is bald, the linguistic conventions that govern the use of the term 'true' likewise leave it unsettled whether or not 'Harry is bald' is true. . . . The notion of truth inherits the vagueness of vague non-semantical terms.[22]

Associated with the nonsemantic vague term 'bald', we have:

72

4.3 McGee and definite truth

If Harry is definitely bald, 'Harry is bald' is definitely true.
If Harry is definitely not bald, 'Harry is bald' is definitely not true.
If it is unsettled whether Harry is bald, it is likewise unsettled whether 'Harry is bald' is true.

And we have an analogue of this for the vague predicate 'true':

(DT) If $[\varphi]$ is definitely true, $[[\varphi]$ is true] is definitely true.
If $[\varphi]$ is definitely not true, $[[\varphi]$ is true] is definitely not true.
If $[\varphi]$ is unsettled, $[[\varphi]$ is true] is unsettled.

Kripke's fixed point construction gives us (DT).[23]

Since McGee rejects the true/false/neither-true-nor-false trichotomy, Kleene's three-valued logic no longer provides an appropriate valuation scheme. Instead, McGee uses van Fraassen's notion of *supervaluation*.[24] We start with a classical first-order language L, with a first-order model A whose domain is D. We extend L to a language $\mathcal{L}$ by adding a one-place predicate $T(x)$. Suppose, in the usual Kripkean way, $\langle S_1, S_2 \rangle$ is an interpretation of $T(x)$, where S_1 is the extension of $T(x)$ and S_2 is the anti-extension of $T(x)$. An unrestricted use of supervaluations runs as follows: We say a sentence is true iff it is true by the ordinary classical valuation scheme in any interpretation $\langle S_1', S_2' \rangle$ that extends $\langle S_1, S_2 \rangle$ and is total (where an interpretation $\langle S_1', S_2' \rangle$ is total if the union of S_1' and S_2' is D). We can then define the minimal fixed point $\mathcal{L}_\rho$ as before.[25]

Now we need not use supervaluations where we take into account *all* total extensions, as we just have.[26] We may consider restrictions on total extensions. McGee restricts the admissible total extensions to those defining maximal consistent sets of sentences. Where Kripke speaks of a sentence being true under the supervaluation interpretation (as opposed to false or without truth value), McGee speaks of a sentence being definitely true under the supervaluation interpretation (as opposed to being definitely untrue or unsettled). We are led to McGee's characterization of sentences that are definitely true: A sentence is definitely true if it is true in any total interpretation $\langle S_1', S_2' \rangle$ that extends $\langle S_1, S_2 \rangle$, where S_1' is a maximal consistent set of sentences disjoint from S_2.[27] Notice, then, that McGee accepts

(MC) The extension of 'true' is a maximal consistent set of sentences.

Let $\mathcal{L}_\rho$ be the language of the minimal fixed point generated by the supervaluational approach. As we saw in connection with Kripke's theory, a good diagonal argument establishes the expressive incompleteness of $\mathcal{L}_\rho$. In the case of Kripke's theory, the diagonal theorem told us that no one-place wff of $\mathcal{L}$ is true of exactly the codes of those wffs false or undefined of their own codes. In McGee's terms, the diagonal theorem tells us that no wff of $\mathcal{L}$ is definitely true of exactly the codes of those wffs definitely untrue or unsettled of their own codes. This result is associated with a Liar sentence:

'Is not definitely true of itself' is not definitely true of itself.

The diagonal result suggests that there are forms of the Liar that McGee's account cannot handle.

McGee does consider the *Definite Liar* paradox, in the form generated by the sentence

(1) (1) is not definitely true.

It might seem, McGee says, that we can produce a Definite Liar paradox by the following reasoning:

> Suppose that the definite liar sentence is unsettled, that is, neither definitely true nor definitely untrue. Then it is definitely true that the definite liar sentence is unsettled, and *a fortiori* it is definitely true that the definite liar sentence is not definitely true. But that the definite liar sentence is not definitely true is just what the definite liar sentence says. So the definite liar sentence is definitely true after all.[28]

But, according to McGee:

> This argument is no good. From the hypothesis that a sentence is unsettled, it by no means follows that it has been settled that the sentence is unsettled. Quite the contrary, if a sentence is unsettled, then we are free to adopt linguistic conventions that settle it.[29]

Now we may ask whether McGee has presented the most straightforward form of the Definite Liar reasoning. Let us accept, as McGee presumably does, that the Definite Liar sentence (1) is unsettled (though we could adopt conventions that settle it). Then it seems to follow at once that

(2) (1) is not definitely true.[30]

But now we have apparently asserted the very sentence that we took to be unsettled. This intuitive reasoning does not move from the hypothesis that a sentence is unsettled to its being settled that it is unsettled. And our linguistic conventions do not change in the course of the reasoning. *So the apparent difference in semantic status between* (1) *and* (2) *still stands in need of explanation.*[31]

4.3 McGee and definite truth

Moreover, we can ask, how free are we to adopt conventions to settle the truth value of the Definite Liar sentence? According to McGee, if (1) is unsettled, we are free to adopt conventions that will settle it. Suppose we adopt a convention according to which (1) is definitely untrue. Then, given that convention, it is definitely true that (1) is definitely untrue and so definitely true that (1) is not definitely true – and now we recover the paradox. Suppose, on the other hand, we adopt a convention according to which (1) is definitely true. Then, as Stephen Yablo remarks,[32] we are led to a contradiction. Given the convention, (1) is definitely true; but then what it says is the case, and so it *isn't* definitely true. The threat of contradiction should prevent us from adopting either convention: both these alternatives must be rejected. So we are not free to adopt either kind of convention; we are *not* free to adopt linguistic conventions that will settle (1). But then it is definitely true that (1) is unsettled, and we have the Definite Liar again. It might be responded that we *can* consistently adopt either kind of convention as long as we give up (DT). But presumably McGee will not find this way out attractive, since it abandons his theory.

Over and above these difficulties for McGee's way out of the Definite Liar, there is the problem posed by the diagonal argument four paragraphs back. It is tempting to put the problem this way: In order to express the complement of the concept of definite truth, we must ascend to a metalanguage. But this way of putting the problem presupposes that the predicates 'assigned the value "true" at the minimal fixed point for $\mathcal{L}_\rho$' and 'definitely true' are coextensive. And for McGee this is not so: The former notion is sharp, while the latter notion is vague. It need not be a settled matter that a sentence is unsettled: We are free, according to McGee, to adopt conventions that will settle it. But still, the minimal fixed point is supposed to express the notion of definite truth as determined by the conventions we have in fact adopted (so that, e.g., Liar sentences are unsettled in the minimal fixed point). So the predicate 'assigned the value "true" at the minimal fixed point for $\mathcal{L}_\rho$' *is* coextensive with 'definitely true relative to the linguistic conventions we have adopted'. So the diagonal argument shows that $\mathcal{L}_\rho$ cannot express the concept *not definitely true relative to the linguistic conventions we have adopted.*

The question now is whether this concept is available to the ordinary speaker. McGee suggests that it is natural to think of 'true' as a vague predicate and natural to divide sentences into those that are definitely true, those that are definitely untrue, and those that are unsettled. So this trichotomy is available to the ordinary speaker, by McGee's own lights. Further, the notion of linguistic convention is surely available. So the construction of this version of the Definite Liar is within the resources of ordinary language. In short, the answers to our two questions are affirmative.

First, there is no avoiding the ascent to a metalanguage; and second, this ascent is prompted by semantic concepts expressible in ordinary language.

Perhaps McGee will respond that we should not aim to capture ordinary language and our ordinary intuitions about the notion of truth. He writes:

> Quite frankly, the philosophical explication of folk semantics does not seem to me a particularly interesting or useful task, in any event. The more important task it seems to me, is to establish the logical basis for a consistent semantics of natural language. The problem of giving voice to the our [sic] preanalytic intuitions about truth is comparatively less important, just as understanding popular misconceptions about space and time is comparatively less important than understanding the actual geometry of space–time.[33]

But what our good diagonal argument shows goes beyond the demonstration of a mismatch between our naive intuitions and a reconstructed theory. From McGee's trichotomy, and the notion of linguistic convention, emerges an intuitive enough semantic concept. This concept and its associated paradoxes are not accommodated by McGee's account. And so the account is too narrow in scope. Moreover, McGee cannot simply set aside the semantic intuitions that give rise to the concept and the paradoxes: *The plausibility of the treatment of 'true' as a vague predicate is grounded in these intuitions.*

We should distinguish two ways in which a proposed account of truth may be forced to a metalanguage. The account may be stated in a theoretical metalanguage, or there may be semantic concepts beyond the reach of the account. Kripke mentions both ways in discussing his own approach:

> The present approach certainly does not claim to give a universal language, and I doubt that such a goal can be achieved. First, the induction defining the minimal fixed point is carried out in a set-theoretic metalanguage, not in the object language itself. Second, there are assertions we can make about the object language which we cannot make in the object language. For example, Liar sentences are *not true* in the object language, in the sense that the inductive process never makes them true; but we are precluded from saying this in the object language by our interpretation of negation and the truth predicate.[34]

Now McGee is very much concerned with the *first* of these ways; that is, he is not content to describe a theory of truth within an essentially richer metalanguage, like the language of set theory.[35] Rather, "one must solve the problem of how to present the semantics of a language within the language itself"; [36] the problem is to provide "a consistent theory of truth for one's own language."[37] McGee is sympathetic to Feferman's attempt:

> Kripke characterized the fixed points model theoretically, by giving a set of models; to do this he required an essentially richer metalanguage. Feferman characterized the fixed points proof theoretically, by giving a set of axioms, and no metalanguage was required.[38]

I am presently arguing that McGee's attempt to provide "the semantics of a language within the language itself" does not succeed: an ascent to a metalanguage is still forced *in the second way,* as it was in the case of Feferman's theory.

According to McGee's account, "Our naive concept of truth has now split into two notions, truth and definite truth."[39] These notions are captured respectively by (MC) and (DT). So McGee is after a Kripkean construction for a language $\mathcal{L}_{T,D}$ obtained from L by adding *two* predicates, T ('true') and D ('definitely true'). Both (MC) and (DT) may be formalized in $\mathcal{L}_{T,D}$. McGee's aim is to show that there is a consistent theory Γ of truth and definite truth in the language of $\mathcal{L}_{T,D}$ that entails (MC) and (DT). McGee intends Γ to be a theory *"that expresses everything that our linguistic conventions have determined about the extension of* T *and the extension of* D."[40]

Let A be a model for L; then to say φ is definitely true under (A, Γ) is to say that $[\varphi]$ is true in every expansion of A to a model of Γ. We build up the desired theory Γ in stages. Given Γ_β, for $\beta < \alpha$, we will define Γ_α as follows. Consider the theory that consists of the formalized version of (DT), the formalized version of (MC), and all the sentences $D([\varphi])$ and $T([\varphi])$, where $\varphi \in \bigcup_{\beta < \alpha} \Gamma_\beta$. We let Γ_α be the set of sentences that are made definitely true by this theory. For small values of α, there will be definite truths outside the extension of D. But eventually the process saturates: for some ordinal, *no* definite truth remains outside the extension of D. So, if we let Γ_∞ be $\bigcup_{\alpha \in OR} \Gamma_\alpha$, then (DT) is satisfied by (A, Γ_∞), and φ is definitely true under (A, Γ_∞) iff $D([\varphi])$ is definitely true under (A, Γ_∞). So Γ_∞ is the desired theory of truth and definite truth.[41]

Thus far, the need for a metalanguage has not been avoided,

> since we have not *given* the theory of truth Γ_∞ at all; we have only *described* the theory. The set of sentences Γ_∞ is, according to recursion theory, an extremely complicated object that we cannot hope to exhibit explicitly. We can give a description of the theory Γ_∞, formulated within an essentially richer metalanguage, by depicting a transfinite recursion which produces Γ_∞, but we cannot present the theory itself. The essentially richer metalanguage is still with us.[42]

But what can be done is to give an effective version of the Kripkean construction. We obtain a theory "that plays the role of Γ_∞ by adding a *recursive* set of axioms to Γ."[43] In this way, McGee claims, we can give a consistent theory of truth for our own language.

However, there remain semantic concepts that cannot be expressed in the language of the fixed point associated with Γ_∞. That is the lesson of our diagonal argument. By a Kripkean fixed-point construction, McGee obtains a language that contains its own definite truth predicate: The extension of D comprises all the definite truths, *as determined by "our linguistic conventions."* But by our diagonal argument, adjusted to the fixed point associated with Γ_∞, there is no predicate of the language whose extension is exactly those sentences that are either definitely untrue or unsettled, according to our linguistic conventions. To express the concept *not definitely true as determined by our linguistic conventions,* a metalanguage is required, on pain of paradox. This is an especially serious lack of expressive power for a language that is supposed to express everything that our linguistic conventions have determined about the notion of definite truth. Moreover, notice that changes in our linguistic conventions about truth and definite truth – at least those compatible with McGee's (MC) and (DT) – will not avoid this expressive incompleteness. The fixed point associated with a new set of conventions may generate a different extension for D. But then an analogous diagonal argument establishes the expressive incompleteness of the language of this fixed point.

4.4. INCONSISTENCY VIEWS

Rescher and Brandom present an altogether different kind of solution to the Liar.[44] According to their view, Liar sentences are both true *and* false. Theirs, then, is an *inconsistency* view, one that has received increasing support in recent years.[45] Rescher and Brandom's broad project is a study of the logic of inconsistency within an extended framework of possible worlds. There are two classical principles governing possible worlds. One is the Law of Excluded Middle (LEM): Given a world w, then for any proposition P, either P obtains in w or ¬P obtains in w. The other is the Law of (non)Contradiction (LC): Given a world w, then for any proposition P, either P or ¬P fails to obtain in w. In the view of Rescher and Brandom, there are possible worlds that violate one or the other, or both, of these principles. A *standard* world is a world in which both principles hold. A *schematic* world is a world in which LEM fails – where there are propositions such that neither they nor their negations hold. More important for our purposes, an *inconsistent* world is one in which LC fails – where there are propositions such that both they and their negations hold.

4.4 Inconsistency views

Given a world w and a proposition P, exactly one of two basic onto-logical situations is reflected in w: (i) the state of affairs purported by P is present in w – symbolically, $[P]_w = +$; or (ii) the state of affairs purported by P is not present in w – symbolically, $[P]_w = -$. So "in *this* regard the ontological situation is orthodoxly two-valued (+ or −) according as P obtains or fails; it is 'on' or 'off'."[46]

It is a "cardinal doctrine" of Rescher and Brandom's analysis that "the ontological status of P and that of ¬P should be seen as strictly independent issues."[47] There are four distinct possibilities for the pair $[P]_w$, $[\neg P]_w$, symbolized by $\{P\}_w$:

$[P]_w$	$[\neg P]_w$	$\{P\}_w$
+	+	++
+	−	+−
−	+	−+
−	−	−−

In an inconsistent world, there will be a proposition P such that $\{P\}_w = ++$; in a schematic world, there will be a proposition P such that $\{P\}_w = --$.

Rescher and Brandom rest their semantics of nonstandard worlds on the following rule:

(R) $|P|_w = T$ iff $[P]_w = +$,
$|P|_w = F$ iff $[\neg P]_w = -$,

where $|P|_w$ is the truth value of the proposition P with respect to the world w.

We are now in a position to look at Rescher and Brandom's treatment of one version of the Liar. They consider the statement

(L) This statement is false.

We obtain

$$|L| = T \text{ iff } |L| = F \text{ iff } |\neg L| = T.$$

By the basic semantic rule R,

$$[L] = + \text{ iff } [\neg L] = +.$$

So the conditions under which L obtains are given by

$$|L| = T \text{ iff } \{L\} = ++.$$

So L can obtain in an inconsistent world. And

given the prospect of such a world, there is no need to reject L as *meaning-less* (= "lacking in truth value") because its realization-as-true is now an

79

available alternative. The paradoxical thesis at issue is smoothly accommodated, in a perfectly viable way, within the resources of a non-standard possible world.[48]

However, as Rescher and Brandom go on to point out, their theory cannot deal with

(L') This statement is not true.

We obtain

$$|L'| = T \text{ iff } |L'| \neq T,$$

or

$$[L'] = + \quad \text{iff } [L'] \neq + \text{ iff } [L'] = -.$$

But this is unacceptable, for recall that Rescher and Brandom insist that the ontological situation, given either by $[P]_w = +$ or by $[P]_w = -$, is "orthodoxly two-valued." So their theory of nonstandard possible worlds cannot accommodate this version of the Liar.

As a consequence, Rescher and Brandom's theory fails to satisfy our criterion. Again, natural language, even "ordinary" natural language, surely does have the resources to formulate (L'). So the theory cannot provide a semantics for natural language, not even "ordinary" natural language. The theory cannot dispense with a metalanguage; and it is not open to Rescher and Brandom to claim that at least they have provided a model of a significant portion of natural language.

Rescher and Brandom do recognize the need to ascend to a metalanguage. According to Rescher and Brandom, we must separate the inconsistent object theory from our consistent discourse about it.[49] We can discuss an inconsistent world in perfectly consistent terms as long as we distinguish between "(1) discourse at the level of an object language . . . and (2) discourse at the theoretical metalevel."[50] But this suggests a way out of the Liar, including versions of it like (L'), along Tarskian lines. Ultimately the Liar is resolved *not* by a logic of inconsistency, but rather by a Tarskian distinction of language levels.

It would seem that a *genuine* inconsistency solution to the Liar must dispense with the object language/metalanguage distinction altogether. Such a line is taken by Graham Priest.[51] Priest writes of his "paraconsistent" approach that "it finally renders the object-language/meta-language distinction unnecessary in any shape or form."[52] But now new difficulties arise. According to Priest, a Liar sentence is both true and false, that is, *paradoxical* (abbreviated by 'p'). Now consider Priest's account of the truth conditions of 'A is true' and 'A is false', summed up by these tables:

A	A is true		A	A is false
t	t		t	f
p	p		p	p
f	f		f	t

Let L be a Liar sentence. Then, according to Priest, the sentence L is both truth and false. Following Priest's truth tables, we have

$$\text{L is true} \leftrightarrow \text{L},$$

and

$$\text{L is false} \leftrightarrow \text{L}.$$

So 'L is true' and 'L is false' are paradoxical. Since, according to Priest's theory, the conjunction of two paradoxical sentences is paradoxical, 'L is true and L is false (i.e., L is paradoxical)' is paradoxical. So every time that Priest asserts that a (Liar) sentence is paradoxical, this assertion is itself paradoxical. Further, since on Priest's theory the negation of a paradoxical sentence is paradoxical, it follows that 'It is not the case that L is paradoxical' is paradoxical. But now we see that every time Priest asserts that L is paradoxical, he could just as well assert that L is not paradoxical. We have, then, a problem with the very language in which Priest expresses his theory. It is not itself immune from paradoxical assertions. Moreover, we do not know how to take Priest's assertion that L is paradoxical, once we understand that it is also assertible that L is not paradoxical.[53]

Priest has responded to these difficulties along the following lines.[54] Consider an assertion that the sentence L is paradoxical. Given that this assertion is itself paradoxical, we should make of it what we should make of any paradoxical sentence: It is both true and false. The fact that it is false does not undercut the fact that it is true. It gives you more information, not less.

It is true that Priest's aim is not to produce a consistent theory, but rather to show how inconsistencies could be tolerated. Let us accept that the assertion that L is paradoxical is itself paradoxical. The question, then, is whether this *can* be tolerated. According to the theory, we are to treat the assertion that L is paradoxical as itself paradoxical. But this is to say, among other things, that L is not paradoxical. The statement that L is paradoxical is coupled with the statement that L is not paradoxical. In stating his theory, Priest will assert the first of these. But why is this in any way privileged? We might just as well assert the second – it is no less a part of Priest's account and, according to Priest, no less informative.

But if we do, we will not succeed in conveying Priest's theory. The further information – that L is not paradoxical – undercuts our ability to convey the theory. And this, I think, is a reason *not* to tolerate the paradoxical nature of the assertion that L is paradoxical.

For reasons that will emerge in subsequent chapters, I do agree with Priest that we should seek to reject a Tarskian division of object language and metalanguage as a way out of the Liar. With the exception of Priest's account, the purportedly non-Tarskian theories we have examined in this and the previous chapter do not escape a Tarskian hierarchy. But the price Priest pays seems to me too high: we do not want the language of our theory of truth to be itself infected with paradox and inconsistency.

Chapter 5

A medieval solution to the Liar

According to Diogenes Laertius, the Liar was authored by Eubulides in the 4th century B.C.[1] Little is known of ancient solutions. Aristotle appears to treat it as a fallacy *secundum quid et simpliciter;*[2] Chrysippus seems to have held that the Liar sentence has no meaning at all;[3] other treatments are alluded to in three entries of Diogenes' catalogue of the writings of Chrysippus.[4]

In contrast, the medieval *insolubilia* literature is a very rich source of attempts to solve the Liar.[5] Some of these resolutions are primarily influenced by Aristotle and attempt to force *insolubilia* into the mold of one or other of several fallacies laid out by Aristotle in *Sophistical Refutations.*[6] Other solutions are distinctively medieval.[7] Still others anticipate, to varying degrees, modern approaches. There are clear anticipations of the following modern views: the Liar sentence is not grammatically well-formed;[8] the Liar sentence, though well-formed, does not express a proposition;[9] the Liar sentence is neither true nor false, but suffers a truth-value gap, or else receives a third truth value;[10] and, finally, restrictions are to be placed on self-reference.[11] Further, it is arguable that there are medieval anticipations of Tarski's solution via a hierarchy of languages,[12] of Russell's type theory[13] and his vicious circle principle,[14] and of the view that Liar sentences are both true and false.[15]

In this chapter, I examine one medieval resolution of the Liar. I shall argue that this resolution has not been adequately captured by modern commentators. Once it has been properly understood, we can forge a new link between it and certain modern solutions not in the preceding list. In this way, we provide further support for the claim that the medieval anticipation of modern treatments of the Liar is complete. But the interest of the medieval resolution goes beyond this, because, though related to recent solutions, it is not reducible to them. This medieval line on the Liar, I shall argue, is original and of independent interest. Its leading

5 A medieval solution to the Liar

ideas form part of the intuitive basis of the positive "singularity" proposal I shall develop in the following chapters.

5.1. AN OUTLINE OF THE OCKHAM–BURLEY–PSEUDO-SHERWOOD SOLUTION

The medieval resolution in question is found in the writings of Ockham, Burley, and Pseudo-Sherwood.[16] Though there are significant differences that I shall discuss later, the core of the approach is common to the three authors, and to this I now turn.

Each considers the following paradoxical situation.[17] Socrates says only 'Socrates says a falsehood'. From either assumption, that Socrates' utterance is true, or that it is false, we obtain a contradiction: this pair of arguments constitutes the two halves of the paradox.

To resolve it, all three authors invoke the rule of the *restringentes:* A part never supposits for[18] the whole of which it is a part.[19] Thus the predicate 'falsehood' in Socrates' utterance does not supposit for Socrates' utterance, but for all other falsehoods. Following Pseudo-Sherwood's terminology, let the name 'A' stand for these other falsehoods. Then, according to Pseudo-Sherwood, Socrates' utterance is equivalent to 'Socrates says a falsehood that is A'. The terminology makes it explicit that Socrates' utterance is not in the extension of the occurrence of 'falsehood' in Socrates' utterance. Since, by hypothesis, Socrates says no other falsehood, what Socrates says turns out to be straightforwardly false.

But the second half of the paradox is an argument that leads from the falsity of Socrates' utterance to a contradiction. Since all three authors take Socrates' utterance to be straightforwardly false, they need to show that this argument is fallacious. Since the argument is differently presented by Pseudo-Sherwood on the one hand, and by Ockham and Burley on the other, and since their respective treatments are not exactly analogous, I shall deal with each in turn.

Pseudo-Sherwood takes the problematic inference to be from ' "Socrates says a falsehood" is false' to 'Therefore, that Socrates says a falsehood is false'.[20] According to Pseudo-Sherwood, Socrates' utterance is to be understood as 'Socrates says a falsehood that is A', and since this is false, the premise is true. If we now fallaciously infer the conclusion, we make the mistake of lifting the restriction on the supposition of the predicate 'falsehood' in Socrates' utterance. The fallacious move is from the true premise

'Socrates says a falsehood that is A' is false

to the false conclusion

That Socrates says a falsehood is false,

where there is no restriction on the predicate 'falsehood' in the conclusion. The inference would be valid if we preserved the restriction – that is, if we drew the conclusion

That Socrates says a falsehood that is A is false.

This conclusion is true, and it follows from the premise. But in our fallacious reasoning, we move from a use of 'falsehood' with a restricted extension (that does not contain Socrates' utterance) to a use of 'falsehood' with an unrestricted extension (that contains all falsehoods including Socrates' utterance). In Pseudo-Sherwood's terms, there is an unwarranted shift in the supposition of the predicate from restricted to unrestricted. The error is to proceed

> from an expression *secundum quid* or an expression with a determination to an expression *simpliciter*. And there is most straightforwardly [a paralogism] *secundum quid et simpliciter*.[21]

Ockham and Burley consider several versions of the fallacious argument. I shall take Ockham's treatment of one example as typical:

> The inference 'Socrates says this falsehood; therefore Socrates says a falsehood' does not hold good, but there is a fallacy *secundum quid et simpliciter*. And this is because in the proposition 'Socrates says a falsehood', the term 'falsehood' cannot supposit for this falsehood – which is that Socrates says a falsehood.[22]

Here the premise of the argument is

Socrates says this falsehood,

where 'falsehood' is unrestricted, and the demonstrative refers to Socrates' sole utterance. Since Socrates' utterance *is* false, the premise is true. The conclusion is Socrates' utterance, in which the predicate 'falsehood' is restricted. The conclusion may be represented as

Socrates says a falsehood that is A.

So we move from a true premise to a false conclusion. There is a transition from an unrestricted use of 'falsehood' in the premise to a restricted use in the conclusion. We commit the fallacy by taking the predicate 'falsehood' in the conclusion to have unrestricted supposition when, in fact, its supposition is restricted. Like Pseudo-Sherwood, Ockham diagnoses the argument as a fallacy *secundum quid et simpliciter.*[23]

There are superficial differences between the two presentations. The argument presented by Pseudo-Sherwood is fallacious if the restriction does not apply in the conclusion, and valid if it does; for the argument presented by Ockham, the reverse is true. But all agree that there is a restriction on 'falsehood' in the conclusion, and in failing to notice this, we mistake a fallacious inference for a valid one.

The present paradox is generated by Socrates' sole utterance 'Socrates says a falsehood'. This proposition is characterized by Ockham and Burley as an *affirmative* insoluble. An example of a *negative* insoluble is Socrates' sole utterance 'Socrates does not say a truth'. Ockham and Burley treat this kind of insoluble in just the same way. Here the predicate 'true' cannot supposit for Socrates' utterance. If we let 'A' stand for all other truths, what Socrates says is equivalent to 'Socrates does not say a truth that is A', which, by hypothesis, is true. Affirmative insolubles are false, but negative insolubles are true. The way in which Ockham and Burley deal with the corresponding fallacious arguments generated by negative insolubles follows the same pattern as before.[24]

5.2. AN INTERPRETATION OF THE OCKHAM–BURLEY–PSEUDO-SHERWOOD SOLUTION

We now have the bare bones of the Ockham–Burley–Pseudo-Sherwood solution. In this section my aim is to articulate it further. This I shall do by clearing up some misconceptions about it.

5.2.1.

One such misconception is that the solution is essentially a ban on self-reference.[25] This interpretation rests on the assumption that the basis of the Ockham–Burley–Pseudo-Sherwood solution is the rule of the *restringentes:* "In no proposition does a part supposit for the whole of which it is a part." In the case of Pseudo-Sherwood, this assumption is correct. Pseudo-Sherwood provides grounds for the *restringentes'* rule, in a fully unqualified form:

> As they say, it seems that the part cannot supposit for the whole. For when the expression is argued [with] in the intellect, the understanding of the predicate and [the understanding] of the subject are first taken separately and afterwards put together [in a sentence or proposition]. And they are put together in the proposition in the way they were taken [at first]. But the

expression 'falsehood' was not taken for the whole, because this composite expression did not exist in the intellect then. Therefore 'falsehood' does not enter into the composition [insofar as it is taken] for this.[26]

Now the argument presented here applies not only to the term 'falsehood' as it occurs in Socrates' utterance 'Socrates says a falsehood', but also to the term 'falsehood' as it occurs in the sentence

(S) '$2+2=4$' is a falsehood

or the term 'sentence' as it occurs in the sentence

(S') '$2+2=4$' is a sentence.

If we apply the restriction to Socrates' paradoxical utterance, then what Socrates is saying is 'Socrates says a falsehood that is A'. So Socrates does not succeed in talking about his very utterance, but only about other falsehoods. It may be plausible to construe this as ruling out self-reference. But there is *nothing* self-referential about the sentences (S) and (S') and yet the *restringentes'* rule applies. That is, the *restringentes'* rule places restrictions within sentences that are not in any natural sense self-referential. The *restringentes'* rule bans self-reference only in a highly attenuated way: Words like 'falsehood' and 'sentence' cannot "refer" to the very sentences in which they occur. And this restriction applies irrespective of whether or not the sentences themselves are self-referential. So, unlike modern approaches that ban self-reference, Pseudo-Sherwood's resolution does not diagnose self-referential sentences as semantically pathological because of their self-referential nature. Rather, the treatment of such sentences arises as a consequence of a *more general rule;* and to describe this rule as a ban on self-reference is strained.

Unlike Pseudo-Sherwood and the *restringentes,* Ockham and Burley limit the scope of the *restringentes'* rule to the insolubles only.[27] So at first glance it may seem plausible to characterize their solution as a ban on self-reference. But such a characterization is demonstrably mistaken. For it is clear from their treatment of negative insolubles that the restrictions that Ockham and Burley place on supposition do not always coincide with applications of the limited *restringentes'* rule. Burley writes:

Nor does the following inference hold: 'That a proposition spoken by Socrates is not true is true; and that a proposition spoken by Socrates is not true is a proposition spoken by Socrates; therefore a proposition spoken by Socrates is true'. For the term 'proposition spoken by Socrates' in the conclusion cannot supposit for the whole 'a proposition spoken by Socrates is not true'. And the term does supposit for this in the minor. Therefore, the inference does not hold good.[28]

Here, the conclusion is

A proposition spoken by Socrates is true.

And according to Burley, the term 'proposition spoken by Socrates' in this conclusion cannot supposit for the proposition

A proposition spoken by Socrates is not true.

The crucial point to notice is that the proposition for which the term in the conclusion cannot supposit is different from the one of which the term is a part. The restriction here is *not* according to the rule of the *restringentes*.[29]

What rule *does* this restriction accord with? Although Burley appeals to the *restringentes'* rule, he also suggests another.[30] This says that the restriction on supposition applies wherever its violation leads to something "self-reflexive with a privative determination." For example, consider the affirmative insoluble 'I say a falsehood'. Suppose we let the term 'falsehood' supposit for my utterance. When we replace the term by this suppositum, we obtain 'I say that I say a falsehood'. But this is self-reflexive with a privative determination, since "here the act of speaking reflects back over the act of speaking with the determination 'falsehood', which is a privative determination."[31] In the case of fallacies associated with affirmative insolubles, this rule and the *restringentes'* rule coincide in their results. But they pull apart in the case of fallacies associated with negative insolubles. In Burley's example, if we ignore his rule, we obtain 'That a proposition spoken by Socrates is not true is true'. Socrates' assertion of this may be taken to be self-reflexive with a privative determination. The restriction Burley places on supposition here is in accordance with his rule, *not* with that of the *restringentes*.

Consider now Ockham's corresponding argument:

> . . . just as the inference 'This is true, and Socrates says it; therefore he says a true proposition other than this' does not hold good, so the inference 'Socrates says the proposition "Socrates does not say a truth," and this is true; therefore Socrates says a truth' does not hold.[32]

The natural way to make out the parallel between these inferences is to restrict the supposition of the term 'truth' in the conclusion of the second inference so that it cannot supposit for the proposition 'Socrates does not say a truth'. Again, it is *not* the *restringentes'* rule that is being applied here. If we replace the term 'truth' in the conclusion by Socrates' utterance, we obtain 'Socrates says that Socrates does not say a truth', which is self-reflexive with a privative determination. Perhaps, then, Ockham is implicitly applying a rule like Burley's – but whatever the rationale, it is not one provided by the *restringentes*.

So Ockham and Burley do not resolve the Liar by a ban on self-reference. Indeed, there is reason to suppose that they would admit directly self-referential sentences. Suppose I say 'This very sentence is a falsehood'. Here is the natural way to apply the Ockham–Burley–Pseudo-Sherwood resolution to this example: The predicate 'falsehood' in my utterance cannot supposit for my utterance, which is then equivalent to 'This very sentence is a falsehood which is A', where 'A' stands for all other falsehoods. But now what I say is clearly false, since my utterance is identified with some falsehood other than it. Nevertheless, in saying what I do, I succeed in talking about my very utterance: I say something false about it. Here, then, there is no problem in my referring to my very utterance. Of course, according to the *restringentes* and Pseudo-Sherwood, the subject term 'this very sentence' cannot supposit for my utterance. But this further restriction plays no role in resolving the paradox, and so Ockham and Burley would have no reason to invoke it.[33]

5.2.2.

A second misconception about the medieval resolution concerns the claim made by Pseudo-Sherwood and Ockham that the Liar is correctly diagnosed as involving a fallacy *secundum quid et simpliciter.* The thought is that, under the influence of Aristotle, medieval authors forced insolubles into a pattern that they do not fit. Paul Spade argues that all medieval solutions along these lines are strained.[34] Marie-Louise Roure claims that Pseudo-Sherwood does not completely succeed in placing his solution within the framework of the fallacy, and even suggests that he may not have been seriously committed to this classification.[35]

The fallacy *secundum quid et simpliciter* arises when an expression used in a restricted way is taken as if it were unrestricted. A leading example of Aristotle's is the inference from 'The Ethiopian is white, with respect to his teeth and eyeballs' to 'The Ethiopian is white, absolutely'. In fallaciously drawing this conclusion, we neglect a restriction attaching to the term 'white': The term 'white' applies to parts of the Ethiopian, but not to the Ethiopian as a whole. The part–whole distinction here, to put it in medieval terms, is between an integral part and an integral whole.[36] And if this is the example we have in mind, it *is* unclear how the Liar argument is an instance of this fallacy.[37] What is the integral part, and what is the integral whole? To fix ideas, take the fallacy associated with the affirmative insoluble 'I say a falsehood'. According to Pseudo-Sherwood, Ockham, and Burley, some occurrences of 'falsehood' within the argument have unrestricted supposition, while others supposit for false-hoods other than Socrates' utterance. That is, the part–whole distinction is between *some* of the falsehoods and *all* of the falsehoods: In the terminology of certain medieval authors, including Burley, the distinction is between a universal part and a universal whole.[38] The question, then, is whether *this* part–whole distinction has a place in fallacies *secundum quid et simpliciter.*

From the twelfth century on, medieval authors distinguished various forms of the fallacy.[39] The example of the Ethiopian suggests one form, but it is not the only one. Ockham writes:

> Nor is the fallacy of inferring an absolute from a relative predication always made by arguing from a determinable taken together with a determination that diminishes [the supposition] to that determination taken absolutely.[40] But that form of argument is only one form that is fallacious in this way. And another form occurs when the argument is from a proposition having a predicate to a proposition of the second adjacent, as for example in the argument 'Socrates is believed in: therefore Socrates exists'.[41]

And Albert of Saxony writes:

> I maintain that there are two principal ways to commit this fallacy. The first occurs when there is an argument from the third adjacent to the second adjacent in the affirmative, or from the third adjacent to the second adjacent in the negative. Example of the first: 'The Antichrist is conceivable; therefore the Antichrist is'.[42]

These example are clearly suggested by Aristotle at the very outset of his discussion of the fallacy:

> Fallacies connected with the use of some expression absolutely or in a certain respect and not in its proper sense, occur when that which is predicated in part only is taken as though it was predicated absolutely. For example, 'If that-which-is-not is an object of opinion, then that-which-is-not is'; for it is not the same thing 'to be something' and 'to be' absolutely.[43]

The examples, then, are unquestionably genuine instances of the fallacy *secundum quid et simpliciter.* Now what we want to know is how they are analyzed by Ockham and Albert.

The answer is found in their theory of *ampliation*. These examples of the fallacy are treated as cases involving ampliated supposition. Ockham maintains that an argument such as 'The Antichrist is not; therefore the Antichrist is not possible' moves from 'is' taken *per se* to ['is'] taken together with a predicate after it, where the predicate is such as to be able to pertain to a term that supposits for a non-being as well as for a being. Whenever the argument goes this way, there is a fallacy *secundum quid et simpliciter* when one argues in the negative, and conversely when one argues in the affirmative. For example, these [inferences] – 'a is producible by God; therefore a is' and 'a is not; therefore a is not producible by God' – contain a fallacy *secundum quid et simpliciter*. Likewise, the [inference] 'The Antichrist is not; therefore the Antichrist is not foreknown by God', and conversely 'The Antichrist is foreknown by God; therefore the Antichrist is'. Thus, since what is not can be foreknown as much as what is, there is a fallacy *secundum quid et simpliciter* in such [inferences].[44]

So in the sentence 'a is', for example, the copula allows the subject to range over only presently existing things. In the sentence 'a is producible by God', the subject term ranges not only over presently existing things, but over all possibly existing things, since it is for these that the predicate 'producible by God' stands. The predicate has the effect of ampliating or extending the supposition of terms to which it is adjoined. This is the case with modal terms in general and with verbs in the past and future tense. In relation to a present-tense copula in a proposition of the second adjacent, the subject term supposits only for presently existing things. In relation to a past-tense or future-tense copula, or a verb of possibility (such as 'can') or predicates that can supposit not only for beings but also for nonbeings (things that do not exist in the present), the subject term can supposit for past, future, or possible things as well.

Now we can diagnose the fallacious inference from 'a is producible by God' to 'a is'. What may escape us is that there is a shift in the supposition of the subject term from all possible things to all presently existing things. We are prone to take the subject term in the conclusion to supposit for a universal whole (all possible things), when in fact it ranges over a part of that universal whole (those possible things that are presently existing).[45]

But this is just how things are with the Liar, according to Ockham, Burley, and Pseudo-Sherwood. When we illegitimately infer the conclusion, we take 'falsehood' to supposit for a universal whole (all the falsehoods), when in fact it supposits for a universal part (some of the falsehoods). Again, there is a term in the conclusion of the fallacious argument that supposits for only a part of the universal whole for which we think it stands. There is, then, no reason to deny that this is indeed a genuine form of the fallacy *secundum quid et simpliciter,* or that Pseudo-Sherwood and Ockham took it this way.

5.2.3.

A third misconception draws a false analogy between this medieval solution and the modern approaches of Russell and Tarski. Several authors treat Ockham's solution in a way that suggests an anticipation of Russell's theory of types or Tarski's hierarchy of languages.[46] According to Marie-Louise Roure, the approaches taken by Pseudo-Sherwood, Burley, and the *restringentes* also bear a resemblance to the theories of Russell and Tarski.[47] I shall focus on Roure's interpretation of Pseudo-Sherwood, Burley, and the *restringentes,* but what I have to say applies equally well to the corresponding interpretation of Ockham.

Roure argues that in the solutions of Pseudo-Sherwood, Burley, and the *restringentes,* we can discern an implicit distinction between two levels, that of the discourse, and that of discourse about the discourse.[48] At the level of the discourse, there is the insoluble itself; for example, Socrates' sole utterance 'Socrates says a falsehood'. This utterance is false, given the restriction on the term 'falsehood'. At the second level of discourse, we reflect on Socrates' utterance. We ask whether, in saying what he did, Socrates says a truth or a falsehood.[49] As we have seen, from the assumption that Socrates' utterance is false, an apparent contradiction is obtained in a variety of ways. These problematic inferences belong to the level of discourse about the discourse: They arise from reflection on the truth value of what Socrates says. Such an inference, Roure concludes, constitutes a paradox at this second level, which is solved by distinguishing restricted and unrestricted occurrences of 'falsehood' within the inference.[50]

I do not find Roure's two-level interpretation plausible. It is true that the medieval line is concerned with two distinct pieces of discourse. There is Socrates' original utterance 'Socrates says a falsehood'. And then there is the argument that leads from the falsity of Socrates' utterance to a contradiction; for example: ' "Socrates says a falsehood" is a falsehood, and Socrates says "Socrates says a falsehood"; therefore, Socrates says a falsehood'.[51] Of course, the argument is *about* Socrates' utterance, and so, in an uninteresting way, it is a "metadiscourse."[52] The question is whether it is any sense a *Tarskian* metadiscourse.

As we have seen, Tarski showed that no classical formal language contains its own truth predicate. The truth predicate for such a language (the object language) is contained in a metalanguage. And the truth predicate for this metalanguage is contained in a further metalanguage: In this way, an infinite hierarchy of formal languages is generated, and with it, infinitely many *distinct* truth predicates.

5.2 An interpretation

Now the key difference between our discourse and "metadiscourse" is that, in the argument, there is an unrestricted occurrence of 'falsehood', whereas in Socrates' utterance there is only a restricted occurrence. This may tempt us into drawing a distinction between two falsity predicates, 'false (that is A)' and 'false (unrestricted)', and correlating different levels of language with these predicates, so that our "metadiscourse" *is* a Tarskian metadiscourse.[53] But this temptation should be resisted. For in the argument, there are *restricted,* as well as unrestricted, occurrences of 'falsehood'. (This is precisely why, according to Ockham, Burley, and Pseudo-Sherwood, such arguments are fallacies). So, if we distinguish falsity predicates in the way suggested, there would be uses of both within a single discourse, and this is not possible on the Tarskian account. The attempt to treat the argument as a Tarskian metadiscourse assumes that it has some definite metalevel to which the uses of 'falsehood' correspond; but the attempt leads to the absurd conclusion that the argument belongs at once to distinct levels, the metalevel *and* the object level. The upshot is that the relation here between "metadiscourse" and discourse bears no resemblance to the relation between a Tarskian metalanguage and object language.

Ockham, Burley, and Pseudo-Sherwood have *no need* of a distinction between levels of discourse. They proceed by placing restrictions on certain occurrences of the semantic predicates[54] and by this alone. This suggests the correct view of their solution: It is a *contextual* solution. It treats the semantic predicates 'true' and 'false' as *context-sensitive,* that is, as terms whose linguistic meaning is fixed, while their extensions vary according to the context of utterance. (Compare the indexical terms 'I', 'you', 'here', 'now'.) The idea is not that there are different truth (and falsity) predicates, one for each level of discourse. Rather it is that there is a single truth predicate and a single falsity predicate, the extensions of which vary according to context.

Pseudo-Sherwood gives particularly clear expression to the contextual idea. He considers this objection to the *restringentes:* "Again, the restricters say that this – that I say a falsehood – is false. Therefore, they grant that this is a supposition of 'falsehood'. And so 'falsehood' supposits for this, even though it is a part of it."[55] Pseudo-Sherwood defends the *restringentes* and, at the same time, his own view as follows:

> In reply to another it must be said that the restricter, when he replies 'a falsehood exists', already the term 'falsehood' in his reply is in another piece of discourse from the one proposed. And he is right to grant that the term 'falsehood' which is in another piece of discourse could supposit for the former one [namely, the first instance of 'I say a falsehood'] but the term 'falsehood' in that piece of discourse [can]not.[56]

5 A medieval solution to the Liar

We find a statement to similar effect in Ockham (where the inference to which he refers is 'Socrates says this falsehood; therefore Socrates says a falsehood'):

> All insolubles should be replied to this way: viz., by denying the inference from a term taken with a demonstrative pronoun that indicates something contained [in what he said] to the term taken without such a pronoun. The only reason is that a common term cannot supposit in that proposition for that inferior, although it could supposit for it in other propositions.[57]

And Burley's general principle expresses the contextual idea, since it restricts certain occurrences of a term and not others, according to context.[58]

Context sensitivity is deeply embedded in the medieval theory of supposition, and the contextual parameters go beyond the modern ones. We can distinguish two levels at which context sensitivity is treated in medieval supposition theory. At the first level of proposition types, there are general principles governing restrictions on supposition. The operative extension of any (singular or predicate) term depends on the propositional context. Parameters of the propositional context are the quantifier, negation, the tense of the verb, and ampliating terms. (One principle may tell us that, in a certain proposition, a given term has confused and distributive supposition; another may tell us that an unampliated term supposits for presently existing things). At the second level of proposition tokens, the environmental context comes into play, and this will include the modern parameters of speaker, time, and place. At this level, a definite extension can be attributed to a token of a term. (For example, the extension may be all things existing at a specific time.) Principles like Burley's and the *restringentes'* belong to the first level. At the second level, tokens of 'true' and 'false' have definite extensions according to the particular context of utterance and the rules of the first level.

Thus far, what picture do we have of the Ockham–Burley–Pseudo-Sherwood solution? It is a nonhierarchical, contextual solution. It is not to be identified with an approach that bans self-reference. It diagnoses liar arguments as fallacies that *are* appropriately placed in the framework *secundum quid et simpliciter*. In the next section, I fill out this picture some more by exploring the connections between this medieval solution and certain modern proposals.

5.3. COMPARISONS AND CONTRASTS WITH SOME MODERN APPROACHES

In his paper "Russell's Mathematical Logic," Gödel notes that Russell's theory of types brings in a new idea for the solution of the paradoxes: "It

94

consists in blaming the paradoxes . . . on the assumption that every concept gives a meaningful proposition, if asserted for any arbitrary object or objects as arguments."[59] Gödel goes on to say that the simple theory of types carries through this idea on the basis of a further assumption, that whenever an object x can replace another object y in a proposition, and preserve meaningfulness, it can do so in any meaningful proposition. This means that objects are grouped into mutually exclusive ranges of significance, or types; each concept is significant for arguments taken from only one such range. In Russell's simple theory of types, each concept is significant "for an infinitely small portion of all objects."[60]

Gödel finds this further assumption unacceptable.[61] His suggestion is to reject it, while retaining the idea that not every concept gives a meaningful proposition for any object as argument:

> It is not impossible that the idea of limited ranges of significance could be carried out without the above restrictive principle. It might even turn out that it is possible to assume every concept to be significant everywhere except for certain 'singular points' or 'limiting points,' so that the paradoxes would appear as something analogous to dividing by zero.[62]

Gödel does not enlarge on this idea. It is helpful to do so by way of an example. Consider again the heterological paradox. A paradox arises when we ask whether or not the term 'heterological' is itself heterological. Following through Gödel's suggestion, we suppose that the concept of heterologicality is significant for any object as argument, except for certain "singular points." One such singular point is the expression 'heterological': If it were not a singular point, the sentence ' "Heterological" is heterological' would generate a paradox. According to Gödel's suggestion, the sentence is meaningless.[63]

Gödel's hope is for a nonhierarchical solution to the paradoxes. In the case of the Liar, the idea is that we locate singularities in our semantic concepts, rather than distinguish levels of language in a hierarchy. Semantic predicates are *univocal* and are not subject to Russellian typical ambiguity. There is just one word 'true' in English, not a hierarchy of distinct predicates 'true$_i$' (the subscript indicating level). Paradox is avoided by a *minimal* restriction on the range of significance of 'true' or predicates constructed from it (like 'heterological').

The Ockham–Burley–Pseudo-Sherwood resolution has much in common with Gödel's suggestion. Ockham, Burley, and Pseudo-Sherwood, like Gödel, aim for a "single-level," nonhierarchical solution to the Liar. And to achieve this, *minimal* restrictions are placed on the extensions of semantic predicates, so that in our fallacious reasoning we are minimally incorrect.

5 A medieval solution to the Liar

There are disanalogies too. Ockham, Burley, and Pseudo-Sherwood place minimal restrictions on *tokens* of semantic predicates; according to the natural way of developing Gödel's idea, it is semantic predicate *types*, denoting semantic concepts, that have singularities. For Gödel, the Liar demonstrates that there are *systematic*, though minor, errors in our understanding of semantic concepts. For Ockham, Burley, and Pseudo-Sherwood, the Liar does not reveal an imperfect grasp of semantic concepts, but rather a minimal misunderstanding about what the concept-word picks out on certain occasions of use. Our mistake is relative to the context of utterance. We do not go wrong in any *principled* way; rather, we make a mistake about what the term picks out, because the empirical circumstances so conspire.

There is a further contrast between the views. A Gödelian singularity does not belong to the *range of significance* of the relevant predicate. But Ockham, Burley, and Pseudo-Sherwood restrict only the *extension* of the predicate: There is nothing outside the range of significance of *any* predicate. For example, the affirmative insoluble 'Socrates says a falsehood' *is* in the range of significance of the token of 'falsehood' occurring within it; the token is false of it. For Gödel, paradoxical sentences, like '"Heterological" is heterological', are meaningless and have no truth value. But for Ockham, Burley, and Pseudo-Sherwood, insolubles are perfectly meaningful and are either true or false.

Gödel's solution is threatened by the Strengthened Liar. If a paradoxical sentence, say '"heterological" is heterological', is meaningless, then it is not true. Thus, the term 'heterological', when predicated of itself, yields a sentence that is not true. But then, 'heterological' *is* heterological. And now we have asserted the very sentence that we originally argued was not true: It seems that it is true after all. So Gödel's claim that the paradoxical sentence is meaningless does not prevent paradox.[64]

The Ockham–Burley–Pseudo-Sherwood line, however, makes no appeal to meaninglessness and does not fall afoul of the Strengthened Liar. It operates with a fully classical bivalent semantics: *All* sentences, *including* the insolubles, are either true or false. The evaluation of insolubles as true or false leads not to the Strengthened Liar, but to other problematic inferences (see Sections 5.1 and 5.2). But these present no new difficulties. As we have seen, Ockham, Burley, and Pseudo-Sherwood treat them in a way that is uniform with their treatment of the original insoluble.

A number of contextual approaches to the Liar have been offered in recent years – most notably by Charles Parsons, Tyler Burge, Haim Gaifman, and Jon Barwise and John Etchemendy.[65] Perhaps the approaches of Parsons and Burge come closest to the Ockham–Burley–Pseudo-Sherwood view. Parsons offers an informal account that, like Burley's, does not limit contextual variation in Liar arguments to the semantic predicates. Such context sensitivity can arise for "quantifiers, 'say', 'mean', and other expressions that involve indirect speech."[66] Parsons writes:

> It seems clear that different occasions of use of a word such as 'say' can presuppose different schemes of interpretation. Moreover, it seems clear that the universe for the quantifiers does not have to be taken as constant for an entire language and even throughout a single discourse, so that this is one dimension with respect to which the schemes of interpretation presupposed in uses of words such as 'say' can differ.[67]

Burge offers a formal theory that is in broad agreement with Parsons's informal account. Burge's formal theory appeals to the indexicality of the truth predicate only, though Burge's indexical view extends to other semantic and epistemic notions.[68] Burge writes:

> In natural language there is a single indexical predicate. We represent this predicate by the schematic predicate expression $[true_i]$. This expression may in particular contexts be filled out by any of an unlimited number of numerical subscripts. Any one of the resulting predicates (formally, there are infinitely many) may represent a particular occurrence of 'true' in a context in which its application is fixed. Thus numerals substituted for 'i' mark not new predicate constants, but contextual applications of the indexical 'true'.[69]

Despite the obvious similarities, there are significant differences between these medieval and modern accounts. Unlike Ockham, Burley, and Pseudo-Sherwood, Parsons and Burge offer a *hierarchical* account. Parsons suggests that there are more and less comprehensive interpretations of uses of natural language, and "a less comprehensive interpretation can be appealed to in a discourse for which a discourse using the more comprehensive interpretation is a metadiscourse."[70] The indices attached to Burge's univocal, indexical truth predicate correspond to levels that are broadly Tarskian in character.[71] Parsons and Burge admit truth-value gaps in a restricted sense,[72] and a hierarchy is generated, on pain of the Strengthened Liar. As we have seen, a hierarchy is not to be forced on the bivalent medieval account, at least not from this direction.

A second major difference is that, according to Parsons and Burge, *no* occurrence of the truth predicate is unrestricted.[73] In contrast, according to the Ockham–Burley–Pseudo-Sherwood line there are restrictions on some, but not all, occurrences of semantical predicates; so, at least prima facie, there is nothing problematic about nonparadoxical, "global" sentences like 'All sentences are either true or not true' or 'God is omniscient'.[74] Further, the evaluations that cannot be expressed by those sentences in which the semantic predicate is restricted *can* be expressed by other sentences in which the restrictions do not apply: Expressive incompleteness is not absolute. On the face of it, then, the Ockham–Burley–Pseudo-Sherwood resolution appears to do justice to Tarski's intuition that natural languages are semantically universal.

Of course, the work of Ockham, Burley, and Pseudo-Sherwood on the insolubles does not constitute a fully developed theory of truth, but it is highly suggestive. I will take up some of their suggestions (though not all of them) in the next chapter. What their work suggests is a contextual, nonhierarchical solution to the Liar that retains classical semantics and respects the intuition that natural language is universal, or at least semantically universal. Ockham, Burley, and Pseudo-Sherwood offer us something "new," and it warrants further investigation.

Chapter 6

A singularity solution to the Liar

The Liar is a product of our ordinary semantic concepts. It shows that we lack a complete grasp of our familiar notions of truth and falsity. Its proper setting is natural language, in which our ordinary semantic terms appear. The Liar is not primarily a "formal" or "technical" problem. If a formal theory of truth is to provide a solution to the Liar, it must be a theory of natural language and, in particular, a theory of our concept of truth.

I argued in Chapters 3 and 4 that a number of recent non-Tarskian treatments of the Liar do not capture our ordinary semantic concepts. For each of these accounts, there are semantic concepts available to the speaker of English that cannot be expressed within the formal theory, on pain of contradiction. Diagonal arguments establish that these semantic concepts can be expressed only in a metalanguage. So the theory does not provide a model of natural language. And a Tarskian hierarchy is forced on the purportedly non-Tarskian account.

This may seem to support a Tarskian resolution of the Liar: If the hierarchy is inevitable anyway, why not accept it from the outset? There are, I believe, a number of reasons why we should reject the Tarskian route, reasons that will emerge in the course of these final chapters. One obvious worry is this: Hierarchical theories do not seem to provide a natural account of our semantic concepts. The Tarskian account of natural language is highly regimented: The stratification of English into a hierarchy of distinct languages is, to borrow a phrase from Russell, "harsh and highly artificial."[1] With Tarski, we may doubt "whether the language of everyday life, after being 'rationalized' in this way, would still preserve its naturalness and whether it would not rather take on the characteristic features of the formalized languages."[2]

I think we can dispense with the hierarchy and provide a natural account of our semantic concepts. My aim in the rest of this book is to develop an account of truth and a solution to the Liar that treats English as a single language. Since the proposal is not hierarchical, there is no unnatural stratification of natural language. And, I shall argue, the proposal does capture our semantic concepts: According to the singularity account, our semantic intuitions stand in need of only minimal correction.

In this chapter, I shall present in an intuitive way the main ideas of the singularity solution. These are drawn in part from the resolution of Ockham, Burley, and Pseudo-Sherwood. In Chapter 7, I present the formal account. The formal account is applied to a variety of Liar-like cases in Chapter 8. In Chapter 9, I return to the problem of universality.

6.1. AN INFORMAL PRESENTATION OF THE SINGULARITY SOLUTION

We may distinguish four main claims of the singularity proposal. According to the first claim, *semantic pathology may be analyzed in terms of the notion of groundedness*. The pathological sentences are those that are ungrounded. A sentence like

(i) '"Snow is white" is true' is true

is grounded because the predications of 'true' within it can be traced back to a sentence free of such predications (namely, the sentence 'Snow is white'). Not so with the Liar sentence

(ii) (ii) is not true

or the Truth Teller sentence

(iii) (iii) is true.

In these ungrounded sentences, 'true' is predicated of a sentence that is not independent of that very predication: (ii) and (iii) are self-referential. Ungrounded sentences need not, though, be self-referential. In the general case, we have systems of sentences in which 'true' is always predicated of sentences themselves involving (the same or other) predications of 'true'. Such is the case not only with the Liar and the Truth Teller, but also with *chains,* like $(\sigma_1)(\sigma_2)$ is true, $(\sigma_2)(\sigma_3)$ is true, $(\sigma_3)(\sigma_4)$ is true, ..., and *loops,* like $(\rho_1)(\rho_2)$ is true, $(\rho_2)(\rho_3)$ is true, ..., $(\rho_n)(\rho_1)$ is true.[3]

The remaining claims go back to the work of Ockham, Burley, and Pseudo-Sherwood. According to the second claim, *a solution to the Liar must be sensitive to contexts of utterance*. A solution to the Liar must deal either with tokens or with sentence types in a context. An adequate account of truth cannot limit itself to sentence types. For one thing, a token of a sentence type may be determinately true or false, while another

100

6.1 An informal presentation

token of the same type may be semantically pathological. Suppose that, on two separate occasions, Joanne says

What Mark is saying is false.

At the time of the first of these utterances, Mark is saying something that has a determinate truth value, say '$7 + 5 = 12$'. At the time of the second, Mark is saying

What Joanne is saying is true.

Joanne's first utterance is determinately true or false, while her second is semantically pathological. Though her utterances are tokens of the same sentence type, they have quite different semantic status. In general, where semantic well-being and pathology are concerned, the context of utterance matters.

Further, it is not enough to limit ourselves to sentence tokens, considered as physical items. Suppose I write on the portable blackboard in room 101

This sentence is written on the blackboard in room 101.

In these circumstances, this sentence token is true. Once the board is wheeled into the corridor, the token is false. If we take the physical token to be the bearer of truth or falsity, we will be forced to conclude that it bears *both* values. Instead, we should account for this shift in truth value by understanding tokens contextually. The same moral may be drawn from sentence tokens containing indexicals. Suppose I write on the board

Someone is reading *Principia Mathematica* now.

Assume that my token survives through at least one period when *Principia* is being read and at least one period when it isn't. Then the truth value of the sentence token shifts with variation in the content of the indexical 'now'.

So we must work either with sentence types in a context or with sentence tokens, understood contextually. The medieval authors work with tokens. In what follows, I shall work with sentence types in a context.

The third main claim of the singularity proposal is this: *The predicates 'true' and 'false' are context-sensitive terms, shifting their extensions according to context.* This places my proposal within the category of *contextual* solutions to the Liar. As we remarked in the previous chapter, contextual approaches to the Liar have been proposed by Parsons, Burge, Barwise and Etchemendy, and Gaifman.[4] These contextual approaches are all motivated by the Strengthened Liar, introduced in Chapter 1.

6 A singularity solution to the Liar

Let us set up a piece of Strengthened Liar reasoning. Aristotle, believing that what Plato has written next door is untrue, writes on the board

(L) The sentence written on the board in room 101 is not true.

But Aristotle is confused about his whereabouts and is himself in room 101. So the sentence is a Liar sentence. Now, we can reason about (L) as follows. Suppose (L) is true. Then what (L) says is the case. So (L) is not true. Suppose, on the other hand, that (L) is false. Then (L) is not true. So (L) is true. Either way we get a contradiction. So (L) is neither true nor false. So (L) is pathological (or undefined, or paradoxical, or gappy, or unstable – here one may insert one's preferred term). However we describe (L)'s semantic status, we can now infer that (L) is not true. But that's what (L) says; so (L) is true, after all.

Any adequate solution to the Liar must account for this intuitive reasoning.[5] Let's examine the argument a little more closely. We may distinguish three stages. First, we reason to the conclusion that (L) is pathological. Second, *given* (L)*'s pathological status,* we infer

(P) (L) is not true.

Third, *given* (P), and *given what* (L) *says,* we infer

(R) (L) is true.

Let an *evaluation* be any sentence σ of the form $T(\rho)$, $F(\rho)$, $\neg T(\rho)$, or $\neg F(\rho)$; ρ is the *evaluated sentence.* Now (P) and (R) are examples of two special kinds of evaluations. When we produce the evaluations (P) and (R), we explicitly reflect on the pathological nature of (L) and evaluate (L) accordingly. Both (P) and (R) are what I shall call *explicit reflections;* when we produce an explicit reflection, we evaluate a pathological sentence qua pathological. The uses of 'true' in (P) and (R) differ from Aristotle's original use in (L). When we utter (P) and (R), we use 'true' in an explicitly reflective way to evaluate a sentence qua pathological; but when Aristotle utters (L), he does not evaluate (L) on the basis of its pathologicality. Strengthened Liar reasoning indicates that we use 'true' in an explicitly reflective way, as well as nonreflectively.

There are two types of explicit reflection. (P) is an example of the first type. Presented with a pathological sentence, we can declare it not true (and not false), simply because it is pathological. That is what we do when we utter (P). Let us call such an explicit reflection a *partial explicit reflection.* In general, a partial explicit reflection σ is always of the form $\neg T(\rho)$ or $\neg F(\rho)$.

(R) is an example of the second type of explicit reflection. In producing (R), we build on the partial explicit reflection (P), taking into account what the pathological sentence itself says. We will call (R) a *complete explicit reflection*. In general, when we utter a complete explicit reflection, we evaluate a pathological sentence *on the basis of a partial explicit reflection and what the pathological sentence says*. A complete explicit reflection can take any of the four forms of an evaluation, namely, $T(\rho)$, $F(\rho)$, $\neg T(\rho)$, or $\neg F(\rho)$. For example, given the "simple Liar"

(S) S is false,

we can carry out the appropriate strengthened reasoning to produce the complete explicit reflection '(S) is not true'. And a complete explicit reflection says that the Truth Teller is false.[6]

Strengthened Liar reasoning shows we have semantic intuitions that lead us to both partial and complete explicit reflections. As we have seen, we evaluate pathological sentences as not true (consider (P)). And we also evaluate certain pathological sentences as true (consider (R)) and others as false (consider a complete explicit reflection on the Truth Teller).

Whether an evaluation is a partial or complete explicit reflection, or neither, is a context-dependent matter. With the three stages of the Strengthened Liar reasoning in mind, we may identify several relevant differences between the contexts of (L), (P), and (R). Clearly there are differences of time and place: First, (R) is uttered later than (P), which is uttered later than (L); and second, neither (P) nor (R) are written on the board in room 101. And third, if we suppose that someone other than Aristotle carries out the strengthened reasoning, there is a difference of speaker too. Still, the familiar contextual parameters of speaker, time, and place do not tell the whole story.

A fourth difference is that (L), (P), and (R) occupy different positions in the Strengthened Liar discourse. In general, the correct interpretation of an expression or a stretch of discourse may depend on the larger discourse in which it is embedded.[7] The first stage of the strengthened reasoning culminates in the evaluation of (L) as pathological. At the second stage, we start out from this subconclusion, that (L) is pathological, established by the first stage of the reasoning. From the subconclusion, we infer (P). At the third stage, we infer (R), in part on the basis of (P). The different positions in the discourse occupied by (L), (P), and (R) are ordered logically as well as temporally.

This points to a fifth difference between the contexts of (L), (P), and (R): There is a difference of relevant information. When Aristotle first utters (L), the information that (L) is pathological is not available to him. But the information is available throughout the second and third stages of the reasoning; indeed, it is made available by the reasoning of the first stage. The reasoning of the second and third stages should be interpreted as incorporating this information. And in turn, the reasoning of the second stage makes available further semantic information, that (L) is not true. This information is utilized at the third stage.[8]

A sixth difference is found in speaker's intentions. When Aristotle first utters (L), his intention is to evaluate an utterance of Plato's. This intention is overridden, given the time and place of Aristotle's utterance: Aristotle has unwittingly landed himself in paradox. At the second and third stages of the reasoning, we have a very different intention, to treat (L) *as* a pathological utterance and evaluate (L) on this basis. This intention is not overridden. On the contrary, the fact that we intentionally take (L) to be pathological leads to our reflective evaluations (P) and (R).[9]

We distinguish, then, three kinds of evaluation: partial explicit reflections (like (P)), complete explicit reflections (like (R)), and the rest (of which (L) is one). Let 'true$_L$' abbreviate 'true in the context of utterance of (L)'; let 'true$_P$' abbreviate 'true in the context of utterance of (P)'; and let 'true$_R$' abbreviate 'true in the context of utterance of (R)'. We may represent Aristotle's pathological utterance as

(L) (L) is not true$_L$.

Corresponding to the predicate 'true$_L$' is the truth schema

s is true$_L$ iff p,

where instances of the schema are obtained by substituting for 'p' any sentence, and for 's' any name of this sentence. Any attempt to evaluate (L) via this schema leads to contradiction. And this is just what is going on at the first stage of the Strengthened Liar reasoning. An attempt is made to evaluate (L) via the truth$_L$ schema. Following Burge, we may discern here a *pragmatic implicature,* that (L) is to be evaluated via the schema for the occurrence of 'true' in (L). This is an instance of a more general implicature; as Burge puts it, "Sentences being referred to or quantified over are to be evaluated with the truth schema for the occurrence of 'true' in the evaluating sentence."[10] When Aristotle utters (L), this implicature is in place. No semantic reasoning about (L) has yet occurred; Aristotle is unaware of the pathological nature of his utterance, and he does not intend to evaluate (L) qua pathological.

The conclusion of the first stage of the Strengthened Liar argument is that (L) is neither true$_L$ or false$_L$: (L) is pathological in its context of utterance. At the second stage, we argue that since (L) is pathological in the context of (L), (L) is not true in the context of (L); that is,

(P) (L) is not true$_L$.

We have seen that the contexts of (L) and (P) differ in a number of respects: there are shifts of discourse position, relevant information, and

6.1 An informal presentation

intentions. Along with these differences, there is a further difference of pragmatic implicature. When we utter (P), we do so on the basis of (L)'s pathologicality: We have just inferred that (L) is pathological, and our intention is to evaluate (L) qua pathological. We recognize that (L) cannot consistently be evaluated via the truth$_L$ schema. The implicature associated with the first stage of the reasoning is now canceled. With the changes in discourse position, relevant information, and intentions, there comes a cancellation of the implicature. Given that we're further along in the reasoning, that more information is available, and that our intentions are different from Aristotle's, we no longer expect the implicature to hold.

Notice that (L) and (P) attribute to the same object the very same property, and yet while (L) is pathological, (P) is true. The difference in semantic status is explained by the differences between their respective contexts of utterance. In the context of utterance of (L), the implicated schema is the truth$_L$ schema; and since (L) does not have truth$_L$ conditions, (L) is pathological in its context of utterance. But (P) is uttered in a context in which the truth$_L$ schema is *not* implicated. So (P) is not pathological in its context of utterance. Rather, (P) is true in its context of utterance, that is, true$_P$, since it *is* the case that (L) is not true$_L$.

In general, whether or not a sentence σ of the form $\neg T(\rho)$ or $\neg F(\rho)$ is a partial explicit reflection is determined by the relevant facts about the context of σ and the context of ρ, facts about speaker, time, place, discourse position, relevant information, intentions, and implicatures. If the facts determine that σ is a partial explicit reflection, then, on our analysis, we interpret the occurrence of 'true' in σ as 'true in the context of the evaluated sentence ρ'. And the partial explicit reflection σ is true in its context of utterance.

Given (P) and given that (L) says that (L) is not true$_L$, we go on to infer

(R) (L) is true$_R$.

This is our complete explicit reflection on (L): We evaluate (L) as true (i.e., true$_R$) because (L) is not true$_L$, and that's what (L) says. We arrive at a final evaluation of (L).[11] In general, whether or not an evaluation σ of a sentence ρ is a complete explicit reflection is a matter determined by the relevant pragmatic facts about the contexts of σ and ρ. If these facts determine that σ is a complete explicit reflection, then we interpret the occurrence of 'true' in σ as 'true in the context of σ'.

So a close examination of Strengthened Liar reasoning suggests a tripartite division of evaluations. An evaluation σ falls into one of three categories according to the relevant facts about the contexts of utterance of σ and the evaluated sentence ρ: σ is a partial explicit reflection, a complete explicit reflection, or neither.[12] The way in which the occurrence of the semantic predicate in the evaluation σ interacts with the context of utterance of σ depends on the nature of the evaluation. An occurrence of 'true' (or 'false') in σ is analyzed as 'true in the context of σ' (or 'false in the context of σ') *except* where σ is a partial explicit reflection; in this case, 'true' ('false') is analyzed as 'true in the context of ρ' ('false in the context of ρ').

Consider now the pathological utterance (L) and the complete explicit reflection (R). The occurrence of 'true' in (L) does not have (L) in its extension because (L) is not true in its context of utterance. But the occurrence of 'true' in our final evaluation (R) *does* include (L) in its extension, since (L) is true in the context of (R). So, according to our analysis of Strengthened Liar reasoning, there is a shift in the extension of 'true' according to context: 'true' is a context-sensitive term.[13]

There is a sharp contrast between the singularity proposal and other contextual approaches. The contextual approaches of Parsons, Burge, Gaifman, and Barwise and Etchemendy all appeal to a hierarchy in some form or other. As we saw in Chapter 5, Parsons, in his discussion of Liar discourses, suggests that there are more and less comprehensive interpretations of uses of natural language, and "a less comprehensive interpretation can be appealed to in a discourse for which a discourse using the more comprehensive interpretation is a metadiscourse."[14] And the indices attached to Burge's univocal, indexical truth predicate correspond to levels that are Tarskian in character.[15] Gaifman writes of his "jump rule" that it is the "rule by which we ascend in the Tarskian hierarchy."[16] Later Gaifman goes on to say: "Tarski's hierarchy can be reconstructed within our framework. The idea is that the application of the Jump Rule moves us up to a higher major level."[17] According to Barwise and Etchemendy, "We can look at the Liar as providing us with a propositional function from situations s to propositions f_s, one that can be used to diagonalize out of any set P of propositions."[18] This generates a sequence of increasingly comprehensive situations. But a universal situation is not reached: "The Liar construction shows that the situations propositions can be about fall short of universality."[19] Though Austinian propositions "can be about extremely comprehensive situations," still "we can . . . step outside such a situation and describe the behavior of its Liar."[20] In contrast to each of these approaches, the singularity proposal is strongly antihierarchical. This will become clear as we turn to the fourth main claim of the singularity account.

The fourth claim is this: In semantically pathological sentences, there are *minimal* restrictions on occurrences of 'true' and 'false'. We have seen that the occurrence of 'true' in (L) is restricted: At least (L) is excluded from its extension. Are there other restrictions, and if so, what are they? How are we to fix the extension of this occurrence of 'true'?

At this point, certain pragmatic principles of interpretation come into play. We turn first to the principle of *Minimality*. According to Minimality, restrictions on occurrences of 'true' (and 'false') are kept to a minimum: We are to restrict the application of 'true' and 'false' only when there is reason to do so. To put things the other way around, the evaluative reach of a given context is to be as comprehensive as possible. Suppose you say "'Snow is white' is true." Should Aristotle's utterance (L) be excluded from the extension of 'true' here? Minimality says no. And this is surely plausible. As we've seen, *within* Aristotle's context of utterance, (L) is pathological; but outside that context, it is true. Since your utterance is quite unrelated to Aristotle's, we have no reason to interpret your utterance as in some way pathologically linked to Aristotle's. Since what (L) says is indeed the case ((L) *isn't* true in its context of utterance), we have no reason to withhold (L) from the extension of 'true' in your utterance. It would be a poor interpretation that implicated your utterance in semantic pathology. In general, speakers do not usually aim to produce pathological utterances, or utterances implicated in pathology.[21] By adopting Minimality, we respect this pragmatic fact.

Further, if we adopt Minimality, we respect a basic intuition about predicates. Intuitively, we take a predicate to pick out everything with the property that the predicate denotes. In general, if an individual has the property denoted by the predicate φ, then the individual is in the extension of φ. The more restrictions we place on occurrences of 'true', the more we are at odds with this intuition. We do expect any solution to a genuine paradox to require some revision of our intuitions. But the more a solution conflicts with our intuitions, the less plausible that solution will be.

For example, the Tarskian stratification of the truth predicate involves massive restrictions on occurrences of 'true'. On a standard Tarskian line, Claire's utterance 'Snow is white' is of level 0; Mark's utterance ' "Snow is white" is true' is of level 1; and so on, through the levels. Mark's use of 'true' in an utterance of level 1 has in its extension all sentences of level 0 *and no others*. So all sentences of level 1 and beyond are excluded from the extension of such a use of 'true'. Gödel remarks of Russell's type theory that "each concept is significant only . . . for an infinitely small portion of objects."[22] A similar point can be made about a standard Tarskian account of truth: An ordinary use of 'true' will apply to only a fraction of all the truths.

Minimality keeps surprise to a minimum: Our uses of 'true' apply to almost all the truths. We are sometimes forced to restrict 'true' – we must, for example, limit the extension of 'true' in Aristotle's pathological utterance (L) by excluding (L) itself. Still, according to Minimality, we are required to exclude only those (pathological) truths that cannot be included.

So my proposal locates what I shall call *singularities* of truth and falsity. For example, (L) is a singularity of the concepts of truth and falsity. (L) is neither true nor false in its context of utterance – (L) is neither in the extension of 'true$_L$' nor in the extension of 'false$_L$'. Attempts to evaluate (L) within its context of utterance fail. In general, a semantically pathological sentence is, in its context of utterance, a singularity of truth and falsity.

Pathological sentences are singularities only in a context-relative way – there is an appropriate reflective context in which the singularity *is* in the extension of 'true' or the extension of 'false'. In the case of our Strengthened Liar discourse, we *can*, from our subsequent reflective context, evaluate (L) as true. It is only within its context of utterance that (L) is a singularity of truth and falsity.

When we fix extensions of occurrences of 'true' in accordance with Minimality, we fix those extensions in a way that is not determined by what the speaker, or we as interpreters, *know*. Such ignorance does not affect the general way in which extensions are determined by Minimality. The relevant empirical and semantic facts may not be available to the speaker or interpreter; nevertheless, these facts in part determine the extension of 'true'.

No occurrence of 'true' is without singularities. Consider again your innocent utterance ' "2 + 2 = 4" is true'. Now suppose you add, not so innocently, 'But this very sentence isn't'. Because of the anaphoric construction here, your pathological addition shares its context of utterance with your original utterance. And so your pathological addition is a singularity of the occurrence of 'true' in your original utterance. It may be that there are no *actual* statements uttered that force restrictions on a given occurrence of 'true' or 'false'; there may be no *actual* singularities. But there are always *possible* anaphoric back references, appropriate pairs of sentence types and contexts. And these will be singularities of the given occurrence of 'true' or 'false'.[23]

We are now in a position to see the anti-Tarskian nature of the singularity proposal. The singularity proposal is not hierarchical. This is a consequence of Minimality. Consider again our Strengthened Liar discourse. On a Tarskian view, the shift from (L) to our reflection (R) would involve an upward shift in language level. But according to the singularity proposal, there are no such levels. Indeed, by Minimality, (R) is *not* excluded from the extension of 'true' in (L): (R) is not a singularity of

6.1 An informal presentation

'true' in (L). (R) is a truth in any context – it is true in any context that (L) is true in (R)'s context of utterance. In particular, (R) is a truth in the context of (L). So, in the extension of 'true$_L$', there is a sentence in which the predicate 'true$_R$' appears. For the Tarskian, this would amount to an unacceptable mixing of language levels. On the singularity proposal, there are no language levels to be unacceptably mixed.

Moreover, there are singularities of the occurrence of 'true' in (R) that are *not* singularities of the occurrence of 'true' in (L). We may add to our reflection (R) the words 'but this very sentence isn't' and produce, ana-phorically, a singularity of 'true' in (R). But by Minimality, this is not a singularity of 'true' in (L). On a Tarskian view, the extension of 'true' in (L) is a proper subset of the extension of 'true' in (R). On the singularity account, neither extension includes the other.

It seems to me an unwarranted Tarskian prejudice to insist that, in moving from (L) to (R), we move to an essentially richer language. Per-haps this prejudice is encouraged by consideration of the utterer's epi-stemic situation. In the context of utterance of (L), Aristotle does not know or believe that (L) is pathological, and so (R) does not express any-thing he knows or believes. Aristotle may come to know or believe (R), but only by transcending the epistemic situation he is in when he utters (L). But as we have already said, what is true or false in a given situation is not determined by what speakers know.

Further, the Tarskian cannot help herself to this epistemic justification of the levels. *For it would be quite possible for Aristotle to produce in-tentionally a pathological token on the board, in full knowledge that he will go on to reflect on that utterance qua pathological.* We may be quite self-conscious about the production of pathological sentences; this is so, for example, when we discuss the Liar. We may produce pathological utterances in full knowledge that, in another (reflective) context, these utterances are true, because pathological in the present context. In this case, there is no shift in what is known, yet still the Tarskian will discern a shift in language levels.

Minimality allows room for any degree of semantic awareness. We may even be omniscient semanticists, producing Liar sentences while in possession of an entire theory of truth. According to Minimality, a use of 'true' applies to all truths except those that are pathological in the given context, whatever the epistemic state of the speaker. In particular, (R) is a truth in the context of utterance of (L), whether Aristotle knows it or not.

Though Minimality is a guiding principle of the singularity proposal, it is not unconstrained. Consider the chain[24]

(1) (2) is false.
(2) (3) is false.
⋮
(n) (n + 1) is false.
⋮

Intuitively, these sentences form a pathological system: each is un-grounded. Now consider this further sentence:

(0) (1) is false.

Should we count this sentence as pathological too? It would better accord with Minimality to treat (0) as a reflection that truly evaluates (1) as false, so that (1) is *not* excluded from 'false' in (0). But since (0) is related to (1) just as each sentence in the chain is related to the next, we have no reason to treat (0) differently from any other sentence in the chain. We should count (0) as pathological too. Here we are applying a principle that we shall call *Symmetry:* To put it somewhat vaguely, we do not treat one sentence as pathological and another not without some reason.[25]

Symmetry applies to loops as well as to chains. Buridan provides us with an example: "Let us posit a case in which Socrates says 'What Plato is saying is false', and nothing else, and Plato on the other hand says 'What Socrates is saying is false', and nothing else."[26] Each utterance makes reference to the other, so as to form a loop:

$$\left(\begin{array}{c}\text{Socrates' utterance, S}\\ \text{Plato's utterance, P}\end{array}\right)$$

We should ascribe the same semantic status to these utterances. Buridan puts it this way: "There is no more reason why Socrates' proposition should be true, or false, than Plato's, or *vice versa,* since they stand in an exactly similar relation to each other."[27]

In the next chapter, we will provide a rigorous characterization of Sym-metry. A key notion there will be the notion of a *symmetrical network*. We can give the rough idea here. There are two kinds of symmetrical net-works: chains and loops. Both chains and loops are infinite sequences of sentences, where each refers to the next. In a chain, no sentence repeats; in a loop, every sentence repeats.

We can represent chains and loops as trees composed of branches and nodes. For example, the sentences (1), (2), ..., (n), ... form an infinite se-quence of sentences, which may be represented as a single-branched tree (see diagram at top of facing page). As we go down this infinite branch, we move from an evaluation to the sentence it evaluates. No sentence

6.1 An informal presentation

$$
\begin{array}{ll}
(1) & \text{[i.e., F(2)]} \\
| & \\
(2) & \text{[i.e., F(3)]} \\
| & \\
(3) & \text{[i.e., F(4)]} \\
\vdots &
\end{array}
$$

repeats on this infinite branch, and this indicates that the sentences (1), (2), ..., (n), ... form a chain. This is one kind of symmetrical network.

The utterances in Buridan's example may also be represented as an infinite, single-branched tree:

$$
\begin{array}{ll}
S & \text{[i.e., F(P)]} \\
| & \\
P & \text{[i.e., F(S)]} \\
| & \\
S & \\
| & \\
P & \\
\vdots &
\end{array}
$$

Both sentences repeat on this infinite branch, and this indicates that P and S form a loop. This is the other kind of symmetrical network.

There are far more complicated symmetrical networks. For example, we can add truth-functional complexity. According to our formal account, the sentences

(φ) ψ is not true and $2+2=4$

and

(ψ) φ is true or $2+2 \neq 4$

form a symmetrical network. Still more complicated symmetrical networks involve both loops and chains, as with this system of sentences:

(1) (2) is true and (1) is not true.
(2) (3) is true and (2) is not true.
$\vdots$
(n) (n+1) is true and (n) is not true.
$\vdots$

However complicated these networks get, the intuitive idea remains the same. A symmetrical network is an infinite sequence of sentences, where each sentence makes reference to the next. And either no members

111

of the sequence repeat, or they all do. Once we have rigorously characterized the notion of a symmetrical network, we can put the principle of Symmetry this way: *All sentences of a symmetrical network are to be treated alike.* Now the infinite length of the sequence indicates pathology. By Symmetry, then, we treat all members of a symmetrical network as pathological.

Consider now an *asymmetrical* network generated by these respective (and simultaneous) utterances of Socrates and Plato:

S′. What I am saying now is true.
P′. What Socrates is saying now is false.

These utterances are *not* symmetrically related. P′ makes reference to S′, but S′ does not make reference to P′. P′ stands above the loop in which S′ is caught. Consider the tree for P′:

$$
\begin{array}{ll}
P' & [\text{i.e., } F(S')] \\
\mid & \\
S' & [\text{i.e., } T(S')] \\
\mid & \\
S' & \\
\mid & \\
S' & \\
\vdots &
\end{array}
$$

P′ does not repeat on this infinite branch: P′ and S′ do not form a symmetrical network. It is no violation of Symmetry to treat these two utterances differently: Symmetry does not constrain Minimality here. Applying Minimality without the constraint of Symmetry, we identify S′ as a singularity of 'true' in S′, but *not* as a singularity of 'false' in P′. S′ cannot but be treated as pathological; but P′ need not be. By Minimality, P′ is treated as a reflection, and S′ *is* in the extension of 'false' in P′.

Notice that P′ is not the result of explicit strengthened reasoning. P′ is a *nonexplicit reflection.* That there are nonexplicit reflections as well as explicit reflections is a consequence of Minimality.

6.2. A GLIMPSE OF THE FORMAL ACCOUNT

We can catch a glimpse of the formal account by way of an example. Consider these respective utterances of Albert and Buridan:

A. A horse is not a goat and this conjunction is not true.
B. What Albert is saying is true.

6.2 A glimpse of the formal account

In the formal account, such utterances are sentences, *where sentences are to be understood as sentence types in a context.* So given an utterance σ, we shall represent it as the ordered pair ⟨sentence type of σ, context of σ⟩. For convenience, we will abbreviate this by '$[\sigma]_\sigma$', where 'σ' within the square brackets stands for the type of utterance σ, and the subscripted 'σ' stands for the context of σ. So '$[A]_A$' denotes Albert's utterance A; '$[B]_B$' denotes Buridan's utterance B. We can also represent A and B in a more structure-revealing way. The sentence type of B may be represented by '$T([A]_A)$'. So we may represent B by '$[T([A]_A)]_B$'. And A may be represented by '$[\neg P\ \&\ \neg T([A]_A)]_A$', where P represents the sentence type of 'A horse is a goat'.

Further, if the type of an utterance σ is truth-functionally complex, the context of its components is taken to be that of σ. So, for example, if σ is representable by $[\rho\ \&\ \tau]_\sigma$, then its components may be represented by $[\rho]_\sigma$ and $[\tau]_\sigma$. The components of Albert's utterance may be represented by '$[\neg P]_A$' and '$[\neg T([A]_A)]_A$'.

The *basic tree* for A is

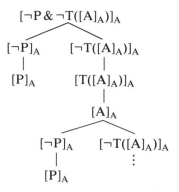

The type of A is a conjunction. The type of the first conjunct may be represented by '$\neg P$', and the type of the second by '$\neg T([A]_A)$'. The two nodes immediately below A are composed of these sentence types paired with the context of utterance of A. The node below $[\neg P]_A$ is (the representation of) the sentence negated. The sentence type associated with this node is not a truth-functional compound or a quantification, and is not the type of an evaluation. Accordingly, the node terminates here. Notice that there is a branch of the basic tree that never terminates. Consider the rightmost branch suggested by our diagram. This branch is infinite, indicating the self-referential character of A.

Next we consider the *pruned tree* for A. Recall the notion of a grounded sentence, described informally in Section 6.1.[28] The pruned tree is obtained from the basic tree as follows: We terminate each branch at the first occurrence of a sentence that is grounded. The pruned tree for A is:

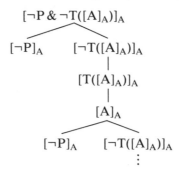

Notice that there is still an infinite branch of the pruned tree; that indicates that A is pathological or ungrounded.

We are now in a position to identify a singularity of 'true' in A. Given the infinite branch on the pruned tree, we say that *the first evaluated sentence on this infinite branch is a singularity of 'true' in* A. The first evaluation on this infinite branch is $[\neg T([A]_A)]_A$; and the first evaluated sentence is, then, $[A]_A$. And so A is a singularity of 'true' in A. The intuition is this: A singularity is a sentence that cannot be evaluated in the given context, since it is ungrounded. The attempt to evaluate the singularity A fails; the failure is indicated by the presence of the infinite branch.

The formal account will allow us to identify further singularities of 'true' in A. Once we have identified them all, we may formally capture the principle of Minimality as it applies to the occurrence of 'true' in A: We exclude from the extension of this occurrence of 'true' only its singularities. And we can characterize Minimality in this fully general way: We exclude from the extension of a given occurrence of 'true' only its singularities.

We now obtain the *evaluated tree* for A from its pruned tree. We first assign an appropriate truth value to all the grounded sentences on the tree. Next, having identified the singularity A, we pair the truth value F with the evaluating sentence immediately above the singularity. This corresponds to the exclusion of the singularity from the extension of 'true' in A: The singularity is *not* true in the context of utterance of A. Then we pair truth values with every sentence of the tree, in the obvious way, according to the truth tables for the sentential connectives. This yields a truth value for A itself. The evaluated tree for A is shown in the diagram at the top of the next page. According to the evaluated tree, A receives the value T. This coincides with the value A receives in an appropriate reflective context.

6.2 A glimpse of the formal account

$$\langle[\neg P\ \&\ \neg T([A]_A)]_A, T\rangle$$

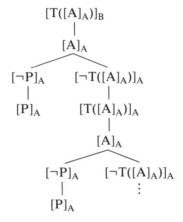

$$\langle[\neg P]_A, T\rangle \qquad \langle[\neg T([A]_A)]_A, T\rangle$$

$$\langle[T([A]_A)]_A, F\rangle$$

Now consider the basic tree for Buridan's utterance B:

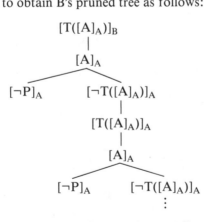

$$[T([A]_A)]_B$$

$$[A]_A$$

$$[\neg P]_A \qquad [\neg T([A]_A)]_A$$

$$[P]_A \qquad [T([A]_A)]_A$$

$$[A]_A$$

$$[\neg P]_A \qquad [\neg T([A]_A)]_A$$

$$[P]_A \qquad \vdots$$

Notice the switch of contextual subscripts between the first and second node.

We may go on to obtain B's pruned tree as follows:

$$[T([A]_A)]_B$$

$$[A]_A$$

$$[\neg P]_A \qquad [\neg T([A]_A)]_A$$

$$[T([A]_A)]_A$$

$$[A]_A$$

$$[\neg P]_A \qquad [\neg T([A]_A)]_A$$

$$\vdots$$

Consider the infinite branch of this pruned tree. All sentences other than B continually repeat: B stands outside this symmetrical network. This is sufficient to characterize Buridan's utterance B as a (nonexplicit) reflection. Once we have identified B as a reflection, we may obtain B's evaluated tree. We terminate the tree at the sentence B evaluates, namely, the sentence A. We pair with A the value provided by A's evaluated tree (i.e., the value T). We then pair with B the appropriate truth value. The evaluated tree for B is

$$\langle [B]_B, T \rangle$$
$$|$$
$$\langle [A]_A, T \rangle$$

According to this analysis, Buridan has produced a true evaluation of Albert's pathological utterance.

6.3. A SUGGESTION OF GÖDEL'S

This concludes the informal presentation of the singularity proposal. To sum up, we treat everyday English not as a hierarchy of languages, but as a single language. We do not divide up truth between infinitely many languages; rather we identify singularities of a single, context-sensitive truth predicate.

Recall Gödel's suggestion, discussed in the last chapter:

> It might even turn out that it is possible to assume every concept to be significant everywhere except for certain 'singular points' or 'limiting points', so that the paradoxes would appear as something analogous to dividing by zero.[29]

Gödel continues:

> Such a system would be most satisfying in the following respect: our logical intuitions would then remain correct up to certain minor corrections, i.e. they could then be considered to give an essentially correct, only somewhat 'blurred', picture of the real state of affairs.[30]

I take my singularity proposal to be very much in the spirit of Gödel's remarks.[31] And we can claim for it the same satisfying feature: Our logical intuitions about 'true' and 'false' are almost correct. The intuition that every sentence is true or false is essentially correct. It is only in pathological or paradoxical contexts that we may mistakenly suppose that certain statements are true or false, when they are neither – and in such cases our applications of 'true' and 'false' require only *minimal* corrections. And ultimately, bivalence is upheld: Any sentence is true or false, in an appropriate reflective context. A second intuition that requires revision is that 'true' is a predicate *constant*. Strengthened Liar discourses suggest that 'true' shifts its extension according to context. But these shifts are kept to a minimum.

6.3 A suggestion of Gödel's

In correcting both these intuitions, we retain a single truth predicate that undergoes minimal changes in its extension according to context. There is no wholesale revision of the notion of truth (or falsity), no division of 'true' into infinitely many distinct predicates, no splitting of everyday English into an infinite hierarchy of languages, and no absolute rejection of bivalence.

In Chapter 9, I claim that the singularity proposal respects another semantic intuition, the intuition that natural languages are semantically universal. Many have taken the Liar to show that we cannot respect this intuition: We must give up any hopes for a universal language. This may seem inevitable, given the split between a language and a theory of truth for that language. If the relation between theory and language is that of Tarskian metalanguage to object language, then certainly universality is lost. But, I shall argue, the singularity theory does not stand to English as metalanguage to object language. The singularity theory can accommodate talk about the theory itself – talk about groundedness, about contexts, even about truth in all contexts. In short, the singularity proposal respects the intuition that English can say everything there is to be said, even about its own semantics. But this is to anticipate. First, we need to develop the formal account itself, and that is our task in the next chapter.

Chapter 7

A formal account of singularities

7.1. PRAGMATIC AND SEMANTIC ASPECTS

We may distinguish two components of the singularity proposal: a pragmatic component and a semantic component. The two main concerns of the pragmatic component have already emerged in the previous chapter. One is the identification of the contextual parameters that play a role in Strengthened Liar reasoning. The other is the articulation of the pragmatic principles of interpretation that guide our treatment of truth. The semantic component is the main topic of the present chapter. Our aim is to give a more precise characterization of semantic well-being, semantic pathology, and singularities. There is of course a good deal of interplay between the pragmatic and semantic aspects of the theory. For example, we will see how the pragmatic principles of Minimality and Symmetry guide the semantic account; and in the other direction, we will see how the semantic account provides for a precise formulation of Symmetry.

But it is important for present purposes to note that the characterization of *explicit* reflections (either partial or complete) is a matter for the *pragmatic* part of our account. In the previous chapter, we characterized explicit reflections in pragmatic terms, via contextual features – in particular, discourse position, relevant information, intentions, and implicatures. The tripartite division between partial explicit reflections, complete explicit reflections, and all other evaluations is a pragmatic division. This division does *not* uniquely determine the semantic account: It does not determine the definition of pathologicality or the extension of occurrences of 'true'. For example, a hierarchical approach and a nonhierarchical approach are each perfectly compatible with the pragmatic characterization of explicit reflections. In this respect, the singularity theory is modular.

I think it is quite misguided to search for a characterization of explicit reflections within the semantic component of the theory. Consider the following chain:

(1) (2) is not true.
(2) (3) is true.
$\vdots$
(2n − 1) (2n) is not true.
(2n) (2n + 1) is true.
$\vdots$

Consider now a further sentence:

(0) (1) is true.

Contrast (0) with the sentence (0′), produced through strengthened reasoning as follows:

> (2) heads a chain, and so (2) is pathological. Since (2) is
> pathological, (2) is not true.
> That's what (1) says; so,
> (0′) (1) is true.

By Symmetry, we treat (0) as a pathological member of an enlarged chain. In contrast, (0′) is true: (0′) is a true complete explicit reflection. Yet there are no *semantic* features that distinguish (0) and (0′). As we saw when we glimpsed the formal account in the preceding chapter, the relevant semantic features of a sentence are articulated via various trees – basic trees, pruned trees, and evaluated trees. These trees exhibit the network of sentences to which the given sentence belongs. Suppose we ignore the pragmatic differences between (0) and (0′). Then the basic, pruned, and evaluated trees for (0′) will be exactly similar to those of (0). The fact that (0′) is a complete explicit reflection cannot be recovered from its semantic features. It is the relevant pragmatic facts about the context of (0′) and the context of the sentence (1) that (0′) evaluates that determine the status of (0′) as a complete explicit reflection. If we want to bring out the difference between (0) and (0′), we cannot dispense with the pragmatic component of our account.

Or consider a partial explicit reflection on (2), produced by strengthened reasoning as follows:

> (2) is a member of an infinitely descending chain, and hence
> (2) is pathological. So,
> (1′) (2) is not true.

Here, (1′) is a partial explicit reflection and is true. In contrast, (1) is a pathological member of an infinite chain. The difference between (1) and (1′) is to be explained pragmatically in terms of the differences between

the context of (1) and the context of (1'). Again, the trees for (1) and (1')
will be exactly similar. The difference between (1) and (1') is not to be explained in terms of their semantic features.

For a third example, consider a Truth Teller sentence:

(T) (T) is true.

As we have seen,[1] we may produce strengthened reasoning about (T) as
follows:

> (T) is pathological, and so:
> (P*) (T) is not true.
> But (T) says of itself that it *is* true, and so, given (P*) and what
> (T) says,
> (R*) (T) is not true.

Here, (P*) is a true partial explicit reflection and (R*) is a true complete
explicit reflection. But we cannot distinguish between (P*) and (R*) on
semantic grounds.

*The situation is very different where nonexplicit reflections are con-
cerned.* For example, consider again the asymmetrical network we introduced in the previous chapter. Socrates and Plato say respectively (and
simultaneously)

(S') What I am saying now is not true.
(P') What Socrates is saying now is true.

The treatment of (P') as a true nonexplicit reflection *is* determined by its
semantic features. In particular, the basic tree for (P') indicates that (P')
stands above the loop in which (S') is caught, so that (P') and (S') are not
members of a symmetrical network. Here, then, Symmetry does not constrain Minimality; and by Minimality, while (S') is pathological, (P') is a
true nonexplicit reflection.[2] We can identify a nonexplicit reflection in virtue of its semantic features, as revealed by the relevant trees. But we cannot identify explicit reflections independently of certain pragmatic facts.

An utterance of any form, evaluations included, will be treated as a
sentence type in a context – recall Section 6.2. Given an evaluation σ, this
is represented as the ordered pair ⟨the sentence type of σ, the context
of σ⟩. And for convenience, we abbreviate this by '$[\sigma]_\sigma$', where 'σ' within
the square brackets stands for the type of σ, and the subscripted 'σ' stands
for the context of σ.

Now, whether or not an evaluation σ is an explicit reflection is a matter
determined by the relevant pragmatic facts. If σ is a partial explicit reflec-
tion, we might represent it by $[\neg T([\rho]_\rho)]^1_\sigma$ or $[\neg F([\rho]_\rho)]^1_\sigma$. And if σ is a
complete explicit reflection, we might represent it by $[T([\rho]_\rho)]^2_\sigma$, $[F([\rho]_\rho)]^2_\sigma$,

$[\neg T([\rho]_\rho)]^2_\sigma$, or $[\neg F([\rho]_\rho)]^2_\sigma$. In these representations, the appropriate superscript is determined by the relevant pragmatic facts about the context of σ and the context of the evaluated utterance ρ – in particular, facts about speaker, time, place, discourse position, relevant information, intentions, and implicatures. These superscripts are established independently of the formal semantic account.

We will import the pragmatically established superscripts into the formal semantic account. In characterizing formally semantic well-being, semantic pathology, and singularities, we will assume that all the pragmatic facts are in. We'll assume that those evaluations that are explicit reflections may be identified as such in advance of the semantic account. When it becomes necessary, these evaluations will be assigned their appropriate superscripts.[3]

7.2. THE REFLECTIVE HIERARCHY AND SINGULARITIES

We now turn to a more formal semantic account. Our main aim is to characterize certain singularities of a given occurrence of 'true' – what we will call its *key singularities*. The first notions we will define – those of a *g-witness,* a *basic tree,* and a *pruned$_0$ tree* – are independent of the pragmatic facts; it is only after we have defined a pruned$_0$ tree that we will need to import the pragmatically established superscripts into our account.

In what follows, we will be largely concerned with the precise characterization of notions like *basic tree, pruned tree,* and *evaluated tree* (glimpsed in the previous chapter). There will be more by way of definitions than theorems. But we will draw out some simple consequences of our definitions and give informal proofs, as needed.

Let L be a first-order quantificational language. The variables range over a nonempty domain D. The primitive predicates of L are defined by relations on D. We assume that, for each object in the domain, there is an object in the domain that names it. We obtain the language $\mathcal{L}$ by adding to L the one-place predicates T and F, to be interpreted respectively as the truth and falsity predicates for $\mathcal{L}$. We may think of $\mathcal{L}$ as the nonsemantic part of English, together with the context-sensitive English predicates 'true' and 'false'.

7.2.1. *The true$_0$ and false$_0$ sentences*

Our first task is to characterize formally the sentences of $\mathcal{L}$ that are grounded in sentences free of semantic predicates. A sentence like

7 A formal account of singularities

" ' "Snow is white" is true' is true" is true

contains embedded occurrences of 'true' but is ultimately grounded in a sentence that is free of semantic predicates – namely, 'Snow is white'. Such grounded sentences will be defined as those that are associated with certain well-founded trees; intuitively, such a tree witnesses the groundedness of a given sentence.

As we noted in Section 6.2, if the type of a sentence γ is truth-functionally complex, the context of its components is taken to be that of γ – the subscript 'γ' is retained in the representation of these components. Parallel remarks apply to instances of quantified sentences.

Definition. A *g-witness* for a sentence σ of $\mathcal{L}$ is a well-founded tree composed of nodes as follows:

(1)   The first node is either $\langle [\sigma]_\sigma, T \rangle$ or $\langle [\sigma]_\sigma, F \rangle$.

(2) (a)(i) If $\langle [T([\rho]_\rho)]_\gamma, T \rangle$ is a node, then $\langle [\rho]_\rho, T \rangle$ is the next node.

   (ii) If $\langle [T([\rho]_\rho)]_\gamma, F \rangle$ is a node, then $\langle [\rho]_\rho, F \rangle$ is the next node.

   (iii) If $\langle [F([\rho]_\rho)]_\gamma, T \rangle$ is a node, then $\langle [\rho]_\rho, F \rangle$ is the next node.

   (iv) If $\langle [F([\rho]_\rho)]_\gamma, F \rangle$ is a node, then $\langle [\rho]_\rho, T \rangle$ is the next node.

   (b)(i) If $\langle [\neg\rho]_\gamma, T \rangle$ is a node, then $\langle [\rho]_\gamma, F \rangle$ is the next node.

   (ii) If $\langle [\neg\rho]_\gamma, F \rangle$ is a node, then $\langle [\rho]_\gamma, T \rangle$ is the next node.

   (c)(i) If $\langle [\rho \vee \tau]_\gamma, T \rangle$ is a node, then either $\langle [\rho]_\gamma, T \rangle$ or $\langle [\tau]_\gamma, T \rangle$ is the next node.

   (ii) If $\langle [\rho \vee \tau]_\gamma, F \rangle$ is a node, then $\langle [\rho]_\gamma, F \rangle$ and $\langle [\tau]_\gamma, F \rangle$ are the next nodes.

   (d)(i) If $\langle [\rho \mathbin{\&} \tau]_\gamma, T \rangle$ is a node, then $\langle [\rho]_\gamma, T \rangle$ and $\langle [\tau]_\gamma, T \rangle$ are the next nodes.

   (ii) If $\langle [\rho \mathbin{\&} \tau]_\gamma, F \rangle$ is a node, then either $\langle [\rho]_\gamma, F \rangle$ or $\langle [\tau]_\gamma, F \rangle$ is the next node.

   (e)(i) If $\langle [\rho \rightarrow \tau]_\gamma, T \rangle$ is a node, then either $\langle [\rho]_\gamma, F \rangle$ or $\langle [\tau]_\gamma, T \rangle$ is the next node.

   (ii) If $\langle [\rho \rightarrow \tau]_\gamma, F \rangle$ is a node, then $\langle [\rho]_\gamma, T \rangle$ and $\langle [\tau]_\gamma, F \rangle$ are the next nodes.

   (f)(i) If $\langle [\exists x\, \varphi(x)]_\gamma, T \rangle$ is a node, then, for some object in the domain, $\langle [\varphi(a)]_\gamma, T \rangle$ is the next node, where 'a' is a name of the object.

122

(ii) If $\langle [\exists x \varphi(x)]_\gamma, F \rangle$ is a node, then, for each object in the domain, $\langle [\varphi(a)]_\gamma, F \rangle$ is one of the next nodes, where 'a' is a name of the object.

(g)(i) If $\langle [\forall x \varphi(x)]_\gamma, T \rangle$ is a node, then, for each object in the domain, $\langle [\varphi(a)]_\gamma, T \rangle$ is one of the next nodes, where 'a' is a name of the object.

(ii) If $\langle [\forall x \varphi(x)]_\gamma, F \rangle$ is a node, then, for some object in the domain, $\langle [\varphi(a)]_\gamma, F \rangle$ is the next node, where 'a' is a name of the object.

(h)(i) If $\langle [\rho]_\gamma, T \rangle$ is a node, and $[\rho]_\gamma$ is an atomic sentence of L, then $[\rho]_\gamma$ is true in L.

(ii) If $\langle [\rho]_\gamma, F \rangle$ is a node, and $[\rho]_\gamma$ is an atomic sentence of L, then $[\rho]_\gamma$ is false in L.

For example, suppose that I am mistaken about my whereabouts and write on the board in room 101 the following pathological sentence:

(A) The sentence written on the board in room 101 is false or snow is white.

(A) is grounded in virtue of the component 'snow is white' (in accordance with Kleene's strong tables).[4] The g-witness for (1) is

$$\langle [F([A]_A) \vee \text{'snow is white'}]_A, T \rangle$$
$$|$$
$$\langle [\text{'snow is white'}]_A, T \rangle$$

Suppose now that, in the same empirical circumstances, I write

(B) The sentence written on the board in room 101 is false and snow is white.

Then my utterance has no g-witness. In general, a semantically pathological sentence has no g-witness. Notice also that since explicit reflections evaluate pathological sentences, they too have no g-witnesses.[5]

We now define the $true_0$ and $false_0$ sentences.[6]

Definition. Let σ be a sentence of $\mathcal{L}$. Then,

σ is $true_0$ iff there is a g-witness with first node $\langle [\sigma]_\sigma, T \rangle$.
σ is $false_0$ iff there is a g-witness with first node $\langle [\sigma]_\sigma, F \rangle$.

For example, (A) is $true_0$. (B), like any pathological sentence, is neither $true_0$ nor $false_0$.

7.2.2. The reflective hierarchy

In an intuitive sense, sentences like (A) and (B) are *reflection-free:* They are not themselves reflections, and the network of sentences to which they belong do not contain reflections. We can go on to produce reflections on ungrounded sentences like (B). For example, recall from the previous chapter Aristotle's pathological utterance

(L) The sentence written on the board in room 101 is not true.

As we saw, we can produce an explicit reflection (R) on (L):

(R) (L) is true.

And we can go further. We can produce a new pathological utterance that involves the reflection (R). For example, we may produce an anaphoric paradox by adding to our reflection (R) the words 'but this very sentence isn't', so as to obtain

(L') (L) is true but this very sentence isn't.

Clearly (R) and (L') are not reflection-free. Each either is, or involves, a reflection, (R). Below we will call (R) a *first-level reflection,* since it is a reflection on a reflection-free sentence. And we will accordingly call (R) and (L') *1-reflective.*

And we can go further still. Via some appropriate strengthened reasoning, we can produce a complete explicit reflection on (L'):

(R') (L') is true.

Since (R') is a reflection on a 1-reflective sentence, we will call (R') a *second-level reflection,* and we'll say that (R') is 2-reflective. And there will be pathological 2-reflective sentences as well: Consider the result of an appropriate anaphoric addition to (R').

And so on. We are led to a hierarchy of sentences that are or involve reflections. At the base level 1 of the hierarchy are sentences that are not, and do not themselves involve, reflections: the true_0 and false_0 sentences, and pathological sentences like (L). On our account, the hierarchy is *cumulative,* so at level 2 we find all the sentences from level 1. But some sentences appear for the first time at level 2. At level 2, we find first-level reflections like (R); and we find 1-reflective sentences like (L'), which are pathological sentences that involve first-level reflections. At level 3, we find for the first time second-level reflections like (R'); and we also find 2-reflective pathological sentences that involve second-level reflections. And so on, through the levels. Let us call this hierarchy *the reflective hierarchy.* Notice that every sentence of $\mathcal{L}$ will appear at some level of this hierarchy – for every sentence, there is an upper limit on the level of the reflections it involves.

The reflective hierarchy captures in a formal way our capacity to produce reflections. To forestall misunderstanding, let me stress that the level of a sentence σ in the reflective hierarchy is *not* a measure of the extension of an occurrence of 'true' in σ: *we are not offering a Tarskian account.*[7] If σ is of a higher level than ρ, this does *not* mean that 'true' in σ has a broader extension than 'true' in ρ. (For example, 'true' in (R) does not have broader extension than 'true' in (L).) As a consequence of Minimality, neither extension includes the other; each occurrence of 'true' has singularities that the other does not (consider appropriate anaphoric paradoxes). Notice another anti-Tarskian feature: Both extensions will contain sentences from every level of the hierarchy. For example, any true reflection from any level of the hierarchy is in each extension. *The level of a sentence in the hierarchy merely indicates the level of the highest reflection that the sentence involves.*

We need the reflective hierarchy in order to characterize the singularities of an occurrence of 'true'. In general, the singularities of 'true' in a sentence σ will depend on the semantic status of σ: for example, on whether σ is true_0, false_0, pathological, or a reflection. And we can only decide the status of σ if we can identify its place in the hierarchy. (Further general remarks about the reflective hierarchy and its relation to English can be found at the end of this chapter.)

We now take the first of a number of steps toward a more precise account of the reflective hierarchy and of singularities.

7.2.3. *Basic trees and pruned$_0$ trees*

We first define the notion of a *basic tree* for sentences of $\mathcal{L}$. Every sentence has a basic tree. If a sentence is a member of a network of evaluations, then this will be exhibited by the basic tree.

Definition. A *basic tree* for a sentence σ of $\mathcal{L}$ is composed as follows:

(1)   The top node of the tree is $[\sigma]_\sigma$.

(2) (a) If $[T([\rho]_\rho)]_\gamma$ is a node, then $[\rho]_\rho$ is the next node.
     (b) If $[F([\rho]_\rho)]_\gamma$ is a node, then $[\rho]_\rho$ is the next node.
     (c) If $[\neg T([\rho]_\rho)]_\gamma$ is a node, then $[T([\rho]_\rho)]_\gamma$ is the next node.
     (d) If $[\neg F([\rho]_\rho)]_\gamma$ is a node, then $[F([\rho]_\rho)]_\gamma$ is the next node.
     (e) If $[\neg \rho]_\gamma$ is a node, then $[\rho]_\gamma$ is the next node.

7 A formal account of singularities

(f) If $[\rho \vee \tau]_\gamma$ is a node, then $[\rho]_\gamma$ and $[\tau]_\gamma$ are the next nodes.

(g) If $[\rho \,\&\, \tau]_\gamma$ is a node, then $[\rho]_\gamma$ and $[\tau]_\gamma$ are the next nodes.

(h) If $[\rho \rightarrow \tau]_\gamma$ is a node, then $[\rho]_\gamma$ and $[\tau]_\gamma$ are the next nodes.

(i) If $[\exists x \,\varphi(x)]_\gamma$ is a node, then, for each object in the domain, $[\varphi(a)]_\gamma$ is one of the next nodes, where 'a' is a name of the object.

(j) If $[\forall x \,\varphi(x)]_\gamma$ is a node, then, for each object in the domain, $[\varphi(a)]_\gamma$ is one of the next nodes, where 'a' is a name of the object.

(k) If $[\rho]_\gamma$ is a node, and $[\rho]_\gamma$ is an atomic sentence of L, then the branch terminates at this node.

The basic tree for my pathological utterance (A) is

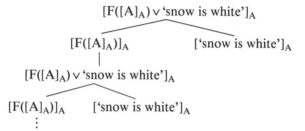

The basic tree for (B) is exactly similar, and it too has an infinite branch.

Given the true$_0$ and the false$_0$ sentences, we can go some way toward evaluating a given basic tree. The first step is to prune the basic tree: We cut away any part of a branch below a true$_0$ or false$_0$ sentence.

Definition. Given a sentence σ, the *pruned$_0$ tree* for σ is obtained from the basic tree for σ by terminating any branch at the first occurrence of a true$_0$ or false$_0$ sentence.

The pruned$_0$ tree for (A) is simply

$$[F([A]_A) \vee \text{'snow is white'}]_A,$$

since (A) is true$_0$. The pruned$_0$ tree for (B) has an infinite branch:

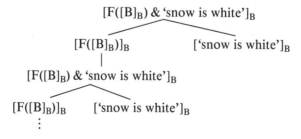

126

7.2 The reflective hierarchy and singularities

An infinite branch of a pruned$_0$ tree indicates pathology. We next characterize two kinds of pathological sentences: those that loop and those that head a chain.

Definitions. Given a sentence σ, let ρ be a sentence that is a node of σ's pruned$_0$ tree. Then, ρ *loops* iff there is an infinite branch of the tree on which ρ repeats; and ρ *heads a chain* iff there is an infinite branch of the tree such that no sentence below ρ repeats.

With respect to the pruned$_0$ tree for the sentence (B), (B) loops. Recall this chain from Chapter 1:

(σ_1) σ_2 is false.
(σ_2) σ_3 is true.
⋮
(σ_{2k-1}) σ_{2k} is false.
(σ_{2k}) σ_{2k+1} is true.
⋮

With respect to the pruned$_0$ tree for the sentence σ_1, σ_1 heads a chain; and so does every other member of this chain.

7.2.4. Reflection-free sentences

We will now provide a characterization of those sentences at the base level of the reflective hierarchy, those that involve no reflections. In our informal discussion, we distinguished two kinds of reflections, explicit and nonexplicit reflections. These require separate consideration.

As we noted in Section 7.1, nonexplicit reflections may be characterized in terms of their semantic features. Recall our treatment of the following utterances of Socrates and Plato:

(S') What I am saying now is not true

and

(P') What Socrates is saying now is true.

While (S') is pathologically looped with itself, (P') stands above this loop; (P') is a nonexplicit reflection in virtue of this semantic feature. In general, *a nonexplicit reflection evaluates a looped sentence but is not itself looped*.

As we also noted in Section 7.1, explicit reflections must be characterized pragmatically. *It is here that we will import the relevant pragmatic facts into our account.* Take a sentence σ and its pruned$_0$ tree. Let ρ be

127

an evaluation that is a node of σ's pruned$_0$ tree. If the relevant pragmatic facts – about the context of ρ and the context of its evaluated sentence – determine that ρ is a partial explicit reflection, then every node composed of ρ is flagged with a superscript 1. If the relevant pragmatic facts determine that ρ is a complete explicit reflection, then every node composed of ρ is flagged with a superscript 2. We will call the tree that results the *pruned$_0^R$ tree for σ*.

For example, consider again the sentence (0) and the complete explicit reflection (0′), from Section 7.1. The pruned$_0$ trees for (0) and (0′) are exactly similar. But since (0′) is a complete explicit reflection, and (0) is not, their pruned$_0^R$ trees are different. The pruned$_0^R$ for (0) is identical to its pruned$_0$ tree:

$$[T([1]_1)]_0$$
$$|$$
$$[\neg T([2]_2)]_1$$
$$|$$
$$[T([2]_2)]_1$$
$$|$$
$$[T([3]_3)]_2$$
$$\vdots$$

The pruned$_0^R$ tree for (0′) is given by

$$[T([1]_1)]_{0'}^2$$
$$|$$
$$[\neg T([2]_2)]_1$$
$$|$$
$$[T([2]_2)]_1$$
$$|$$
$$[T([3]_3)]_2$$
$$\vdots$$

The superscript 2 at the top node embodies the pragmatic facts about the context of (0′) and the context of the evaluated sentence (1).

For another example, recall (1′) from Section 7.1. This is a partial explicit reflection on sentence (2) of our infinitely descending chain. Its pruned$_0$ tree is exactly similar to that of (1). But its pruned$_0^R$ tree is different, and is shown as the figure at the top of the next page. The superscript 1 at the top node embodies the pragmatic facts about the context of (1′) and the context of the evaluated sentence (2).

We are now in a position to characterize the sentences at the base level of the reflective hierarchy, the reflection-free sentences.

$$[\neg T([2]_2)]^1_{1'}$$
$$|$$
$$[T([2]_2)]_{1'}$$
$$|$$
$$[T([3]_3)]_2$$
$$\vdots$$

Definition. A sentence σ is *reflection-free* iff

(a) σ is $true_0$ or $false_0$, or

(b) (i) No evaluation with superscript 1 or 2 is a node of σ's $pruned^R_0$ tree, and

(ii) If ρ is an evaluation on any infinite branch of σ's $pruned_0$ tree, then ρ either loops or heads a chain.

If a sentence σ is reflection-free, then neither explicit nor nonexplicit reflections appear on its $pruned^R_0$ (or $pruned_0$) tree. Explicit reflections are ruled out by clause (b)(i). Nonexplicit reflections are excluded by clause (b)(ii).

Definition. Let σ be a reflection-free sentence. The sentences of an infinite branch of σ's $pruned_0$ tree form a *reflection-free symmetrical network*.

Consider again my utterance (B). We saw that the $pruned_0$ tree for (B) has an infinite branch. The sentences on this branch form a reflection-free symmetrical network, and every sentence in this network loops. Or consider σ_1. We saw that the $pruned_0$ tree for σ_1 is composed of a single infinite branch. The sentences on this branch form a reflection-free symmetrical network, and every sentence in this network heads a chain. It is easy to show that all the members of a reflection-free symmetrical network either loop or head a chain.

Now we can give a characterization of the pragmatic principle of Symmetry, limited to the reflection-free sentences.

(Limited) Principle of Symmetry. *All members of a reflection-free symmetrical network are to be treated alike, as pathological.*

Next, we capture precisely the notion of pathologicality for reflection-free sentences, via the notion of groundedness.

Definition. A reflection-free sentence σ is *grounded* if σ is $true_0$ or $false_0$, and *ungrounded* if the $pruned_0$ tree for σ is unfounded.

7 A formal account of singularities

7.2.5. Key singularities of reflection-free sentences

We are finally in a position to identify certain singularities of occurrences of 'true' or 'false' in an ungrounded, reflection-free sentence. We will be particularly interested in the *key singularities*. As we will see, the key singularities have the following feature. *The exclusion of the key singularities from the extensions of occurrences of 'true' or 'false' in a sentence generates a truth value for the sentence.*

Some terminology: Call a sentence *prime for the propositional calculus* if the most structure-revealing symbolization of it in the propositional calculus is a sentence letter. (So, for example, if I say, 'All humans are mortal', my utterance is prime for the propositional calculus.) Given an occurrence O of 'true' or 'false', *the prime container of O* is the largest sentence that contains O and is prime for the propositional calculus.

> **Definition.** Let σ be an ungrounded, reflection-free prime container of an occurrence O of 'true' or 'false'. The *key singularities* of O are the first evaluated sentences occurring on the infinite branches of σ's pruned_0 tree.[8]

For example, consider the sentences

(C) (D) is true and $2+2=4$,
(D) (C) is true.

The first conjunct of (C), call it (C1), is the prime container of the occurrence of 'true' in (C). (C1)'s pruned_0 tree is

$$[T([D]_D)]_C$$
$$|$$
$$[D]_D$$
$$|$$
$$[T([D]_D) \,\&\, 2+2=4]_C$$

$$[T([D]_D)]_C \qquad [2+2=4]_C$$
$$\vdots$$

The first evaluated sentence occurring in the only infinite branch is (D). So (D) is the key singularity of 'true' in (C1). The intuition is this: A singularity is a sentence that cannot be evaluated in the given context. The attempt to evaluate the singularity (D) fails: The failure is indicated by the presence of the infinite branch. Notice that the exclusion of the key singularity (D) from the extension of this occurrence of 'true' determines a truth value (false) for (C1) and for (C). This exclusion is justified by Symmetry. (C1) and (D) are members of a symmetrical network, since every sentence of the infinite branch repeats. So, by Symmetry, both (C1) and (D) are treated as pathological. Clearly, if (C1) is pathological, it must be excluded from the extension of 'true' in (C1) itself. And so (D) must be excluded too. Notice that (C1) is also a singularity, though not a key singularity, of 'true' in (C1).[9]

7.2.6. The $true_1$ and $false_1$ sentences

We now describe a way of establishing a truth value for a reflection-free sentence σ. Consider σ's pruned$_0$ tree. There are three steps:

STEP 1. Pair each true$_0$ or false$_0$ sentence with the appropriate truth value.

STEP 2. Consider each infinite branch, if there are any. The first occurrence of either $[T([\rho]_\rho)]_\gamma$ or $[F([\rho]_\rho)]_\gamma$ in each infinite branch is paired with the value F, and the branch terminates here.

Note that this step corresponds to the exclusion of a key singularity from the extension of an occurrence of 'true' or 'false' in σ. The exclusion is justified by Symmetry. We can generalize the reasoning in the previous paragraph. Since σ and ρ are members of a symmetrical network, both σ and ρ are to be treated alike, as pathological. Since σ is pathological, σ is not in the extension of any occurrence of 'true' or 'false' in σ itself. By Symmetry, neither is ρ: ρ is also excluded from the extension of occurrences of 'true' or 'false' in σ.

STEP 3. By Steps 1 and 2, we obtain a tree all of whose terminal nodes are paired with a truth value. We go on to obtain a fully evaluated tree by associating truth values with all other sentences of the pruned tree, in the following way:[10]

    (1) (i) $[T([\rho]_\rho)]_\gamma$ is true if $[\rho]_\rho$ is true.
        (ii) $[T([\rho]_\rho)]_\gamma$ is false if $[\rho]_\rho$ is false.
       (iii) $[F([\rho]_\rho)]_\gamma$ is false if $[\rho]_\rho$ is true.
       (iv) $[F([\rho]_\rho)]_\gamma$ is true if $[\rho]_\rho$ is false.
    (2) (i) $[\neg\rho]_\gamma$ is false if $[\rho]_\gamma$ is true.
        (ii) $[\neg\rho]_\gamma$ is true if $[\rho]_\gamma$ is false.
    (3) (i) $[\rho \vee \tau]_\gamma$ is true if $[\rho]_\gamma$ or $[\tau]_\gamma$ is true.
        (ii) $[\rho \vee \tau]_\gamma$ is false if $[\rho]_\gamma$ and $[\tau]_\gamma$ are false.

7 A formal account of singularities

(4) (i) $[\exists x\,\varphi(x)]_\gamma$ is true if, for some object in the domain, $[\varphi(a)]_\gamma$ is true, where 'a' is a name of the object.

(ii) $[\exists x\,\varphi(x)]_\gamma$ is false if, for each object in the domain, $[\varphi(a)]_\gamma$ is false, where 'a' is a name of the object.

Definition. Given a reflection-free sentence σ, the *evaluated$_0$ tree* for σ is the result of applying the just cited procedure to σ's pruned$_0$ tree.

It is easy to show that the procedure we have just described determines a truth value for the sentence σ. Suppose, toward a contradiction, that no truth value is determined for σ. Then the evaluated$_0$ tree must have an infinite branch. This branch must pass through an initial $[T([\rho]_\rho)]_\gamma$ or $[F([\rho]_\rho)]_\gamma$. And this is a contradiction, since infinite branches are terminated at such sentences.

We can regard this procedure as embodying the reasoning that leads to the reflective evaluation of a pathological sentence. The evaluated$_0$ tree for (C1) in our previous example is simply

$$\langle [\text{C1}]_\text{C}, \text{F} \rangle.$$

The termination of the infinite branch at this node corresponds to our step of identifying (D) as the key singularity of (C1) and excluding (D) from the extension of the occurrence of 'true' in (C1). *The pairing of the value* F *with* (C1) *corresponds to a final reflective evaluation of* (C1) *as false.* (C1) says (D) is true, and (D) is *not* true, because it is pathological in its context of utterance.

We now define the true$_1$ and the false$_1$ sentences:

Definition. A sentence σ is a *true$_1$ sentence* iff the first node of the evaluated$_0$ tree for σ is $\langle \sigma, T \rangle$.

A sentence σ is a *false$_1$ sentence* iff the first node of the evaluated$_0$ tree for σ is $\langle \sigma, F \rangle$.

(C1) is false$_1$. It is easily checked that Aristotle's pathological utterance (L) is a true$_1$ sentence, while the Truth Teller is a false$_1$ sentence.

7.2.7. Higher levels of the reflective hierarchy

We have now characterized the first level of the reflective hierarchy: At level 1 are the true$_1$ and the false$_1$ sentences. These sentences are the reflection-free sentences. We now turn to the higher levels. Recall our intuitive remarks in Section 7.2.2. At level 2 of the hierarchy, we find first-level reflections like (R), and pathological sentences that involve first-level reflections (and no higher reflections). At level 3, we find second-level reflections, and pathological sentences that involve second-level reflections (and no higher reflections). And so on. Just as we described the first level of the hierarchy as comprising the $true_1$ and $false_1$ sentences, so we will describe level α of the hierarchy as comprising the $true_\alpha$ and $false_\alpha$ sentences.

We will proceed as follows: Given the $true_\beta$ and $false_\beta$ sentences, $1 \leqslant \beta < \alpha$, we go on to show how to define the $true_\alpha$ and $false_\alpha$ sentences.

First we define the notion of a $pruned_\beta$ tree for a sentence σ:

Definition. Given a sentence σ and an ordinal $\beta < \alpha$, the *pruned$_\beta$ tree for σ* is obtained from the basic tree for σ by terminating any branch at the first occurrence of a $true_\beta$ or $false_\beta$ sentence.

For example, consider again our reflection (R) on Aristotle's pathological utterance (L):

(R) (L) is true.

The $pruned_1$ tree for (R) is as follows:

$$[T([L]_L)]_R$$
$$|$$
$$[L]_L$$

The tree is terminated at the second node, since (L) is a $true_1$ sentence.

For a second example, recall the pathological sentence (L′) produced by an anaphoric addition to (R):

(L′) (L) is true but this very sentence isn't.

The $pruned_1$ tree for (L′) is

$$[T([L]_L) \,\&\, \neg T([L']_{L'})]_{L'}$$

$$[T([L]_L)]_{L'} \qquad [\neg T([L']_{L'})]_{L'}$$
$$| \qquad\qquad\qquad |$$
$$[L]_L \qquad\qquad [T([L']_{L'})]_{L'}$$
$$|$$
$$[T([L]_L) \,\&\, \neg T([L']_{L'})]_{L'}$$

$$[T([L]_L)]_{L'} \qquad [\neg T([L']_{L'})]_{L'}$$
$$| \qquad\qquad\qquad \vdots$$
$$[L]_L$$

The presence of an infinite branch indicates the pathological nature of L′.

7 A formal account of singularities

Now, to define the $true_\alpha$ and $false_\alpha$ sentences, we must concern ourselves with reflections on the $true_\beta$ and $false_\beta$ sentences, for any $\beta < \alpha$. And here, once more, we will import the pragmatic facts into our account. We introduce the notion of a $pruned_\beta^R$ tree, just as we introduced the notion of a $pruned_0^R$ tree.

Take a sentence σ and its $pruned_\beta$ tree. Let ρ be an evaluation that appears on σ's $pruned_\beta$ tree. If the relevant pragmatic facts – about the context of ρ and the context of its evaluated sentence – determine that ρ is a partial explicit reflection, then every node composed of ρ is flagged with a superscript 1. If the relevant pragmatic facts determine that ρ is a complete explicit reflection, then every node composed of ρ is flagged with a superscript 2. We will call the tree that results the *$pruned_\beta^R$ tree for σ*.

The $pruned_1^R$ tree for (R) is

$$[T([L]_L)]_R^2$$
$$|$$
$$[L]_L$$

The pragmatic facts about the context of (R) and the context of (L) determine that (R) is a complete explicit reflection on (L), and these facts are embodied in the superscript 2 that attaches to the evaluation at the top node.

The $pruned_1^R$ tree for (L') is

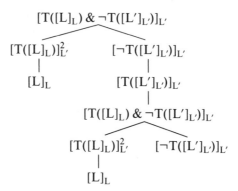

Here the pragmatic facts about the context of (L') and the context of (L) determine that the evaluation of (L) contained in (L') is a complete explicit reflection.

We next define the notion of a β-level reflection:

Definition. r is a *β-level reflection* (for $\beta \geq 1$) iff r is an evaluation of a $true_\beta$ or a $false_\beta$ sentence, but r is not itself $true_\beta$ or $false_\beta$.

134

7.2 The reflective hierarchy and singularities

For example, consider the complete explicit reflection (R). The sentence that (R) evaluates, namely, (L), is $true_1$. But (R) is not itself $true_1$ or $false_1$, since (R) is not reflection-free – as is easy to check. So (R) is a first-level reflection. For another example, consider a partial explicit reflection on (L): Since this is neither $true_1$ nor $false_1$, this too will be a first-level reflection. And a nonexplicit reflection on (L) – an evaluation of (L) that does not itself loop – is also neither $true_1$ nor $false_1$, and so is a first-level reflection.

We next define the notion of a β-*reflective sentence*. The intuitive idea was introduced in Section 7.2.2. A β-reflective sentence may be a β-level reflection (or compounded from such a reflection); or it may be a pathological sentence involving a β-level reflection. In either case, no higher reflections are involved.

Definition. A sentence σ is β-*reflective* iff the following holds for σ's pruned$_\beta^R$ tree:

(a) At least one node of the tree is a β-level reflection.

(b) If ρ is an evaluation on any infinite branch, then ρ does not have superscript 1 or 2, and ρ either loops or heads a chain.

Notice that any node of σ's pruned$_\beta^R$ tree that is a β-level reflection is a member of a finite branch; the branch will terminate at the next node, since the evaluated sentence is $true_\beta$ or $false_\beta$. This captures the idea that a reflection is grounded in semantic facts about the sentence it evaluates.

Another idea we want to capture is this: A β-reflective sentence cannot involve a reflection on a pathological sentence that is not $true_\beta$ or $false_\beta$. Now, any infinite branch of σ's pruned$_\beta$ tree contains such pathological sentences. But by clause (b), no explicit nor nonexplicit reflection can appear on an infinite branch.

It's straightforward to check that (R) is 1-reflective. (R) is not $true_1$, but the sentence that (R) evaluates, namely, (L), *is* $true_1$. So if we consider the pruned$_1^R$ tree for (R), we find that clause (a) is satisfied. And clause (b) is vacuously satisfied, since the pruned$_1^R$ tree has no infinite branches. In general, it's easy to see that any first-level reflection is 1-reflective.

(L') is also 1-reflective. Clause (a) is satisfied, since the evaluation of (L) contained in (L') is not $true_1$, but (L) is. Clause (b) is satisfied, since every evaluation on the infinite branch of (L')'s pruned$_\beta^R$ tree loops.

Definition. Let σ be a β-reflective sentence. Given any infinite branch of σ's pruned$_\beta$ tree, the sentences of that branch form a β-*level symmetrical network*.

7 A formal account of singularities

It's easy to check that all the members of a β-level symmetrical network either loop or head a chain.

We can now state the pragmatic principle of Symmetry in a more general form.

Principle of Symmetry. *For any β, all members of a β-level symmetrical network are to be treated as pathological.*

Next we capture the *pathological β-reflective* sentences, via the notion of ungroundedness.

Definition. Let σ be β-reflective. Then

σ is *grounded* iff σ's pruned$_\beta$ tree is a well-founded tree.
σ is *ungrounded* iff σ's pruned$_\beta$ tree is an unfounded tree.

7.2.8. The key singularities of β-reflective sentences

We may now identify the *key singularities* of a given occurrence of 'true' (or of 'false') in a general way.

Definition. Let σ be an ungrounded, β-reflective prime container of an occurrence O of 'true' or 'false'. The *key singularities* of O are the first evaluated sentences that occur an any infinite branch of σ's pruned$_\beta$ tree.

For example, consider the following pair of sentences:

(E) (G) is true.
(G) (R) is true and (E) is false.

Sentence (G) is 1-reflective, since it involves the first-level reflection (R). (E) is in turn 1-reflective, as a look at its pruned$_1^R$ tree will confirm. It's easy to see that (G) is a key singularity of the occurrence of 'true' in (E). And (E) is a key singularity of the occurrence of 'false' in (G). The pruned$_1$ tree for the prime container of the occurrence of 'false' in (G) looks like this:

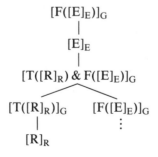

And the first evaluated sentence that appears on the infinite branch of this pruned$_1$ tree is (E).

7.2.9. The true$_\alpha$ and false$_\alpha$ sentences

At this point, we describe a procedure that determines a truth value for a β-reflective sentence σ, by converting σ's pruned$_\beta^R$ tree into an *evaluated$_\beta$* tree. The procedure is very like the one that establishes a truth value for a reflection-free sentence in Section 7.2.6. One new feature is this: Explicit reflections may occur on σ's pruned$_\beta^R$ tree. In particular, explicit partial reflections may occur. Any such partial explicit reflection is true, since it says of a pathological sentence that it is not true (or not false) in its context of utterance.

The procedure is as follows. Given a β-reflective sentence and its pruned$_\beta^R$ tree, we take the following steps:

STEP 1. (a) The first occurrence on a branch of a node of the form $[\neg T([\rho]_\rho)]_\gamma^1$ or $[\neg F([\rho]_\rho)]_\gamma^1$ is paired with the value T, and the branch terminates here.

(b) Each true$_\beta$ or false$_\beta$ sentence is paired with the appropriate truth value.

STEP 2 and STEP 3. Just as before, in Section 7.2.6.

Definition. Given a β-reflective sentence σ, the *evaluated$_\beta$ tree for σ* is the result of applying this procedure to σ's pruned$_\beta^R$ tree.

It is easily shown that a truth value for σ is established by this procedure.[11]

For an example, consider (R). We have seen that (L) is true$_1$, and that (R) is 1-reflective. The application of Step 1 yields

$$[T([L]_L)]_R^2$$
$$|$$
$$\langle [L]_L, T \rangle$$

Step 2 is empty here, since there are no infinite branches. The result of Step 3 is

$$\langle [T([L]_L)]_R^2, T \rangle$$
$$|$$
$$\langle [L]_L, T \rangle$$

This is the evaluated$_1$ tree for (R). (R) is paired with the value T, as we would expect.

137

7 A formal account of singularities

For another example, consider (L′). As we have seen, (L′) is 1-reflective. Step 1 yields

$$[T([L]_L) \mathbin{\&} \neg T([L']_{L'})]_{L'}$$

$$[T([L]_L)]^2_{L'} \qquad\qquad [\neg T([L']_{L'})]_{L'}$$
$$| \qquad\qquad\qquad\qquad |$$
$$\langle [L]_L, T \rangle \qquad\qquad [T([L']_{L'})]_{L'}$$
$$|$$
$$[T([L]_L) \mathbin{\&} \neg T([L']_{L'})]_{L'}$$

$$[T([L]_L)]^2_{L'} \qquad [\neg T([L']_{L'})]_{L'}$$
$$| \qquad\qquad\qquad \vdots$$
$$\langle [L]_L, T \rangle$$

The result of Step 2 is

$$[T([L]_L) \mathbin{\&} \neg T([L']_{L'})]_{L'}$$

$$[T([L]_L)]^2_{L'} \qquad\qquad [\neg T([L']_{L'})]_{L'}$$
$$| \qquad\qquad\qquad\qquad |$$
$$\langle [L]_L, T \rangle \qquad \langle [T([L']_{L'})]_{L'}, F \rangle$$

And Step 3 gives us the evaluated$_1$ tree for (L′):

$$\langle [T([L]_L) \mathbin{\&} \neg T([L']_{L'})]_{L'}, T \rangle$$

$$\langle [T([L]_L)]^2_{L'}, T \rangle \qquad \langle [\neg T([L']_{L'})]_{L'}, T \rangle$$
$$| \qquad\qquad\qquad\qquad |$$
$$\langle [L]_L, T \rangle \qquad\qquad \langle [T([L']_{L'})]_{L'}, F \rangle$$

The pathological sentence (L′) is paired with the value T, which corresponds to a reflective evaluation of (L′).

Finally, consider the partial explicit reflection (1′), from Section 7.1:

(1′) (2) is not true,

where (2) is a pathological member of an infinitely descending chain. It is easy to check that (1′) is 1-reflective. Here Step 1(a) produces this evaluated$_1$ tree for (1′), simply

$$\langle [\neg T([2]_2)]^1_{1'}, T \rangle.$$

Now we define the true$_\alpha$ and the false$_\alpha$ sentences.

Definition. (a) A sentence σ is a *true$_\alpha$* sentence iff σ is true$_1$, or there is an ordinal β, where $1 \leqslant \beta < \alpha$, such that σ is β-reflective and the first node of the evaluated$_\beta$ tree for σ is $\langle [\sigma]_\sigma, T \rangle$.

138

(b) A sentence σ is a *false$_\alpha$* sentence iff σ is false$_1$, or there is an ordinal β, where $1 \leqslant \beta < \alpha$, such that σ is β-reflective and the first node of the evaluated$_\beta$ tree for σ is $\langle [\sigma]_\sigma, F \rangle$.

So (R), (L'), and (1') are each true$_2$ (and true$_3$, and true$_4$, etc.).

7.2.10. Summary

We have now completed the characterization of our cumulative reflective hierarchy. At level 1 are the true$_1$ and false$_1$ sentences. These are the reflection-free sentences, and include not only the true$_0$ and the false$_0$ sentences but also pathological sentences – like (L) – that do not involve reflections. At level α are the true$_\alpha$ and false$_\alpha$ sentences. These are the reflection-free sentences and the β-reflective sentences, for all $\beta < \alpha$. A sentence at level α is *grounded* (*ungrounded*) iff it is a grounded (ungrounded) reflection-free sentence (see 7.2.4) or a grounded (ungrounded) β-reflective sentence, $\beta < \alpha$ (see 7.2.7). Among the grounded sentences at level α are the β-level reflections, for $\beta < \alpha$ (see 7.2.7). For suppose that σ is a β-level reflection. Then σ is β-reflective. Consider the pruned$_\beta$ tree for σ: It is composed of a single finite branch that terminates at the sentence σ evaluates. And so σ is a grounded β-reflective sentence. This accords with our intuition that reflections are grounded in semantic facts about the pathological sentences they evaluate.

Most crucially for our purposes, we have identified the key singularities of the ungrounded sentences at level α. The ungrounded sentences at level α are the ungrounded reflection-free sentences and the ungrounded β-reflective sentences, for $\beta < \alpha$. And we have identified the key singularities of the ungrounded reflection-free sentences (see 7.2.5) and the key singularities of the β-reflective sentences (see 7.2.8). The exclusion of the key singularities gives rise to the evaluation of these ungrounded sentences as true$_\alpha$ or false$_\alpha$.

7.3. ENGLISH AND THE REFLECTIVE HIERARCHY

Let me close this chapter with some general remarks about the significance of the reflective hierarchy for our semantic concepts. (Here I will in part be returning to points mentioned in Section 7.2.2.) I have argued in the previous chapter that we have semantic intuitions that produce reflections. Given a pathological sentence, we can reflect on it and evaluate it as true or false. And from such a reflection, we can produce new pathological sentences (e.g., by anaphoric constructions). And we can in turn reflect on these pathological sentences. The reflective hierarchy is intended as a formal articulation of these semantic intuitions.

These intuitions lead us to say that Aristotle's pathological utterance (L) is true: (L) isn't true, because pathological, in its context of utterance, and that's what (L) says. The evaluated$_0$ tree for (L) embodies this reasoning and tells us that (L) is true$_1$. To say that (L) is true$_1$ is to say something important about (L): That, in a suitably reflective context, (L) is true.

But to say that (L) is true$_1$ is *not* to say that the occurrence of 'true' in (L) is coextensive with 'true$_1$'. The reflective hierarchy is *not* intended as any kind of Tarskian representation of our semantic concepts. It does not embody a hierarchical account of the truth predicate of English. That would violate Minimality. We argued in the previous chapter that the extension 'true' in our explicit reflection (R) is not wider than that of 'true' in (L). Now (R) is a true$_2$ sentence, while (L) is a true$_1$ sentence. But the fact that (R) is of a higher level in the hierarchy does *not* imply that 'true' in (R) has a broader extension that 'true' in (L). Each of these occurrences of 'true' applies to all the truths except its singularities. And since each occurrence of 'true' has singularities that the other does not, neither extension includes the other.

We can extend this sort of consideration to the reflective hierarchy generally. Given a true$_\beta$ sentence ρ and a true$_\alpha$ sentence σ, where $\beta < \alpha$, it is *not* the case that an occurrence of 'true' in σ has a broader extension than an occurrence of 'true' in ρ. The level of a sentence in the reflective hierarchy does not provide a measure of the extension of occurrences of 'true' in the sentence.

So the hierarchy of truth predicates 'true$_1$', 'true$_2$', ..., 'true$_\alpha$', ... should not be understood as representing a stratification of the English predicate 'true'. Still, we might ask what the relation is between the predicate 'true' of English and the predicate constant 'true$_\alpha$ for some α'. A full answer to this question will have to wait until Chapter 9, when we return to the problem of universality. But let me anticipate a little. As we noted at the outset of Section 7.2, we might regard our object language $\mathcal{L}$ as the non-semantic part of English together with the context-sensitive predicates 'true' and 'false'. We can think of 'true$_\alpha$ for some α' as the truth predicate for this object language – in its extension are all the true sentences of $\mathcal{L}$. And we may suppose that this predicate is contained in the language of our theory. Does this mean that the language of our theory is a Tarskian metalanguage for the object language $\mathcal{L}$? In Chapter 9, I shall argue that it *isn't*.

On our singularity account, the English predicate 'true' is a context-sensitive term. In a given context, the predicate applies to all the truths except its singularities. Now the truths of the singularity theory are *not* identified as singularities, and so Minimality requires that we include the truths of the theory in the extension of an occurrence of 'true'. So there are sentences in the extension of any occurrence of the context-sensitive predicate 'true' that are not in the extension of the predicate 'true$_\alpha$ for some α'. We cannot, then, regard the language of the theory as a Tarskian metalanguage for $\mathcal{L}$. And we cannot regard the truth predicate 'true$_\alpha$ for some α' as representing our English predicate 'true'. Again, this is just the briefest sketch of the fuller discussion in Chapter 9.

Let me turn to another point about the hierarchy. Given the nature of our account, we would like to be able to identify the singularities of an occurrence of 'true'. We have gone some distance in this direction. Given an occurrence of 'true' in a sentence σ of $\mathcal{L}$, we have a way of identifying its key singularities. But to do this, we needed the reflective hierarchy. The identification of the key singularities depended on the notion of the appropriate pruned tree, and this in turn depended on the level of σ in the hierarchy.

So we have (at least) two ways in which the reflective hierarchy is significant. First, it articulates the semantic intuitions that produce reflections. And second, it is needed for the identification of singularities. Once we have a way of identifying singularities, we can spell out precisely what Minimality says. Ideally, given an occurrence of 'true', we would like to identify all its singularities, not just its key singularities. That is one of our aims in the next chapter. And we will see that, for the identification of these further singularities, the reflective hierarchy remains indispensable.

Chapter 8

Applications and further singularities

In Section 8.1, we apply our formal account to a variety of Liar-like examples. In Section 8.2, we investigate further the singularities of a given occurrence of 'true'.

8.1. APPLICATIONS OF THE FORMAL ACCOUNT

Example A. Consider a familiar empirical case adapted from Kripke.[1] Suppose Nixon says

(1) All of Dean's utterances about Watergate are not true.

And suppose Dean asserts

(2) Everything Nixon says about Watergate is not true.

Each of these utterances includes the other in its scope. This need not mean that we are unable to assign truth values to (1) and (2). Under certain empirical assumptions, we can. If, for example, Dean has made at least one $true_0$ statement about Watergate, call it '$[d]_d$', then it is easy to check that (1) is grounded and $false_0$. For then (1) has a g-witness whose first node is $\langle[1]_1, F\rangle$ (see diagram at top of facing page, where 'D' abbreviates 'is an utterance of Dean's about Watergate'). If, further, every other statement of Nixon's about Watergate is $false_0$, then it is easily checked that (2) is grounded and $true_0$.

But suppose that all Watergate-related statements made by Nixon and Dean, other than (1) and (2), are $false_0$. Then (1) and (2) are pathologically tangled: Each depends for its truth value on the truth value of the other. There are no g-witnesses for (1) and (2): They are ungrounded. We are now interested in the basic trees for (1) and (2). Let our domain of discourse be sentences (i.e., sentence types in a context); let '$[a]_a$', '$[b]_b$', '$[c]_c$', ... be arbitrary names of sentences. Let 'N' abbreviate 'is an utter-

142

$$\langle [\forall x(Dx \to \neg Tx)]_1, F \rangle$$

$$\langle [D([d]_d) \to \neg T([d]_d)]_1, F \rangle$$

$$\langle [N([d]_d)]_1, T \rangle \qquad \langle [\neg T([d]_d)]_1, F \rangle$$

$$\langle [T([d]_d)]_1, T \rangle$$

$$\langle [d]_d, T \rangle$$

continuation of
g-witness for $[d]_d$

ance of Nixon's about Watergate', and 'D' abbreviate 'is an utterance of Dean's about Watergate'. Then the basic tree for (1) is

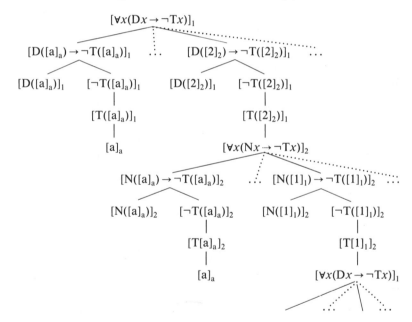

The basic tree for (2) is exactly similar.

Consider the basic tree for (1). Given our empirical assumptions, every sentence other than (2) is either not an utterance of Dean's about Watergate or is false$_0$. So, with the exception of $[D([2]_2) \to \neg T([2]_2)]_1$, the second node of each branch is true$_0$: In each case, the conditional is built from either an antecedent that is false$_0$ or a consequent that is true$_0$. So the pruned$_0$ tree for (1) looks like this:

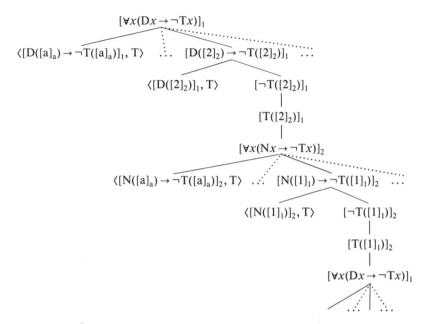

The pruned$_0^R$ tree for (1) is identical to its pruned$_0$ tree – there are no pragmatic features that indicate that any evalution on this pruned$_0$ tree is an explicit reflection. It's easy to check that (1) is reflection-free. The pruned$_0$ tree for (1) contains one infinite branch, on which (1) and (2) repeat. So (1) and (2) are members of a symmetrical network. The pruned$_0$ tree (and the pruned$_0^R$ tree) for (2) is exactly similar.

Consider the infinite branch of (1)'s pruned$_0$ tree. The first evaluated sentence that occurs in this branch is (2) – this sentence, then, is the key singularity of 'true' in (1). We pair the node $[T([2]_2)]_1$ with the value F – this step corresponds to the exclusion of (2) from the extension of 'true' in (1). The justification of the exclusion of (2) is via Symmetry. (1) and (2) are members of a symmetrical network. So, by Symmetry, they are to be treated alike. Now (1) is pathological in the context of (1), and so (2) is also pathological in the context of (1). So (2) is not in the extension of 'true' in (1).

We may now obtain the evaluated$_0$ tree for (1) (see diagram at top of facing page). So (1) is true$_1$. The evaluated$_0$ tree for (2) is exactly similar; (1) is the key singularity of 'true' in (2), and (2) is true$_1$.

Let us see how the analysis here captures our intuitions about this case. We capture the intuition that (1) and (2) are pathological: On our account, (1) and (2) are ungrounded. Our treatment of (1) and (2) makes no appeal to levels; there is no unnatural Tarskian stratification of the truth

$$\langle[\forall x(Dx \to \neg Tx)]_1, T\rangle$$

$$\langle[D([a]_a) \to \neg T([a]_a)]_1, T\rangle \quad \therefore \quad \langle[D([2]_2) \to \neg T([2]_2)]_1, T\rangle \ \dots$$

$$\langle[D([2]_2)]_1, T\rangle \qquad \langle[\neg T([2]_2)]_1, T\rangle$$

$$\langle[T([2]_2)]_1, F\rangle$$

predicate. Instead, semantic pathology is treated by the identification and exclusion of singularities. In this way, our intuition that an occurrence of 'true' applies to anything that is true requires only slight correction. In accordance with Minimality, *minimal* restrictions are placed on the occurrences of the truth predicate in (1) and (2).[2]

There is a further intuition about (1) that we capture. Although (1) is pathological, we can go on to reflect on it, as follows. Since all of Dean's statements about Watergate are not true (since they are either false or pathological) and since that's what (1) says, (1) is true. This intuition is also captured. According to our formal account, (1) is true$_1$. This deliverance of the evaluated$_0$ tree embodies our strengthened reasoning. According to our formal account, (1) is neither true$_0$ nor false$_0$, but *is* true$_1$. This captures the semantic intuitions that allow us to evaluate even pathological sentences as true.

Example B. Suppose a policeman testifies

(3) Nothing the prisoner says is true.

The prisoner says

(4) Something the policeman says is true.[3]

Now we can apparently establish that either the policeman says something other than (3) or the prisoner says something other than (4). We can argue as follows. Suppose, toward a contradiction, that (3) is true. Then nothing the prisoner says is true, and so (4) must be false. So nothing the policeman says, (3) included, is true – and we have a contradiction. So (3) is false. So something the prisoner says is true. This truth is either (4) or something else. If it is (4), then the policeman says something true, and so the policeman says something other than (3). If it is something else, then the prisoner says something other than (4). So we conclude that either the policeman says something other than (3) or the prisoner says something other than (4). But this conclusion is clearly unacceptable – it is perfectly possible that the policeman says only (3) and the prisoner says only (4).

8 Applications and further singularities

Let us consider first the case in which the policeman and the prisoner say nothing other than (3) and (4), respectively. The basic trees for (3) and (4) each contain an infinite branch on which both (3) and (4) repeat. It is easily checked that these infinite branches are the only infinite branches on the pruned$_0$ trees for (3) and (4) – since all other branches terminate at true$_0$ sentences. The presence of these infinite branches indicate that (3) and (4) are ungrounded. Notice that the pruned$_0^R$ tree for (3) is identical to the pruned$_0$ tree for (3) – there are no pragmatic features that indicate that any evaluation on the pruned$_0$ tree for (3) is an explicit reflection. (And the pruned$_0^R$ tree and the pruned$_0$ tree for (4) are likewise identical.) It's easily checked that (3) and (4) are reflection-free. The evaluated$_0$ tree for (3) is as follows (where 'Pr' abbreviates 'is said by the prisoner'):

$$\langle [\forall x(\mathrm{Pr}x \to \neg Tx)]_3, \mathrm{T}\rangle$$

$$\langle [\mathrm{Pr}([a]_a) \to \neg T([a]_a)]_3, \mathrm{T}\rangle \quad \therefore \quad \langle [\mathrm{Pr}([4]_4) \to \neg T([4]_4)]_3, \mathrm{T}\rangle \ \cdots$$

$$\langle [\mathrm{Pr}([4]_4)]_3, \mathrm{T}\rangle \qquad \langle [\neg T([4]_4)]_3, \mathrm{T}\rangle$$

$$\langle [T([4]_4)]_3, \mathrm{F}\rangle$$

The node $\langle [T([4]_4)]_3, \mathrm{F}\rangle$ represents the exclusion of (4) from the extension of the occurrence of 'true' in (3): (4) is the key singularity of 'true' in (3). Given the empirical circumstances, we may argue that nothing the prisoner says is true (because the only thing the prisoner says is pathological), and so (3) is true. This final reflective evaluation of (3) is captured by the formal theory: According to its evaluated$_0$ tree, (3) is true$_1$.

The evaluated tree for (4) is as follows (where 'Pol' abbreviates 'is said by the policeman'):

$$\langle [\exists x(\mathrm{Pol}x \ \& \ Tx)]_4, \mathrm{F}\rangle$$

$$\langle [\mathrm{Pol}([a]_a) \ \& \ T([a]_a)]_4, \mathrm{F}\rangle \ \therefore \ \langle [\mathrm{Pol}([3]_3) \ \& \ T([3]_3)]_4, \mathrm{F}\rangle$$

$$\langle [\mathrm{Pol}([3]_3)]_4, \mathrm{T}\rangle \qquad \langle [T([3]_3)]_4, \mathrm{F}\rangle$$

(3) is the key singularity of 'true' in (4). We may argue that (4) is false, because it says that something the policeman says is true, but the only thing the policeman says is pathological. This evaluation of (4) is captured by the theory: According to its evaluated$_0$ tree, (4) is false$_1$.

As with (1) and (2), there are empirical circumstances in which (3) and (4) are grounded. For example, suppose the policeman utters something other than (3) that is true$_0$, and that the prisoner says nothing other than (4). Then it is easy to check that (4) is true$_0$ and (3) is false$_0$.

8.1 Applications of the formal account

Recall that from the fact that the policeman says (3) and the prisoner says (4), it seemed to follow that one of them must say something else besides. Where does the reasoning go wrong? Let 'true$_{c_3}$' abbreviate 'true in the context of utterance of (3)', and 'true$_{c_4}$' abbreviate 'true in the context of (4)'. Then associated with (3) is the truth schema

T_3 s is true$_{c_3}$ iff p;

and associated with (4) is the truth schema

T_4 s is true$_{c_4}$ iff p.

We obtain instances of these schemata by replacing 'p' by a sentence (i.e., a sentence type in a context) and 's' by a name of that sentence. A pragmatic implicature is present throughout the reasoning, that the sentences (3) and (4) may be evaluated via their associated truth schemas. It is the evaluation of (3) and (4) via their implicated schemas that invalidates the argument.

For example, we reason that, if (3) is true, then nothing the prisoner says is true. On our analysis, this piece of reasoning may be represented as follows: If (3) is true$_{c_3}$ then nothing the prisoner says is true$_{c_3}$. This inference depends on T_3; we use the instance of T_3 obtained by replacing 's' by a name of (3) and 'p' by (3) itself. Once made fully explicit, the intuitive reasoning goes like this:

(i) 'Nothing the prisoner says is true' is true. (Assumption)

(ii) s is true iff p. (Schema T_3)

(iii) 'Nothing the prisoner says is true' is true iff nothing the prisoner says is true. (Instance of schema T_3)

So,

(iv) Nothing the prisoner says is true.

In our terms, this reasoning may be represented by

(i) 'Nothing the prisoner says is true$_{c_3}$' is true$_{c_3}$. (Assumption)

(ii) s is true$_{c_3}$ iff p. (Schema T_3)

(iii) 'Nothing the prisoner says is true$_{c_3}$' is true$_{c_3}$ iff nothing the prisoner says is true$_{c_3}$. (Instance of schema T_3)

So,

(iv) Nothing the prisoner says is true$_{c_3}$.

But this unrestricted use of T_3 is illegitimate. T_3 may not apply to a sentence involving the predicate 'true$_{c_3}$'; the sentence may be ungrounded, like (3) under certain empirical assumptions.

147

8 Applications and further singularities

We show that the unrestricted use of T_3 is illegitimate by providing an instance of it that is false. In fact, (iii) itself is such an instance, if we assume that the policeman and the prisoner say only (3) and (4), respectively. For then the left-hand side of the biconditional (iii) is false, since (3) is pathological in its context of utterance and not true_{c_3}; but the right-hand side is true, since it is indeed the case that nothing the prisoner says is true_{c_3}.

Example C. We may give a similar account of our version of Curry's paradox, the purported proof of the existence of God presented in Chapter 1. Let us construct an empirical version of sentence (7) of Chapter 1. Suppose I see the sentence 'God exists' written on the board next door and proceed to write what I take to be a trivial truth:

(5) If the sentence written on the board in room 101 is true, then God exists.

But I am mistaken about my whereabouts – I am in fact in room 101. As we saw in Chapter 1, we have a version of the Truth Teller from which we are apparently able to establish the existence of God. The argument makes essential use of the schema

T_5 s is true_{c_5} iff p.

It is the unrestricted use of this schema that is illegitimate. We cannot assume that we can apply the schema to sentences that themselves involve the predicate 'true_{c_5}'. Indeed, as we will now see, the instantiation of T_5 to my utterance (5) provides a false instance of the schema.

Let 'A' be a name of the sentence type of 'God exists'. Then the pruned_0 tree for (5) is as follows (where 'v' represents the truth value of 'God exists'):

$$[5]_5 \qquad (= [T([5]_5) \to A]_5)$$
$$[T([5]_5)]_5 \qquad \langle [A]_5, v \rangle$$
$$[5]_5$$
$$[T([5]_5)]_5 \qquad \langle [A]_5, v \rangle$$
$$\vdots$$

It's easy to see that (5) is reflection-free – there are no pragmatic facts to indicate otherwise. Since this pruned_0 tree has an infinite branch, (5) is ungrounded. The first evaluated sentence on this infinite branch is (5) itself – and so (5) is a singularity of the occurrence of 'true' in (5). The evaluated_0 tree for (5) is

$$\langle [5]_5, T \rangle$$

$$\langle [T([5]_5)]_5, F \rangle \qquad \langle [A]_5, v \rangle$$

So (5) is evaluated as $true_1$, in virtue of a false antecedent – (5) is not $true_{c_5}$.

Now the argument that purports to establish the existence of God appeals to this instance of T_5:

> 'If the sentence written on the board in room 101 is true, then God exists' is true iff if the sentence written on the board in room 101 is true, then God exists.

This may be represented by

> 'If the sentence written on the board in room 101 is $true_{c_5}$, then God exists' is $true_{c_5}$ iff if the sentence written on the board in room 101 is $true_{c_5}$, then God exists.

But according to our account, this biconditional is false: The left-hand side is false, since (5) is not $true_{c_5}$, while the right-hand side is true, since it is a conditional with a false antecedent.

Example D. Suppose Jane says

(6) All of Ian's utterances are true.

And suppose that everything Ian says is $true_0$, except for one pathological utterance:

(7) (7) is not true.

(7) is reflection-free, and $true_1$. (6), on the other hand, is not reflection-free: It is easily checked that there is an infinite branch of (6)'s $pruned_0$ tree on which $[T([7]_7)]_7$ repeats, but $[T([7]_7)]_6$ does not. So (6) is neither $true_1$ nor $false_1$.

The $pruned_1$ tree for (6) is as follows (where 'I' abbreviates 'is an utterance of Ian's'):

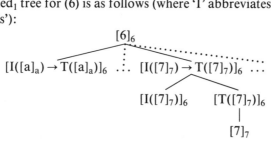

Since the $pruned_1$ tree is finite, there are no key singularities of 'true' in (6). (6)'s $evaluated_1$ tree is

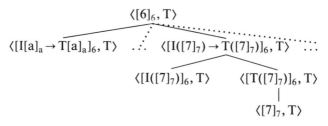

And so (6) is true$_2$. We treat Jane's utterance (6) as nonexplicitly reflective with respect to Ian's pathological utterance (7). This respects the intuition behind Minimality: Since Jane's utterance is not pathologically linked to Ian's, we have no reason to restrict 'true' in (6) by excluding (7) from its extension.

For a slightly more elaborate version of this case, suppose again that Ian utters sentences that are only true$_0$, except for one pathological utterance ρ. Suppose that, like (7), ρ is unrelated to (6): More precisely, (6) does not occur in the basic tree for ρ. Suppose further that ρ involves reflections; let the highest such reflection evaluate a true$_{23}$ or a false$_{23}$ sentence. This 23d-level reflection may be explicit or nonexplicit. (If it is explicit, then the pruned$^R_{23}$ tree for ρ will differ from its pruned$_{23}$ tree.) Now ρ is 23-reflective and either true$_{24}$ or false$_{24}$. And (6) is 24-reflective and true$_{25}$ or false$_{25}$.

Example E. Consider this simple chain of sentences, from Chapter 1:

(σ_1) σ_2 is false.
(σ_2) σ_3 is true.
$\vdots$
(σ_{2k-1}) σ_{2k} is false.
(σ_{2k}) σ_{2k+1} is true.
$\vdots$

The basic tree and the pruned$_0$ tree for (σ_1) is

$$[F([\sigma_2]_{\sigma_2})]_{\sigma_1}$$
$$|$$
$$[T([\sigma_3]_{\sigma_3})]_{\sigma_2}$$
$$|$$
$$[F([\sigma_4]_{\sigma_4})]_{\sigma_3}$$
$$\vdots$$

And this is also the pruned$^R_0$ tree: There are no pragmatic facts that indicate that any of these evaluations are explicit reflections. It's easy to check that the sentences $\sigma_1, \sigma_2, ..., \sigma_k, ...$ form a symmetrical network.

8.1 Applications of the formal account

The evaluated tree for (σ_1) is simply

$$\langle [F([\sigma_2]_{\sigma_2})]_{\sigma_1}, F \rangle.$$

σ_2 is the key singularity of the occurrence of 'false' in σ_1. σ_1 is false$_1$. This accords with a reflective evaluation of σ_1.

Here we may anticipate the discussion of the next section. σ_1 is pathological in its context, and so σ_1 is not in the extension of 'false' in σ_1. Since $\sigma_1, \sigma_2, \ldots, \sigma_k, \ldots$ form a symmetrical network, then by Symmetry, they are all to be treated alike, as pathological. So $\sigma_2, \ldots, \sigma_k, \ldots$ are also pathological in the context of σ_1 – none of them are in the extension of 'false' in σ_1. That is, $\sigma_2, \ldots, \sigma_k, \ldots$ are all singularities of 'true' in σ_1, though only σ_2 is a key singularity. There are singularities beyond the key singularities, and these are the subject of Section 8.2.

Example F. We turn to a case involving loops and chains, a case mentioned in Chapter 6. Consider the following network of sentences:

(1) (2) is true or (1) is not true.
(2) (3) is true or (2) is not true.
$\vdots$
(n) (n + 1) is true or (n) is not true.
$\vdots$

The basic tree and the pruned$_0$ tree for (1) is

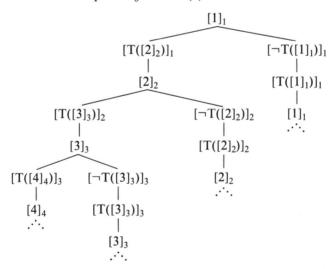

None of the evaluations on this tree are explicit reflections, and it is easily checked that (1) is reflection-free. Notice that the sentences of the left-most infinite branch form a reflection-free symmetrical network.

151

The evaluated$_0$ tree for (1) is

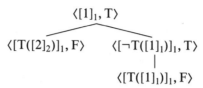

So (1) is true$_1$. The node $\langle[T([2]_2)]_1, F\rangle$ corresponds to the identification of (2) as the key singularity of the occurrence of 'true' in the first disjunct of (1). The node $\langle[T([1]_1)]_1, F\rangle$ corresponds to the identification of (1) as the key singularity of the occurrence of 'true' in the second disjunct of (1).

Again, we may anticipate our exploration of singularities in the next section. Notice that (1), (2), (3), ..., (n), ... are members of a symmetrical network. By Symmetry, they are all to be treated alike, as pathological. Now (1) is pathological in its context of utterance and so is not in the extension of the occurrences of 'true' in (1). But then, by Symmetry, neither are (2), (3), ..., (n), ... All members of this symmetric network are singularities of the occurrences of 'true' in (1).

Example G. Finally, we consider a case in which an occurrence of 'true' has infinitely many key singularities. Consider the sentences

(1) $\forall n\,(n+1)$ is true.
(2) (1) is not true.
(3) (1) is not true.
$\vdots$
(n) (1) is not true.
$\vdots$

The basic tree and the pruned$_0$ tree for (1) is

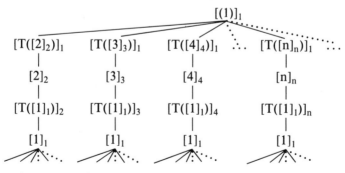

The evaluated$_1$ tree for (1) is

$$\langle [1]_1, F \rangle$$

$$\langle [T([2]_2)]_1, F \rangle \quad \langle [T([3]_3)]_1, F \rangle \quad \langle [T([4]_4)]_1, F \rangle \; \therefore \; \langle [T([n]_n)]_1, F \rangle \; \therefore$$

So (1) is false$_1$. The occurrence of 'true' in (1) has infinitely many key singularities ((2), (3), ...), and their exclusion from the extension of 'true' in (1) is justified in the usual way by Symmetry.

(1) is the key singularity of the occurrences of 'true' in (2), (3), ..., (n), ... For example, the evaluated$_0$ tree for (2) is

$$\langle [2]_2, T \rangle$$
$$|$$
$$\langle [T([1]_1)]_2, F \rangle$$

All of (2), (3), ..., (n), ... are true$_1$. Again, this captures our reflective evaluations of these pathological sentences. It is easy to check that the pruned$_0$ tree for (2) has an infinite branch on which each of (2), (3), ..., (n), ... appear. So these sentences are members of a symmetrical network. To anticipate the next section, it is straightforward to show that these sentences are all singularities of 'true' in (2) (and of 'true' in (3), ..., (n), ..., and of 'true' in (1)).

8.2. FURTHER SINGULARITIES

Once we have identified the key singularity (or key singularities) of a given occurrence of 'true', we may establish a truth value for the prime container of that occurrence. So the key singularities are of special interest. But it is natural to ask, are there other singularities, and, if so, what are they?

It is already clear that the answer to the first part of our question is in the affirmative. Consider a two-person loop. Suppose that, at time t_1, Claire and Joanne say, respectively,

(C) What Joanne is saying at t_1 is true.
(J) What Claire is saying at t_1 is true.

(C) is ungrounded, and is neither true nor false in its context of utterance. So (C) is a singularity (though not a key singularity) of the occurrence of 'true' in (C). In general, an ungrounded sentence is a singularity (though not necessarily the key singularity) of the occurrence(s) of 'true' or 'false' within it. As we have seen (in the previous chapter and in the previous section), it is this fact, together with Symmetry, that justifies the exclusion of a key singularity from the associated extension of 'true'. For example, it is easily checked that (J) is a key singularity of 'true' in (C). Since (C) and (J) are members of a symmetrical network (as is also easily checked), (C) and (J) are to be treated alike, as pathological. By Symmetry, it cannot be that (J) has a truth value in the context of (C), while (C) does not. So (J) too is neither true nor false in the context of (C); (J) is not in the extension of 'true' in (C).

Consider now a three-person loop. Suppose Sigi, Ranit, and Noa say, respectively,

(S) What Ranit is saying is not true.
(R) What Noa is saying is not true.
(N) What Sigi is saying is not true.

By the reasoning of the previous paragraph, (S) and (R) are singularities of the occurrence of 'true' in (S). But so is (N): since (S) and (N) are members of a symmetrical network, and (S) is a singularity of 'true' in (S), so is (N). We may notice, then, that all members of the symmetrical network to which (S) belongs are singularities of 'true' in (S).

When we were interested in the key singularities of an occurrence of 'true', we limited our attention to the prime container of that occurrence. Now we are interested in *all* the singularities; we consider the *entire sentence* that contains the occurrence of 'true'. From now on, when we speak of *the* sentence that contains the occurrence of 'true', we are speaking of the entire sentence, rather than any of its components. Of course, the prime container and the sentence need not coincide: The type of the sentence may be a truth-functional compound. For example, suppose Ian says

(I) What Tricia is saying is true, and what Mark is saying is also true.

Suppose further that Tricia's utterance (T) and Mark's utterance (M) are each looped with (I). Then (I) is ungrounded. So (I) is a singularity (though not a key singularity) of both occurrences of 'true' in (I). Recall this feature of the singularity account: The context of any truth-functional component of a sentence is the sentence itself. So the occurrences of 'true' in (I) are coextensive: Both are represented by 'true in the context of (I)'. It follows that (T), the key singularity of the first occurrence of 'true' in (I), is a singularity of the second occurrence too; and (M), the key singularity of the second occurrence of 'true', is also a singularity of the first. Our example indicates that we will not succeed in identifying the singularities of an occurrence of 'true' if we attend only to its prime container.

The considerations of the last three paragraphs suggest this general result.

8.2 Further singularities

Proposition 8.1. *Let σ be the sentence that contains an occurrence O of 'true' (or 'false'), and suppose that σ is ungrounded. Then every member of a symmetrical network to which σ belongs is a singularity of O.*

The proof is simple. Since σ is ungrounded, σ is a singularity of O. Suppose σ and ρ are members of a symmetrical network. Then ρ is also a singularity of O; for, by Symmetry, it cannot be that ρ has a truth value in the context of σ, if σ does not.

For another illustration, consider a simple chain:

(1) (2) is true.
(2) (3) is true.
  ⋮
(n) (n + 1) is true.
  ⋮

Now, (1) is an ungrounded reflection-free sentence. If we consider the $pruned_0$ tree for (1), we will see that (1), (2), ..., (n), ... are all members of a symmetrical network. By Proposition 8.1, these are singularities of the occurrence of 'true' in (1).

In fact, by Proposition 8.1, there are some further singularities of 'true' in (1). Any chain can be extended – we can always add more links. In the present case, we may add the sentence

(0) (1) is true.

And to this extended chain, we can add

(−1) (0) is true,

and so on. Now, by Proposition 8.1, these additional sentences will also be singularities of 'true' in (1). If, for example, we consider the $pruned_0$ tree for (0), we will see that (0), (1), ..., (n), ... are members of a symmetrical network. In particular, then, (0) and (1) are members of a symmetrical network; and so, by Proposition 8.1, (0) is a singularity of 'true' in (1).

This suggests the following definition of *ungrounded ancestor*.

Definition. *Let σ be an ungrounded, α-reflective sentence. γ is an ungrounded ancestor of σ iff γ is α-reflective, σ is a node of γ's $pruned_α$ tree, and γ is not a member of σ's $pruned_α$ tree.*

It is easily checked that if γ is an ungrounded ancestor of σ, then γ and σ are members of a symmetrical network. So if O is an occurrence of 'true' (or 'false') in σ, then, by Proposition 8.1, γ is a singularity of O. In

155

particular, (0) is an ungrounded ancestor of (1) and a singularity of 'true' in (1). Similarly, (1) is an ungrounded ancestor of (2) and a singularity of 'true' in (2). In general, given any sentence (m) of the chain, the sentence (m), its ungrounded ancestors, and $(m+1)$, $(m+2)$, ... are all singularities of 'true' in (m).

Not all ungrounded sentences have ungrounded ancestors. Recall the two-person loop in which Claire and Joanne are caught. For Claire's utterance (C) to have an ungrounded ancestor, (C) must have an *immediate* ungrounded ancestor – that is, a reflection-free sentence γ whose pruned$_0$ tree has a branch that looks like this:

$$[\gamma]_\gamma$$
$$|$$
$$[C]_C$$
$$\vdots$$

But there is no such sentence γ, on pain of contradiction. The sentence γ would have to take one of three forms, as follows:

(a) The type of γ is a truth-functional compound, and the type of C is a component; for example, the type of γ is a conjunction, and the type of C is one of the conjuncts. But then $[C]_C$ does not appear as one of the next nodes – $[C]_\gamma$ appears instead.[4]

(b) The type of γ is a quantification. Then the next nodes are all of the form $[\varphi(a)]_\gamma$, and so none are $[C]_C$.

(c) γ is an evaluation of the form $[T([C]_C)]_\gamma$ or $[F([C]_C)]_\gamma$. Here, the next node is $[C]_C$. But now γ is not reflection-free, since γ appears on an infinite branch of its pruned$_0$ tree but does not repeat or head a chain.

We may conclude that (C) has no immediate ungrounded ancestor and so has no ungrounded ancestors. A similar argument establishes that (J) has no ungrounded ancestors. (Nor do (S), (R), and (N).) Intuitively, we cannot extend loops the way we can extend chains.

Note that the argument that shows that (C) has no ungrounded ancestors cannot be generalized to all looped sentences. Consider this variant of our two-person loop:

(C*) What Joanne is saying at t_1 is true and snow is white.
(J*) The first conjunct of what Claire is saying at t_1 is true.

Here it is easy to check that (C*) is an (immediate) ungrounded ancestor of the first conjunct of (C*). The argument of the previous paragraph does generalize to those looped utterances that (like (C) and unlike the first conjunct of (C*)) are not components of larger utterances.

8.2 Further singularities

So far, we have considered sentences that are singularities in virtue of membership in a symmetrical network. There is another kind of singularity, which we will call *anaphoric singularities*. These are singularities associated with anaphoric versions of the Liar. For example, suppose Claire utters (C) and then, a little later at t_2, adds, 'But this very sentence isn't'. Given the anaphoric back reference, this pathological addition is a singularity of the occurrence of 'true' in (C). In general, if σ is the entire sentence containing a given occurrence O of 'true' (or 'false'), an *anaphoric singularity of O* is an ungrounded sentence ρ represented by '$[\rho]_\sigma$', where the contextual subscript is established anaphorically. As we noted in Chapter 6, each of our context-sensitive uses of 'true' have anaphoric singularities. Notice that, by Minimality, Claire's addition is not a singularity of 'true' in (J) – here, Symmetry does not constrain Minimality.

Each such anaphoric singularity is associated with its own symmetrical network(s). Suppose Claire's pathological addition at t_2 is

(C') But what Mark is saying at t_2 isn't.

And suppose that what Mark is saying at t_2 is

(M') What Claire is saying at t_2 is true.

Since (C') and (M') are members of a symmetrical network, and (C') is a singularity of 'true' in (C), so is (M'). It is easy to establish the following general proposition:

Proposition 8.2. *Let σ be the sentence containing an occurrence O of 'true' (or 'false'). Let σ' be an anaphoric singularity of O. Then every member of a symmetrical network to which σ' belongs is a singularity of O.*

The proof is obvious: If σ' and ρ are members of a symmetrical network, then, by Symmetry, since σ' is a singularity of O, so is ρ.

Let us sum up our findings thus far about singularities. Let σ be the sentence that contains an occurrence O of 'true' (or 'false'). Then the following are singularities of O:

(i) all members of symmetrical networks to which σ belongs.

(ii) all members of symmetrical networks to which anaphoric singularities of O belong.

Key singularities of O are included under (i). Anaphoric singularities of O are included under (ii). If σ is grounded, O will not have singularities of type (i).

8 Applications and further singularities

Since anaphoric singularities are always possible, there is a wide range of possible sentence types in a context that are singularities of O. But if we restrict our attention to actual singularities, the class of sentences falling under (i) or (ii) might be quite small, and perhaps empty. Consider again our two-person loop. Suppose there are no actual pathological additions to Claire's utterance (C); the occurrence of 'true' in (C) has no actual anaphoric singularities. Then the actual singularities of 'true' in (C) that fall under (i) or (ii) are just (C) and (J). Or suppose I say, ' "Snow is white" is true', and suppose that there are no actual anaphoric singularities of the occurrence of 'true' in my utterance. Then this occurrence of 'true' has no actual singularities that fall under (i) or (ii).

We have not identified all the singularities of a given occurrence of 'true'. For example, suppose we form the truth predicate 'true in the context of (C)'. Now consider the sentence

This sentence is not true in the context of (C).

This sentence is a singularity of the occurrence of 'true' in (C). Every context-sensitive occurrence of 'true' will have such singularities. Still, these singularities involve explicit talk about contexts. Recall that we take our formal language $\mathcal{L}$ to represent the nonsemantic part of English, together with the context-sensitive predicates 'true' and 'false'. The formation of predicates like 'true in the context of (C)' is beyond the scope of $\mathcal{L}$. So I think that the following claim is plausible: Given a context-sensitive occurrence O of 'true' or 'false', all the singularities of O that are sentences of $\mathcal{L}$ are accommodated by (i) and (ii).

In the next chapter, we will enrich the language $\mathcal{L}$ in various ways. For one, we will admit into the language talk about contexts. Then we will need to adjust the foregoing claim to accommodate singularities beyond those we have characterized here.

Chapter 9

Semantic universality

There is a familiar danger threatening any account of the Liar: The proposal may appeal to semantic concepts that themselves generate new paradoxes that the proposal cannot handle. The singularity theory has appealed to the semantic notions of groundedness, singularity, and truth (and falsity) in a context. Can the singularity proposal accommodate *these* semantic notions? In this chapter, I argue that it can: These notions can be incorporated into the object language for which the singularity theory provides an account.

There is another related danger. There may be things that can be said that cannot be said in the object language, on pain of paradox. Perhaps we can diagonalize out of the object language to an essentially richer metalanguage. Perhaps the language of the theory itself stands as a Tarskian metalanguage to the object language. Then semantic paradox is ultimately avoided in the Tarskian way, and this undermines any anti-hierarchical approach, like the singularity approach. I shall suggest that the singularity proposal avoids this danger. I shall argue that the language of the singularity theory is *not* a Tarskian metalanguage for the object language: There is no diagonalizing out of the object language. I shall conclude that the singularity proposal does justice to the intuition that a natural language like English is semantically universal.

9.1. GROUNDEDNESS (AND "SINGULARITY" IN ONE SENSE)

The notion of groundedness is a central notion of the singularity theory. Yet the notion may appear to give rise to paradox. For example, the sentence

(1) (1) is ungrounded

159

appears to be ungrounded. Now, if (1) is ungrounded, then (1) is true. But how can a sentence be both ungrounded and true? Or consider a case adapted from Herzberger.[1] Suppose I say

(2) All my grounded utterances are interesting.

We might seem to be able to produce a paradox as follows. Since my utterance is about only grounded utterances, it is grounded. But if it is itself grounded, then it is about itself and included in the scope of its own quantifier, and so is ungrounded.

I shall argue that there is nothing paradoxical about (1) or (2): on the analysis I offer, both sentences are ungrounded and yet have a determinate truth value. This should not be surprising. It is a prominent feature of the singularity theory that ungrounded sentences, sentences without a truth value in certain contexts, do have a truth value in other contexts. So, according to the singularity account, there is nothing contradictory about an ungrounded sentence having a truth value.

Our present aim is to extend the formal theory so that it can accommodate an object language that expresses its own concept of grounding. Thus far, we have thought of our object language as the nonsemantic part of English, together with the context-sensitive semantic predicates 'true' and 'false'. We will now extend the object language to include its own grounded predicate. This will allow us to attribute to the speaker of English the concept of semantic pathology (which, remember, we analyze as ungroundedness). The attribution is natural enough, since the ordinary speaker can quickly recognize the pathological nature of Liar sentences. Indeed, we might find it plausible to attribute to a speaker the concept of groundedness itself, since the concept is easily conveyed in an intuitive way (say, via a few simple examples).

We expand the language $\mathcal{L}$ to the language $\mathcal{L}'$ by adding the one-place predicate 'G'. Recall from 7.2.10 the characterization of the grounded and ungrounded sentences of level α.

Definition. A sentence σ of level α is *grounded* iff σ is a grounded reflection-free sentence or a grounded β-reflective sentence, $\beta < \alpha$.

A sentence σ of level α is *ungrounded* iff σ is an ungrounded reflection-free sentence or an ungrounded β-reflective sentence, $\beta < \alpha$.

We fix the extension of 'G' as follows:

G(σ) iff σ is a grounded sentence of level α, for some α.

Notice that the definition of grounded now has wider application, since we have expanded the language $\mathcal{L}$ to include 'G'. The extension of the predicate 'G' will include sentences containing the predicate 'G'. So we

need an account of the evaluation of sentences containing 'G'. This requires us to extend some of our definitions.

To the definition of a basic tree, we add this clause:

If $[G([\rho]_\rho)]_\gamma$ is a node, then $[\rho]_\rho$ is the next node.

The definition of a g-witness is left unchanged. No sentence involving
'G', not even a sentence of the form '$2+2=4$ or ρ', has a g-witness. So
the $true_0$ and $false_0$ sentences remain the same, and the definition of a
$pruned_0$ tree is unchanged.

We now define *an evaluated$_0$ tree for a reflection-free* σ as the tree obtained from σ's $pruned_0$ tree by the following steps:

STEP 1. As before.

STEP 2. Consider each infinite branch. Terminate the branch at the first
node of the form $G(\rho)$ (if there is such a node), and pair $G(\rho)$ with the
value F.

The idea behind Step 2 is obvious: Since ρ is a node of an infinite
branch, ρ is ungrounded – and so an evaluation of it as grounded is false.
Once we have carried out Step 2, the nodes of the form $G(\rho)$ that we
have not yet considered, those without a paired F, appear only on finite
branches. In these cases, then, ρ is grounded, and the evaluation of it as
grounded will be true. This is the idea behind Step 3.

STEP 3. Consider any remaining branches that contain a node (or nodes)
of the form $G(\rho)$, where $G(\rho)$ is not paired with the value F. Terminate
each such branch at the first such node, and pair this sentence with the
value T.[2]

STEP 4. Previous Step 2 (in Section 7.2.6).

STEP 5. Previous Step 3 (in Section 7.2.6).

Next, we revise our definition of *an evaluated$_\beta$ tree for a β-reflective* σ:
It is the tree obtained from σ's $pruned_\beta$ tree by the following steps:

STEP 1. As before (in Section 7.2.9).

STEPS 2–5. Just as in the previous paragraph.

This completes the extensions of our definitions.

Suppose σ is β-reflective and σ's $pruned_\beta$ tree is well-founded. It is
straightforward to check that the evaluated$_\beta$ tree for $G(\sigma)$ is simply

$$\langle G(\sigma), T \rangle.$$

Suppose again that σ is β-reflective, but σ's pruned$_\beta$ tree is unfounded. Now the evaluated tree for σ is

$$\langle G(\sigma), F \rangle.$$

These evaluated$_\beta$ trees provide the appropriate truth values for $G(\sigma)$, given the extension we have fixed for 'G'.

A comment is in order. We do not treat 'grounded' as a context-sensitive term. Whether or not a sentence is grounded is not something that changes with the context. An ungrounded sentence may be without a truth value in one context, and true or false in another. But according to our definition of ungroundedness, a sentence σ is ungrounded *simpliciter*. A sentence is ungrounded if there is an α such that the sentence is an ungrounded sentence of level α.

Let us return to sentence (1), namely,

(1) (1) is ungrounded.

The basic tree and the pruned$_0$ tree for (1) are the same:

$$
\begin{array}{c}
[1]_1 \quad \text{(i.e., } [\neg G([1]_1)]_1) \\
| \\
[G([1]_1)]_1 \\
| \\
[1]_1 \\
\vdots
\end{array}
$$

The evaluated$_0$ tree for (1) is

$$
\begin{array}{c}
\langle [1]_1, T \rangle \\
| \\
\langle [G([1]_1)]_1, F \rangle
\end{array}
$$

The pruned$_0$ tree shows that (1) is ungrounded. The evaluated$_0$ tree shows that (1) is true (in fact, true$_1$): (1) is not in the extension of 'grounded' in (1). That is, (1) is a true, ungrounded sentence. There is nothing paradoxical here.

Now consider again my utterance (2):

(2) All my grounded utterances are interesting.

Suppose that my utterance (2) is β-reflective. It is easily checked that the pruned$_\beta$ tree for (2) is unfounded, and so (2) is ungrounded. Consider the evaluated$_\beta$ tree for (2). There will be infinitely many branches leading from (2) to a node of the form $\langle Gx \,\&\, Mx \to Ix, v \rangle$, where G abbreviates 'is grounded', M abbreviates 'is an utterance of mine', I abbreviates 'is interesting', and v is either T or F. If x is grounded and an utterance of mine, then by our revised definition of an evaluated$_\beta$ tree, v will coincide with the value of Ix. If x is ungrounded or not an utterance of mine, then, by our definition of an evaluated$_\beta$ tree, $v = T$, since the antecedent of the conditional is associated with the value false. In particular, this is so where we instantiate to (2). The relevant portion of σ's evaluated$_\beta$ tree looks like this:

$$\langle [G([2]_2)\ \&\ M([2]_2) \to I([2]_2)]_2, T\rangle$$

$$\langle [G([2]_2)\ \&\ M([2]_2)]_2, F\rangle \qquad \langle [I([2]_2)]_2, v\rangle$$

$$\langle [G([2]_2)]_2, F\rangle \qquad \langle [M([2]_2)]_2, T\rangle$$

The evaluated$_\beta$ tree for (2) will assign a definite truth value to (2), depending on the interest of my grounded utterances: (2) will be true$_\alpha$ or false$_\alpha$, for $\alpha > \beta$. (2) is ungrounded, yet it has a definite truth value. Again, there is no paradox.

The admission of the grounded predicate into our object language allows the representation of certain talk about singularities. Once apprised of the notion of singularity, we can say things like

(3) Aristotle's pathological utterance (L) is a singularity

or

(4) All Liar sentences are singularities.

On what is perhaps the most natural reading of these sentences, we are using the term 'singularity' in an absolute sense, not in a context-relative sense: By 'singularity', we mean 'neither in the extension of "true" or of "false" in some context of utterance'.[3] According to our analysis, this notion of singularity is coextensive with the notion of ungrounded: The sentences that are not in the extension of 'true' or of 'false' in some context of utterance are exactly the ungrounded sentences. So we can represent this notion of singularity in terms of the predicate G, the grounded predicate of $\mathcal{L}'$. In general, 'ρ is a singularity' is represented formally by '$\neg G([\rho]_\rho)$'. For example, we may represent sentence (3) as $[\neg G([L]_L)]_3$.

9.2. TRUTH IN A CONTEXT (AND "SINGULARITY" IN A SECOND SENSE)

According to the singularity proposal, 'true' and 'false' are context-sensitive terms. We speak of sentences being true in a context or false in a context; sentences may be neither true nor false in one context and determinately true or false in another. I want now to suggest a way in which we can extend our object language to encompass talk about truth and falsity in a context. It might seem that such an enrichment of our object language will inevitably lead to new paradoxes – an obvious candidate is the "Superliar" generated by my utterance

(X) This sentence is not true in any context.

I shall argue later that such paradoxes may be resolved along singularity lines.[4]

An evaluation may relativize 'true' to a specific context. Given a particular context of utterance c_1, I may say

(5a) 'John is hungry' is true in context c_1.

Notice first that my utterance (5a) is about a sentence *type,* the type of 'John is hungry'. We already have a way of representing sentence types in a context: For example, given utterances ρ and γ, $[\rho]_\gamma$ represents a sentence of the type ρ in the context of γ. We now introduce a way of representing sentence types *simpliciter:* We let $[\rho]$ represent the sentence type of ρ. In particular, ['John is hungry'] represents the sentence type of 'John is hungry'.

Notice second that my utterance (5a) may itself be uttered in a quite different context from c_1, say c_2. Here, 'true' as it occurs in (5a) is not tied to the context of utterance of (5a); rather, 'true' is explicitly relativized to the context c_1. So it will be inappropriate to represent (5a) by $[T([\text{'John is hungry'}])]_{c_2}$, since this representation ties the occurrence of 'true' in (5a) to my context of utterance c_2. A natural first stab at representing (5a) might be this:

$$[[T([\text{'John is hungry'}])]_{c_1}]_{c_2}.$$

But the representation can be simplified. Given that our concern is the evaluation of (5a), we should notice that the actual context of utterance c_2 of (5a) is irrelevant to the semantic status of (5a). (5a) is true, false, or pathological according as the sentence type of 'John is hungry' paired with the context c_1 constitutes a sentence that is true in c_1 or false in c_1. So, for our purposes, it will be adequate to represent (5a) as

$$[T([\text{'John is hungry'}])]_{c_1}.$$

To anticipate the formal account, the g-witness for (5a) is

$$\langle [T([\text{'John is hungry'}])]_{c_1}, v \rangle$$
$$|$$
$$\langle [\text{'John is hungry'}]_{c_1}, v \rangle$$

where v is the truth value of the sentence composed of the type of 'John is hungry' paired with the context c_1. This sentence is found at the bottom node of the tree, since, as we will see, in the formal theory the ongoing contextual subscript carries over to the sentence type. As is appropriate, the truth value of this sentence determines the truth value for (5a).

(5a) is about a sentence type. Suppose now that Mary utters a sentence of the type 'John is hungry' in context c_3. Contrast (5a) with my utterance

(5b) Mary's utterance is true in context c_1.

Unlike (5a), (5b) is about a sentence, not a sentence type. We will represent (5b) as

$$[T(['John is hungry']_{c_3})]_{c_1}.$$

Again anticipating the formal account, the g-witness for (5b) is

$$\langle [T(['John is hungry']_{c_3})]_{c_1}, v \rangle$$
$$|$$
$$\langle ['John is hungry']_{c_3}, v \rangle$$

where v is the truth value of Mary's utterance, namely, the sentence composed of the type of 'John is hungry' paired with the context c_3. Here the truth value of (5b) depends on the truth value of Mary's utterance, not on the truth value of the sentence formed by pairing the sentence type of 'John is hungry' with the context c_1.

Instead of relativizing 'true' to a specific context, an evaluation may involve quantification over contexts, as in

(6) '2 + 2 = 4' is true in any context of utterance.

Like (5a), (6) is about a sentence type. And as with (5a) and (5b), the actual context of my utterance does not matter to the evaluation of (6). This particular context of utterance is but one of the contexts over which the quantifier ranges. So the context of my utterance should play no special role in our representation of (6). My utterance (6) may be represented as

$$\forall c_\alpha [T(['2+2=4'])]_{c_\alpha},$$

where c_α is a variable ranging over contexts. As we will soon see, the g-witness for (6) is given by

$$\langle \forall c_\alpha [T(['2+2=4'])]_{c_\alpha}, T \rangle$$

$$\langle [T(['2+2=4'])]_{c_1}, T \rangle \quad \langle [T(['2+2=4'])]_{c_2}, T \rangle \quad \cdots$$
$$| \qquad\qquad\qquad\qquad |$$
$$\langle ['2+2=4']_{c_1}, T \rangle \qquad\qquad \langle ['2+2=4']_{c_2}, T \rangle \quad \cdots$$

9 Semantic universality

Again, the contextual subscript carries over to the sentence type. As is appropriate, the truth value of (6) depends on the truth value of each sentence obtained by pairing the type of '$2+2=4$' with a context.

The introduction into our language of talk about contexts, whether about particular contexts or quantification over contexts, requires the extension of some of our definitions. We will need to extend the definition of a g-witness, a basic tree, Step 3 of the procedure for obtaining an evaluated tree, and the definition of a singularity. These extended definitions must be sensitive to a new kind of phenomenon, alluded to in the past several paragraphs. Suppose I say

(7) 'John is hungry' is true in context c_1 and '$2+2=4$' is true in any context.

Suppose the context of my utterance is c_2. Then we might represent the top three nodes of the basic tree for (7) this way:

$$[[T(['John\ is\ hungry'])]_{c_1} \& \forall c_\alpha[T(['2+2=4'])]_{c_\alpha}]_{c_2}$$

$$[[T(['John\ is\ hungry'])]_{c_1}]_{c_2} \qquad [\forall c_\alpha[T(['2+2=4'])]_{c_\alpha}]_{c_2}$$

The second node of each branch contains two successive contextual subscripts – one is of the form $[[\ldots]_{c_i}]_{c_j}$, the other of the form $[Q c_\alpha[\ldots]_{c_\alpha}]_{c_k}$, where Q stands for the universal or existential quantifier. Given a node of either form, we will call the outermost contextual subscript *redundant*, in line with the idea that, in cases like (7) (and (5a), (5b), and (6)), the actual context of utterance is irrelevant to the evaluation of the sentence. We will add the following clause to the definitions of a g-witness and of a basic tree.

Clause for redundant contextual subscripts. If a node is of the form $[[\ldots]_{c_i}]_{c_j}$, then the next node is $[\ldots]_{c_i}$; and if a node is of the form $[Q c_\alpha[\ldots]_{c_\alpha}]_{c_k}$, then the next node is $Q c_\alpha[\ldots]_{c_\alpha}$.

According to this clause, the first five nodes of the basic tree for (7) will look like this:

$$[[T(['John\ is\ hungry'])]_{c_1} \& \forall c_\alpha[T(['2+2=4'])]_{c_\alpha}]_{c_2}$$

$$[[T(['John\ is\ hungry'])]_{c_1}]_{c_2} \qquad [\forall c_\alpha[T(['2+2=4'])]_{c_\alpha}]_{c_2}$$
$$| \qquad\qquad\qquad\qquad |$$
$$[T(['John\ is\ hungry'])]_{c_1} \qquad \forall c_\alpha[T(['2+2=4'])]_{c_\alpha}$$

We turn now to the extensions of our definitions.

9.2 Truth in a context

G-witness. To the definition of a g-witness, we add the clause for redundant contextual subscripts. The definition is further extended as follows:

(2)(a)(i) If $\langle[T([\rho]_\rho)]_\gamma, T\rangle$ is a node, then $\langle[\rho]_\rho, T\rangle$ is the next node; if $\langle[T([\rho])]_\gamma, T\rangle$ is a node, then $\langle[\rho]_\gamma, T\rangle$ is the next node.

The other parts of clause (2)(a) are similar. (According to these clauses, when we come to a sentence type without an associated context, the ongoing contextual subscript is retained.)

(2)(f)(i)′ Given ρ, a sentence or a sentence type, if $\langle\exists c_\alpha[\varphi(\rho)]_{c_\alpha}, T\rangle$ is a node, then, for some context, $\langle[\varphi(\rho)]_{c_k}, T\rangle$ is the next node, where 'c_k' is a name of the context.

(f)(ii)′ Given ρ, a sentence or a sentence type, if $\langle\exists c_\alpha[\varphi(\rho)]_{c_\alpha}, F\rangle$ is a node, then, for each context, $\langle[\varphi(\rho)]_{c_k}, F\rangle$ is one of the next nodes, where 'c_k' is a name of the context.

(2)(g)(i)′ Given ρ, a sentence or a sentence type, if $\langle\forall c_\alpha[\varphi(\rho)]_{c_\alpha}, T\rangle$ is a node, then, for each context, $\langle[\varphi(\rho)]_{c_k}, T\rangle$ is one of the next nodes, where 'c_k' is a name of the context.

(g)(ii)′ Given ρ, a sentence or a sentence type, if $\langle\forall c_\alpha[\varphi(\rho)]_{c_\alpha}, F\rangle$ is a node, then, for some context, $\langle[\varphi(\rho)]_{c_k}, F\rangle$ is the next node, where 'c_k' is a name of the context.

Basic tree. To the definition of a basic tree, we add the clause for redundant contextual subscripts. The definition is further extended as follows:

(2)(a) If $[T([\rho]_\rho)]_\gamma$ is a node, then $[\rho]_\rho$ is the next node; if $[T([\rho])]_\gamma$ is a node, then $[\rho]_\gamma$ is the next node.

(2)(i)′ Given ρ, a sentence or a sentence type, if $\exists c_\alpha[\varphi(\rho)]_{c_\alpha}$ is a node, then, for each context, $[\varphi(\rho)]_{c_k}$ is one of the next nodes, where 'c_k' is a name of the context.

(2)(j)′ Given ρ, a sentence or a sentence type, if $\forall c_\alpha[\varphi(\rho)]_{c_\alpha}$ is a node, then, for each context, $[\varphi(\rho)]_{c_k}$ is one of the next nodes, where 'c_k' is a name of the context.

Step 3 of the procedure for obtaining an evaluated$_\beta$ tree. The 4th clause in step 3, dealing with quantification, is extended as follows:

(4) (i)′ Given ρ, a sentence or a sentence type, $\exists c_\alpha[\varphi(\rho)]_{c_\alpha}$ is true if, for some context, $[\varphi(\rho)]_{c_k}$ is true, where 'c_k' is a name of the context.

(4)(ii)′ Given ρ, a sentence or a sentence type, $\exists c_\alpha[\varphi(\rho)]_{c_\alpha}$ is false if, for each context, $[\varphi(\rho)]_{c_k}$ is false, where 'c_k' is a name of the context.

9 Semantic universality

Key singularities. We can now extend our characterization of key singularities to include those generated by "decontextualized" uses of 'true', like 'true in context c', or 'true in any context'. We turn first to the case in which 'true' (or 'false') is relativized to a particular context c.

Let σ be an ungrounded, β-reflective prime container of 'true (or false) in context c'. ρ is a *key singularity of 'true in context* c' (*and of 'false in context* c') if $[T([\rho]_\rho)]_c$ or $[F([\rho]_\rho)]_c$ is the first evaluating sentence that occurs on an infinite branch of σ's pruned$_\beta$ tree.

Second, we consider cases of quantification over contexts.

Let σ be an ungrounded, β-reflective prime container of 'true (false) in any (some) context'. ρ is a *key singularity of 'true in context* c' (*and of 'false in context* c') if $[T([\rho]_\rho)]_c$ or $[F([\rho]_\rho)]_c$ is the first evaluating sentence that occurs on an infinite branch of σ's pruned$_\beta$ tree.

Again, key singularities are of special interest, since their exclusion from the extension of the relevant truth predicate determines a truth value for σ.[5] Notice that the attempt to evaluate a key singularity ρ of 'true in context c' as true (or false) in context c fails: This is indicated by the infinite branch. That is, ρ is pathological in the context c; in particular, ρ is excluded from the extension of 'true in context c'.

Further singularities. Recall that, in the previous chapter, we identified singularities other than key singularities. We said that if σ is the sentence that contains an occurrence O of 'true' (or 'false'), then the following are singularities of O:

(i) all members of symmetric networks to which σ belongs;
(ii) all members of symmetric networks to which anaphoric singularities of O belong.

Now that we have enriched the object language with talk of contexts, we can identify further singularities of O. Let 'c' denote the context of utterance of σ, so that 'true (false) in context c' is coextensive with the occurrence O of 'true' ('false').

Proposition 9.1. *Let ρ be a key singularity of 'true in context* c' *or 'false in context* c'. *Every member of every symmetrical network to which ρ belongs is a singularity of O.*

The proposition is easily established. ρ is a key singularity of 'true (false) in context c', and so a singularity of O. By Symmetry, all members of symmetrical networks to which ρ belongs are also singularities of O.

9.2 Truth in a context

So we can add to our list a third kind of singularity of O:

(iii) the "decontextualized" singularities identified by Proposition 9.1.

Among these decontextualized singularities will be the ungrounded ancestors of the key singularities of Proposition 9.1.[6] These ungrounded ancestors will include not only some ungrounded containers of 'true (false) in context c', but also some ungrounded containers of 'true (false) in any (some) context'; for example,

(X) This sentence is not true in any context

is one such ungrounded ancestor, as we will see later. Also among the decontextualized singularities are ungrounded sentences tied anaphorically to occurrences of 'true (false) in context c'. For example, after saying '(X) is not true in context c', I may utter the sentence

And neither is this very sentence.

This perverse addition is itself a key singularity of 'true in context c', and so a singularity of O.

This completes the presentation of the extended definitions. We now provide some illustrative examples.

Example 1. Consider again the sentence

(6) '$2+2=4$' is true in any context of utterance.

Sentence (6) is analyzed as

$$\forall c_\alpha [T([`2+2=4'])]_{c_\alpha}.$$

The g-witness for (6) is

$$\langle \forall c_\alpha [T([`2+2=4'])]_{c_\alpha}, T \rangle$$

$$\langle [T([`2+2=4'])]_{c_1}, T \rangle \qquad \langle [T([`2+2=4'])]_{c_2}, T \rangle \quad \cdots$$

$$\langle [`2+2=4']_{c_1}, T \rangle \qquad \qquad \langle [`2+2=4']_{c_2}, T \rangle \quad \cdots$$

We conclude that (6) is true_0. (Notice the application of (2)(g)(i)'; and also of (2)(a)(i) of the g-witness definition – '$2+2=4$' is a sentence type not associated with a context, so in the final node of each branch, the previous contextual subscript is retained.)

Example 2. Consider again Aristotle's pathological utterance (L) (introduced in Chapter 6). Now consider

(8) (L) is true in some context.

Intuitively, (8) is true because there is a context in which (L) is true; consider, for example, an appropriate reflective context, such as the explicitly reflective context of the reflection (R) from Chapter 6. Sentence (8) is represented by

$$\exists c_\alpha [T([L]_L)]_{c_\alpha}.$$

The basic tree (and pruned$_0$ tree) for (8) is

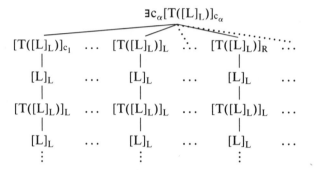

Now, it's easily checked that the evaluated$_0$ tree for $[T([L]_L)]_L$ is simply

$$\langle [T([L]_L)]_L, F \rangle.$$

So $[T([L]_L)]_L$ is false$_1$. It's also easily checked that $[L]_L$ is true$_1$. So the evaluated$_1$ tree for (8) is

$$\langle \exists c_\alpha [T([L]_L)]_{c_\alpha}, T \rangle$$

$$\langle [T([L]_L)]_{c_1}, T \rangle \quad \cdots \quad \langle [T([L]_L)]_L, F \rangle \quad \cdots \quad \langle [T([L]_L)]_R, T \rangle \quad \cdots$$

$$\langle [L]_L, T \rangle \quad \cdots \qquad \qquad \cdots \quad \langle [L]_L, T \rangle \quad \cdots$$

In the contexts other than the context of (L), (L) is reflectively evaluated as true, either explicitly, as in the context of the explicit reflection (R), or implicitly, as in the context c_1. So (8) is true$_2$, as we would expect: There are contexts in which (L) is true. And the numerical subscript on 'true$_2$' indicates that the contexts in which (L) is true are reflective with respect to (L).

Example 3. Suppose I say

(9) This sentence is not true in the present context of utterance.

Let the context of my utterance be denoted by 'c_9'. Then we may represent (9) by

$$[\neg T([9]_{c_9})]_{c_9}.$$

The basic tree (and the pruned$_0$ tree) for (9) is

$$[\neg T([9]_{c_9})]_{c_9}$$
$$|$$
$$[T([9]_{c_9})]_{c_9}$$
$$|$$
$$[\neg T([9]_{c_9})]_{c_9}$$
$$\vdots$$

It is straightforward to check that (9) is a key singularity of 'true in context c_9'. The evaluated$_0$ tree for (9) is

$$\langle[\neg T([9]_{c_9})]_{c_9}, T\rangle$$
$$|$$
$$\langle[T([9]_{c_9})]_{c_9}, F\rangle$$

So (9) is true$_1$.

A variant of this example indicates how we can accommodate a second way of talking about singularities (see note 2, this chapter). Consider

(10) (10) is a singularity.

On what is perhaps the most natural reading of (10), we mean that (10) is a singularity of 'true' and of 'false' in the context of (10): We read 'singularity' as 'neither true nor false in the present context'. Let the context of (10) be c_{10}; then (10) may be represented by

$$[\neg T([10]_{c_{10}}) \,\&\, \neg F([10]_{c_{10}})]_{c_{10}}.$$

It is easy to check that (10) *is* a singularity of 'true in context c_{10}' and of 'false in context c_{10}', and that (10) is true$_1$. The paradox generated by (10) is resolved along singularity lines.

Example 4: The Superliar. Let us now return to the Superliar generated by my utterance

(X) This sentence is not true in any context.

It is a consequence of the singularity account that the Superliar sentence (X) is a singularity of occurrences of 'true' in any context. This response to the Superliar is of a piece with our resolution of other versions of the Liar. (X) is analyzed as

$$\forall c_\alpha[\neg T([X]_X)]_{c_\alpha}.$$

The basic tree for (X) is given by

171

$$\forall c_\alpha [\neg T([X]_X)]_{c_\alpha}$$

$$[\neg T([X]_X)]_{c_1} \qquad [\neg T([X]_X)]_{c_2} \qquad \therefore$$

$$[T([X]_X)]_{c_1} \qquad\qquad [T([X]_X)]_{c_2} \qquad \ldots$$

$$\forall c_\alpha [\neg T([X]_X)]_{c_\alpha} \qquad \forall c_\alpha [\neg T([X]_X)]_{c_\alpha} \qquad \ldots$$

The evaluated$_0$ tree for (X) is

$$\langle \forall c_\alpha [\neg T([X]_X)]_{c_\alpha}, T \rangle$$

$$\langle [\neg T([X]_X)]_{c_1}, T \rangle \qquad \langle [\neg T([X]_X)]_{c_2}, T \rangle \qquad \therefore$$

$$\langle [T([X]_X)]_{c_1}, F \rangle \qquad \langle [T([X]_X)]_{c_2}, F \rangle \qquad \ldots$$

Consider the bottom nodes, where the second member of each ordered pair is F. These indicate that (X) is a key singularity of 'true$_{c_1}$', of 'true$_{c_2}$', and so on, for 'true' in any context. (This may be checked against the extended definition of a key singularity.) On our analysis, the Superliar is defused by the identification of singularities. In particular, (X) is identified as a singularity of occurrences of 'true' in any context. Further, given the top node of the evaluated$_0$ tree, we can say that (X) is true$_1$.

Still, the Superliar (X) presents a special problem. Consider the following intuitive reasoning:

> Given any context c, (X) cannot be true in that context. For suppose that (X) is true in context c. Then, in context c, it is the case that (X) is not true in any context. So, in particular, (X) is not true in context c – and we have a contradiction. So (X) is not true in any context. But that's what (X) says. So
> (Y) (X) is true, after all.

This reasoning is represented by the evaluated$_0$ tree for (X). The bottom nodes of the tree represent our evaluation of (X) as a singularity of truth in any context. And the top node of the tree evaluates our final evaluation (Y) of (X) as true.

But now, we cannot produce reflections on (X) the way we did with, say, Aristotle's pathological utterance (L). Suppose we treat our final evaluation (Y) as a reflection. Then the reflective context of utterance of (Y) provides an instance of the quantification in (X), and our final evaluation of (X) leads us back to contradiction.

9.2 Truth in a context

And yet our reasoning appears valid. There is no reason to suppose that we *are* led back to contradiction – our reasoning appears valid, and our evaluation (Y) seems true. We see that if we take the use of 'true' in our final evaluation (Y) as a context-sensitive use, then the intuitively valid argument is invalidated. So we should regard the use of 'true' in (Y) as *context-independent*. Here, we are adopting the same strategy we adopted with regard to our strengthened reasoning about the Liar. We do not block intuitively valid reasoning by ad hoc restrictions – rather we look for an analysis that respects the reasoning. By adopting this strategy, we are more likely to provide an account of *our* semantic usage, an account that describes how *our* semantic concepts work.

The intuitive reasoning about (X) shows that we are able to stand back from all contexts and evaluate the sentence (X) on the basis of its semantic status in every context. The Superliar reasoning tells us that our ordinary usage does not restrict quantification over contexts. We can quantify over all contexts, and we can evaluate sentences that involve such quantification.

Similar remarks can be made about (6). We can reason as follows:

Given any context, '$2+2=4$' is true in that context. So '$2+2=4$' is true in any context. But that's what (6) says; and so (6) is true.

Again, our final evaluation of (6) as true is context-independent; we evaluate (6) on the basis of its semantic status in every context. As with (X), our intuitive reasoning about (6) is represented by the evaluated$_0$ tree for (6).

Now, with any theory of context-sensitive terms, there is an inevitable separation of theory and object language. The singularity theory is no exception. Though the singularity theory is a theory of context-sensitive terms, the theory does not itself contain context-sensitive terms. As theorists, we evaluate in a context-independent way the sentences of the object language, via the appropriate evaluated$_\beta$ trees.

The Superliar indicates in a specially dramatic way that, as ordinary speakers, we can evaluate the sentences of our language in a context-independent way. Our final evaluation of (6) illustrates the same point, albeit less dramatically. Our ordinary semantic usage extends to a context-independent perspective. In general, given the notion of truth (falsity) in a context, we have the means for providing such context-independent evaluations of any of our utterances. We can assess the semantic status of an utterance in all relevant contexts of utterance and provide an absolute evaluation of the utterance on this basis.

For another example, consider a Liar sentence uttered in context c of the type 'This sentence is not true'. If we "decontextualize" this sentence, understanding it as 'This sentence is not true in context c', we can evaluate it as true, since the sentence is not true in context c. Again, our final evaluation is context-independent. Such decontextualized evaluations of the sentences of the object language are represented by the deliverances of the evaluated$_\beta$ trees of our theory – these evaluations are obtained by stepping back from the contexts of the utterances of the object language. Our context-independent uses of 'true', as in (Y), may be represented by 'true$_\alpha$ for some α': Its extension is composed of the sentences of the object language whose appropriate evaluated$_\beta$ trees yield the value T.

So there are uses of 'true' that are context-independent. Just as we must separate the object language from the language of the theory, so we must keep distinct context-sensitive uses of 'true' and context-independent uses of 'true'. We have taken the object language to be that portion of English in which uses of 'true' (and 'false') are context-sensitive. We have found that we can enrich the object language with the semantic terms 'grounded', 'singularity', and 'true (false) in a context'. This enriched object language displays a good deal of semantic universality. But when we use 'true' in a context-independent way, as we do in our final evaluation (Y) of (X), or in our final evaluation of (6), we go beyond what we can say in the object language. For we have adopted a context-independent perspective, as we do when we develop a theory of our context-sensitive semantic predicates. This lends some plausibility to the theory: its context-independent perspective and the evaluations it yields are to be found in ordinary usage.

9.3. THE OBJECT LANGUAGE AND THE LANGUAGE OF THE THEORY

We have just distinguished the object language from the language of the theory. The question naturally arises: What is the relation between the two languages? According to the orthodox response, the language of the theory stands as Tarskian metalanguage to the object language. This is *not* so in the case of the singularity theory. Now, it *is* the case that the language of the theory contains a truth predicate for the object language: The extension of 'true$_\alpha$ for some α', or more conveniently 'true$_{obj}$', comprises exactly the sentences of the object language that are true from the context-independent perspective. And it *is* the case that 'true$_{obj}$' is not a predicate of the object language. Context-independent uses of 'true' are not to be found in the object language: In the object language, uses of 'true' and 'false' are context-sensitive uses. The sentence

(Y′) (X) is true$_{obj}$

is a true sentence of the language of the theory. Further, the application of the predicate 'true$_{obj}$' is in certain ways wider than context-sensitive uses of 'true' within the object language. Any context-sensitive use of 'true' will have true singularities ((X) is always one of them), and these are all in the extension of 'true$_{obj}$'. All this might seem to suggest that the language of the singularity theory is a Tarskian metalanguage for the object language. However, the application of 'true$_{obj}$' is also *narrower* in certain ways than context-sensitive uses of 'true'. There are truths in the extension of context-sensitive uses of 'true' that are not in the extension of 'true$_{obj}$'. Let us see why this is so.

According to the singularity theory, paradox is avoided by the identification and exclusion of singularities. Intuitively, the theory works by saying what is *excluded from* the extension of context-sensitive occurrences of 'true', *not* by saying what is included; we take a "downward" route rather than an "upward" route. Now, no truth of the theory is identified by the theory as a singularity. So, by Minimality, any truth of the theory is in the extension of ordinary context-sensitive occurrences of 'true'. To speak metaphorically, our ordinary context-sensitive uses of 'true' arch over the theory of that usage: Such uses include in their extension all true sentences of the singularity theory. But the extension of 'true$_{obj}$' does not: For example, it will not include any sentence that itself involves the predicate 'true$_{obj}$'. So, given the predicate 'true$_{obj}$' and any context-sensitive use of 'true', we cannot say that the extension of one is more comprehensive than that of the other.

Now the language of the singularity theory, call it '$\mathcal{L}_0$', may be regarded as a classical formal language. In the usual diagonal fashion, we can generate from this formal language a Tarskian hierarchy of formal languages, each containing the truth predicate for the preceding language. But none of the truths expressible in these languages are identified as singularities by the singularity theory. And so our ordinary context-sensitive uses of 'true' arch over not only the truths of the singularity theory, but also all the truths expressed by the languages of this hierarchy. Truths of *any* language of the hierarchy are in the extensions of ordinary context-sensitive occurrences of 'true'. There is no stratification of our ordinary context-sensitive truth predicate. A context-sensitive use of 'true' applies to *all* truths of English, nontheoretical *and* theoretical, except for its singularities. The singularity solution is not hierarchical. We do not diagonalize beyond the reach of our ordinary truth predicate.

Since any context-sensitive use of 'true' includes in its extension the truths of the singularity theory (and of the associated Tarskian hierarchy), there is no special difficulty in evaluating sentences of the theory via a context-sensitive use of 'true'. Once we are apprised of the singularity theory, there is an increase in the stock of sentences we may explicitly evaluate. I may write on the board

(11) '(L) is a true$_1$ sentence' is true.

My use of 'true' here is an ordinary context-sensitive use, and the theoretical sentence is in its extension. Similarly with

(12) '(X) is true$_{obj}$' is true.

Although the singularity theory, at the lowest level of the hierarchy, does not contain the resources for explicitly evaluating its own sentences, or those of higher levels, it *does* have the resources for quantifying over *all* contexts. The scope of the theory with respect to the sentences it can explicitly evaluate is limited to the sentences of the object language: the sentences that contain no semantic terms, together with those that contain context-sensitive uses of 'true' and 'false' (and in the expanded version, those sentences that contain uses of 'grounded', 'singularity', and 'truth (falsity) in a context'). But the scope of the theory with respect to the contexts that are quantified over is *not* limited. The theory cannot represent my utterances (11) and (12). But this is because the sentences I evaluate in (11) and (12) are beyond the evaluative scope of the theory, by Tarski's theorem. It is not because the contexts of my utterances are beyond the scope of the theory. To represent (11) and (12) formally, we need the resources of the formal language at the next level of the hierarchy. For now we must represent a more comprehensive object language, one in which we evaluate sentences of the singularity theory.

$\mathcal{L}_0$ is the language of the singularity theory. Let $\mathcal{L}_1$ be a suitable formal metalanguage for $\mathcal{L}_0$, containing the predicates 'true in $\mathcal{L}_0$' and 'false in $\mathcal{L}_0$'. We can express an expanded singularity theory in the language $\mathcal{L}_1$, a theory that can accommodate the evaluations (11) and (12). We extend the definition of a g-witness by supplementing clause (2)(h):

(iii) If $([\rho]_\gamma, T)$ is a node, and $[\rho]$ is a sentence of $\mathcal{L}_0$, then $[\rho]$ is true (i.e., true in $\mathcal{L}_0$).
(iv) Similarly for falsity.

We add the following clause to the definition of a basic tree:

If ρ is a sentence of $\mathcal{L}_0$, the branch terminates at this node.

And finally we adjust Step 1 of the procedure for obtaining an evaluated$_\beta$ tree for a β-reflective sentence, from its pruned$_\beta$ tree:

STEP 1. If the terminal node of a branch is a true$_\beta$ or false$_\beta$ sentence, or true in $\mathcal{L}_0$ or false in $\mathcal{L}_0$, the appropriate truth value is associated with that node.

9.3 Object language and language of the theory

Consider now our evaluation (11). Let 'A' abbreviate a name of the sentence type '(L) is a true_1 sentence'. The g-witness for (11) is

$$\langle [T([A])]_{11}, T \rangle$$
$$|$$
$$\langle [A]_{11}, T \rangle$$

(Notice that since no context is associated with the theoretical sentence type A, its contextual subscript in the bottom node is retained from the previous one. This is not to say that I could not utter A in some context – then its contextual subscript will be the context of my utterance.) A similar analysis may be given of (12).

Now the uses of 'true' in (11) and (12) do have singularities. This must be so because of the possibility of anaphoric paradoxes. Such paradoxes are resolved in the usual way. Consider, for example,

(13) '(L) is a true_1 sentence' is true but (13) is not.

The basic tree (and the pruned_0 tree) for (13) is

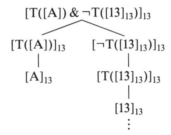

It is easily checked that (13) is reflection-free. The evaluated_0 tree for (13) is

$$\langle [T([A]) \,\&\, \neg T([13]_{13})]_{13}, T \rangle$$

$$\langle [T([A])]_{13}, T \rangle \qquad \langle [\neg T([13]_{13})]_{13}, T \rangle$$
$$| \qquad\qquad\qquad |$$
$$\langle [A]_{13}, T \rangle \qquad \langle [T([13]_{13})]_{13}, F \rangle$$

So the extended theory accommodates explicit direct talk about the theory. The uses of 'true' involved in the evaluation of sentences of the theory are subject to paradox (e.g., anaphoric paradox), and these are resolved in the way characteristic of the singularity theory.

The language $\mathcal{L}_1$ contains a truth predicate, call it 'true_{obj+}', for the expanded object language that includes evaluations of the singularity theory. The predicate 'true_{obj+}' applies to the sentences of the expanded object language that are true from the context-independent perspective. The extension of 'true_{obj+}' properly includes the extension of 'true_{obj}'; sentences like (11) and (12) are in the extension of 'true$_{obj+}$' but are not in the extension of 'true$_{obj}$'.[7]

We must in turn ascend to a metalanguage for $\mathcal{L}_1$ to evaluate sentences of $\mathcal{L}_1$ – and so on, through a hierarchy of languages. We can consider the general case of the language at level δ in the hierarchy. The extended definitions will look like this:

Extended definition of a g-witness. We add to clause (2)(h) as follows:

(h)(iii) If $([\rho]_\gamma, T)$ is a node, and $[\rho]_\gamma$ is a sentence of $\mathcal{L}_\eta$ ($\eta < \delta$), then $[\rho]_\gamma$ is a true sentence of $\mathcal{L}_\eta$.

(h)(iv) Similarly for falsity.

Extended definition of a basic tree. We add the following clause:

If σ is a sentence of $\mathcal{L}_\eta$ ($\eta < \delta$), the branch terminates at this node.

Extended procedure for obtaining an evaluated$_\beta$ tree. We adjust Step 1 to include nodes that are sentences of $\mathcal{L}_\eta$ ($\eta < \delta$):

Pair such a node with the appropriate truth value, according to whether the sentence is true-in-$\mathcal{L}_\eta$ or false-in-$\mathcal{L}_\eta$.

Again, there is no special problem about the evaluation of the sentences of any of these languages by a context-sensitive use of 'true'; by Minimality, none of these sentences are excluded from the extension of a context-sensitive use of 'true'. Take a sentence S that is true in the language $\mathcal{L}_{\delta+1}$, and suppose also that S is beyond the scope of $\mathcal{L}_\delta$ and all languages of lower levels. Suppose that I am apprised of $\mathcal{L}_{\delta+1}$, so that S is within my evaluative scope. Then I can say

(14) S is true,

where my use of 'true' is an ordinary context-sensitive use. Now my utterance can be formally represented only by a theory expressible in a language richer than $\mathcal{L}_{\delta+1}$, such as $\mathcal{L}_{\delta+2}$, a formal metalanguage for $\mathcal{L}_{\delta+1}$. Again, this is because S is not evaluable within $\mathcal{L}_{\delta+1}$ (and not because the context of my utterance is beyond the scope of $\mathcal{L}_{\delta+1}$ or indeed of any language at a lower level). My use of 'true' in (14) may be associated with paradox (e.g., anaphoric versions of the Liar) – and these are resolved in the usual way, via singularities. We offer a singularity solution to the liar, *not* a hierarchical solution. There is a Tarskian hierarchy of formal languages starting out from $\mathcal{L}_0$, but we do not invoke this hierarchy to resolve the Liar. Rather, the Liar is resolved by the identification and exclusion of singularities.

9.3 Object language and language of the theory

We might keep pushing beyond the hierarchy. Consider an even stronger Superliar:

(Sup) (Sup) is not true in any context or at any level of the hierarchy.

Sentence (Sup), like (X), is a singularity of every context. There's a pull toward evaluating (Sup) as true, since it isn't true in any context, on pain of contradiction, and it isn't true at any level of the hierarchy, on pain of contradiction. This forces us out of the hierarchy, since we're quantifying over all its levels. In order to formally represent (Sup), we would need to go to a theory rich enough to quantify over all levels of the hierarchy.

Though its higher reaches may be unclear,[8] this Tarskian route will never lead to a universal theory. We might try to obtain a universal truth predicate by forming the predicate 'true in some context or at some level of the hierarchy'. But such attempts to capture all the truths fails, because a sentence like (Sup) can always be constructed to force us higher still. The search for a universal predicate along Tarskian lines must fail: We can always diagonalize out. For this kind of reason, the Liar is sometimes taken to be *a kind of diagonal argument*. This is so on a Tarskian view like that of Burge and Parsons. And recall again Barwise and Etchemendy: "We can look at the Liar as providing us with a propositional function from situations s to propositions f_s, one that can be used to diagonalize out of any set P of propositions."[9] As we noted in Chapter 6, we obtain a series of nested situations. But a universal situation is not reached: "The Liar construction shows that the situations propositions can be about fall short of universality."[10] But I think it is misguided to draw the moral that the Liar is a diagonal argument.

Tarski's theorem applies to any well-constructed classical formal language. And a Tarskian hierarchy is always forthcoming. This is a matter of mathematical theorems. No solution to the Liar is going to deny these theorems; they are quite neutral with respect to ways out of the Liar. But we should not assume uncritically that these formal Tarskian hierarchies explicate *our* concept of truth. In particular, we should not assume that the formal hierarchy generated from the singularity theory explicates our concept of truth, any more than a hierarchy generated from a formal language for chemistry explicates our concept of truth.[11] The singularity theory, at the base, *is* a theory of our concept of truth: It says that our concept of truth has singularities, that our uses of the truth predicate are context-sensitive, and so on. The higher levels of the hierarchy are not theories of truth the way that the ground level is a theory of our concept of truth. The languages of the hierarchy do serve a purpose though. We have seen that we may evaluate sentences of the singularity theory via our ordinary context-sensitive truth predicate; but we need a richer language to represent such an evaluation. Similarly, we may evaluate sentences of the formal language for chemistry via our context-sensitive truth predicate; but we need a richer language than the formal language for chemistry to represent the evaluation. In general, a language of either hierarchy, generated from the singularity theory or from chemistry, provides a representation of the application of our context-sensitive truth predicate to the sentences of languages at lower levels. But the levels do *not* correspond to any stratification of our ordinary context-sensitive truth predicate.

The singularity solution abandons the Tarskian route. Since the Tarskian is offering a stratified account of our predicate 'true', questions about the extent of the hierarchies and quantification over the levels present special difficulties. Of course, these are substantial questions, quite independently of any particular proposal about 'true' in English. But they present no special difficulty for the singularity account. According to the singularity account, an ordinary context-sensitive use of 'true' applies "almost everywhere," failing to apply only to those truths that are pathological in its context of utterance. By Minimality, when we use 'true' we point to as many truths as can be pointed to from our context of utterance. These truths include all the truths of chemistry and of the Tarskian hierarchy that can be generated from that theory; and it will also include all the truths of the singularity theory and of the hierarchy that can be generated from it, however far this extends.

The intuitive picture is this: We distinguish two mutually exclusive perspectives, one context-sensitive, the other context-independent. Each of these perspectives is incomplete from the evaluative point of view, though in different, complementary ways. Any context-sensitive use of 'true' applies to all true sentences of the language of the singularity theory and to all true sentences of all higher languages of the hierarchy. But still, such a use of 'true' has singularities (such as the Superliar sentence (X) and anaphoric versions of the Liar). Even if you are an omniscient semanticist, with a complete grasp of the singularity theory, still your context-sensitive uses of 'true' will have singularities. On the other hand, a context-independent use of 'true', as in our final evaluation (Y) of the Superliar sentence (X), includes in its extension all true singularities (including (X)). But this context-independent use of 'true' is subject to diagonalization. The use of 'true' in (Y) is represented by 'true_{obj}', and this predicate does not include in its extension truths of the language of the singularity theory or of the languages higher in the hierarchy. Even if, from your context-independent perspective, you have a complete grasp of the truth values of every sentence of the object language, still your concept of truth for the object language is subject to diagonalization. In sum, truths that are beyond the reach of one perspective are within the reach of the other. But neither perspective alone captures them all.[12]

9.4. UNIVERSALITY

In Chapter 1 we saw that, according to Tarski, natural languages are universal: "If we can speak meaningfully about anything at all, we can also speak about it in colloquial language."[13] In particular, we saw that Tarski held that natural languages are semantically universal. I think we are now in a position to see that the singularity theory goes a long way toward accommodating these intuitions.

First, the object language admits a high degree of semantic universality. The object language contains the context-sensitive semantic predicates 'true' and 'false'. Further, as we have seen in this chapter, we can express in the object language the semantic notions of groundedness, singularity (in each of two senses), and truth (falsity) in a context.

Second, the singularity theory is not expressed in a Tarskian metalanguage for our object language. Many have thought that the goal of a universal language is unattainable, since the Liar shows that there are things that cannot be said in the object language, but only in an essentially richer metalanguage.[14] Certainly, the contemporary theories of truth we discussed in Chapters 3 and 4 were unable to avoid an ascent to a metalanguage. But things are different with the singularity account. According to the singularity proposal, sentences of the theory are within the evaluative scope of the context-sensitive truth predicate of the object language.

There is one sense in which a natural language like English is not semantically universal or closed: We should not expect to find a *universal* truth predicate, one that applies to *all* the truths. Suppose there were such an unrestricted truth predicate, call it 'true$_U$'. Then the Liar returns. For we can form the sentence 'This sentence is not true$_U$'; and when we ask whether this sentence is true$_U$ or not, we are landed in contradiction.

Now, according to the singularity theory, every context-sensitive occurrence of 'true' has singularities: anaphoric versions of the Liar are always possible. Even the predicate 'true in some context' has singularities, as is witnessed by the Superliar sentence (X). And the context-independent truth predicates of the singularity theory and the associated Tarskian hierarchy are all subject to diagonalization. There is no universal truth predicate. Still, each occurrence of the context-sensitive predicate 'true' in our object language is taken to apply to *all* truths except its singularities. Given a context-sensitive use of 'true', its application extends to true reflective evaluations of its singularities and to truths of the singularity theory and the associated Tarskian hierarchy. I would suggest that, on the singularity proposal, *each context-sensitive occurrence of the truth predicate is as close to universal as it can be without contradiction.*[15]

Similarly, on the singularity account, a *global* utterance like

(GL) Every sentence is true or not true

is as close to global as it can be. Here 'true' is (minimally) restricted: Apart from anaphoric singularities, the utterance (GL) itself is a singularity of the occurrences of 'true', since (GL) is ungrounded. Notice that the singularity approach places *no* restrictions on the quantifier. This is all to the good: Intuitively, when you utter (GL), you quantify over *all* sentences. The global nature of the universal quantification is respected by the singularity account. And (GL) itself is not beyond our evaluative reach. In the way typical of the singularity approach, (GL) may be reflectively evaluated as true.

Another aspect of the intuition that English is semantically universal is this: Every sentence of our language may be evaluated, as true or as false, *within* the language. In evaluating the sentences of our language, we are never forced outside our language. I believe that the singularity theory does full justice to this. Our ability to evaluate a pathological sentence like Aristotle's utterance (L) is captured by the theory: Reflective contexts are provided for. We can evaluate global sentences like (GL). We can evaluate even the Superliar sentence (X) within our language, for our account admits context-independent uses of 'true'. The singularity approach allows us to step back from, and quantify over, contexts of utterance: Context-independent uses of 'true' are accommodated. In general, for each singularity, there is a sentence of our language that evaluates it. Further, the sentences of the theory (and the associated hierarchy) may be evaluated in our language, since these sentences are within the scope of our ordinary context-sensitive uses of 'true'. The singularity account distinguishes our context-dependent and context-independent uses of 'true', and every true sentence falls within the range of at least one of these uses. No sentence of our language is beyond the reach of our semantic concepts.

The singularity theory, I am claiming, does justice to Tarski's intuition that natural languages are semantically universal. This is not to claim that there is a 'universal' context, a single context that embraces all possible truths and all possible evaluations. Every stretch of semantic discourse has its evaluative gaps: Our semantic predicates either have singularities or are subject to diagonalization. The present discourse is no exception – my uses of 'true' have their singularities, too. But what cannot be expressed within one stretch of semantic discourse can always be expressed in another. We can say everything there is to say, but not all at once.

Notes

1. See Curry 1941 and 1942. Compare the following presentation with that in Boolos and Jeffrey 1989, p. 186. Boolos and Jeffrey point out that this argument runs parallel to a proof of Löb's theorem. See also Barwise and Etchemendy 1987, p. 23.
2. Hughes 1982, p. 57.
3. In line with other medieval authors, Buridan takes 'God exists' to be a stock example of a true sentence.
4. The sequence $\sigma_1, \sigma_2, \ldots$ is an example of a simple chain, where no member of the sequence has any truth-functional or quantificational complexity. It is easy to see that it is always possible to assign consistent truth values to the members of a simple chain. For example, assign the value true to the first sentence and assign to the second sentence the value that the first sentence assigns it; subsequently, one can always continue to assign truth values consistent with previous assignments.
5. Kripke 1975, in Martin 1984, pp. 54–5.
6. This view is found in the medieval literature on the Liar. It is the second opinion considered by Heytesbury 1335, and the eighth opinion considered by Paul of Venice 1499, in bk. II, chap. 15. I shall make use of an unpublished translation by Marilyn Adams of Paul's Treatise on Insolubles; the translation is of the Venice 1499 edition. All page references to Paul's Treatise will be to Adams's translation. Paul Vincent Spade considers Cajetan's attribution of this view to John Dumbleton 1335–40 to be a misunderstanding of Dumbleton's view; see Spade 1975, p. 117.

    The view is found in the modern literature too. See, e.g., Bar-Hillel 1957; Prior 1958; Garver 1970, in Martin 1970; and Kneale 1971.
7. "Paul's Treatise," p. 5.
8. In the medieval literature, this is the approach of the *cassantes*. Cassation is the fifth view discussed by Paul, and the sixth considered by Bradwardine 1321–4, in Roure 1970, pp. 205–326.

    One modern proponent of this view is Fitch 1970, in Martin 1970, pp. 75–7.

9. The view of the *restringentes* may be regarded as an anticipation of the approach that bans self-reference. (For more on the *restringentes,* see Chapter 5.) The *restringentes'* rule is "In no proposition does a part supposit for the whole of which it is a part" ("Paul's Treatise," p. 23).

   Some authors applied this rule to all sentences. See the anonymous author in Spade 1969 (text X in Spade 1975). The same wholesale application of the *restringentes'* rule is found in another anonymous author: see Braakhuis 1967.

   Others applied the rule to the insolubles only. Spade cites Walter Burley, probably before 1320, in Roure 1970; William of Ockham (hereafter Ockham) 1488, III, 3, chaps. 38, 45; Ockham, before 1328; Sexgrave, before 1333; Roseth, before 1337. See Spade 1982.

   The denial of self-reference as a solution to the Liar has had some support in the modern literature. For one example, Frederic B. Fitch writes, "The problem is to find a theory of types which eliminates the 'vicious' sorts of self-reference that lead to the mathematical and semantical paradoxes but not those sorts of self-reference that seem to be such an important part of philosophical logic" (1946, pp. 71–2).

10. A ban on self-reference is unacceptable for other reasons too. There are many cases of apparently harmless self-referential sentences (consider 'This sentence has five words' or 'This sentence is in English'). This point is made in the medieval literature; see, e.g., the tract by Pseudo-Sherwood, in Roure 1970, p. 252, par. 4.02. It is standard in the contemporary literature; see, e.g., Hart 1970.

    It might be replied that we should place *limited* restrictions on self-reference. But this requires some way of distinguishing "good" and "bad" cases of self-reference. And it is hard to see how this can be done in any noncircular way. This difficulty may have been recognized by medieval writers. It is arguable that Paul of Venice recognizes it when he rejects Peter of Ailly's ban on self-reference for proper mental sentences. Paul finds no reason for restricting the signification of terms occurring in mental sentences and not in spoken or written or improperly mental sentences. (See Paul's Treatise, pp. 17–20. For Peter of Ailly's restricted ban on self-reference, see Spade 1980, paragraph 272ff, especially 279–83.) The difficulty is certainly recognized in the contemporary literature. (See, e.g., Fitch 1946; Hart 1970; and Martin 1970, pp. 91–112.)

11. This is the seventh opinion in Thomas Bradwardine's list; see Spade 1975, p. 107. Bochvar 1939 introduced a third value "paradoxical" in order to solve the Liar. Other differently motivated three-valued systems have been developed by Łukasiewicz ("indeterminate"; 1920, 1930), both in McCall 1967; and by Kleene ("undecidable"; 1952). Brian Skyrms calls Liar sentences "neuter" (1970a and b).

12. See the sixth opinion discussed by Paul of Venice. A number of contemporary authors appeal to truth gaps. A notable theory of truth that allows truth gaps is that of Kripke 1975. See also Martin 1967, 1968, 1976, 1977; van Fraassen 1968, 1970; and Martin and Woodruff 1975.

13. Van Fraassen 1968, 1970. Kripke 1975 is also influenced by Strawson's doctrine.
14. Van Fraassen 1970, in Martin 1970, p. 16.
15. See Martin 1970, in Martin 1970, p. 93.
16. See Martin 1976, p. 286.
17. Fine 1974; Zadeh 1975; McGee 1990. For more on Zadeh's account, see Chapter 3; and for more on McGee's, see Chapter 4.
18. McGee 1990, p. 217.
19. Russell 1959, p. 82. See also Russell 1908, in van Heijenoort 1967, where he gives a similar analysis: "When a man says 'I am lying', we may interpret his statement as: 'There is a proposition which I am affirming and which is false.' All statements that 'there is' so-and-so may be regarded as denying that the opposite is always true; thus 'I am lying' becomes 'It is not true of all propositions that either I am not affirming them or they are true'; in other words, 'It is not true for all propositions p that if I affirm p, p is true'. The paradox results from regarding this statement as affirming a proposition, which must therefore come within the scope of the statement" (p. 154).
20. Russell 1908, in van Heijenoort 1967, p. 154.
21. Ibid., p. 155.
22. Bocheński 1961 has suggested that an anticipation of Russell's vicious circle principle may be found in the work of d'Ailly (p. 245). Bocheński cites this passage from d'Ailly: "*It is impossible for the understanding to form a universal mental sentence properly so called that signifies every mental sentence to be false.* For instance, a mental sentence 'Every sentence is false', or 'Every mental sentence is false', and this where we understand the subject to supposit for [that sentence] itself. This is clear, because [if it were possible, the sentence] would signify itself to be false, which violates the conclusion (par. 282). Therefore, if the understanding should form some such sentence, its subject supposits not for [that sentence] itself but for any [sentence] other than it" (Spade 1980, par. 297). It is clear that d'Ailly's examples are very like those that exercised Russell. The mental sentence 'Every mental sentence is false' does involve *all* of a collection (all the mental sentences) and is itself one of the collection – so it is the kind of instance vetoed by at least Russell's first formulation of the vicious circle principle. Moreover, d'Ailly's diagnosis of such sentences is very like Russell's. Compare d'Ailly's claim that we cannot form the mental sentence 'Every mental sentence is false', "where we understand the subject to supposit for [that sentence] itself" (Spade 1980, par. 297).

    So the examples discussed by Russell and d'Ailly are similar, and so are their respective diagnoses. Nevertheless, I believe their resolutions are different. D'Ailly's resolution is based on the rule of the *restringentes*. He applies the rule to the mental sentence 'Every mental sentence is false' and concludes that the subject does not supposit for that very mental sentence, but for all others. Now this appeal to the *restringentes'* rule does *not* imply that we cannot legitimately speak about *all* mental sentences; it implies only that we cannot do so in *insoluble* sentences. In fact, d'Ailly *does* think that the *restringentes'* rule applies to all mental sentences, not just to those that threaten paradox (Spade 1980, par. 313ff). But others, like Burley and Ockham, restrict the application of the rule to insolubles only. So it is possible to preserve d'Ailly's treatment of apparently insoluble mental sentences and yet permit mental sentences about all mental sentences. This shows, I think, that the spirit of d'Ailly's resolution is different from that of Russell's. The *restringentes'* rule is closer to a ban on self-reference than to a Russellian veto of vicious circles. The basic idea is the placing of minimal restrictions on the supposition of terms in certain sentences, not the identification of certain totalities as illegitimate.

23. Russell 1908, in van Heijenoort 1967, p. 155.
24. Russell 1959, p. 82.
25. Ibid. See also Russell 1908, in van Heijenoort 1967, p. 164.
26. Russell 1959, pp. 82–3. See also Russell 1908, in van Heijenoort 1967, p. 166.
27. Tarski 1930–1, in Tarski 1983, pp. 152–278. See also Tarski 1944, in Linsky 1952, pp. 13–47.
28. Aristotle, *Metaphysics,* Γ, 7, 27.
29. Tarski 1944, in Linsky 1952, p. 15.
30. Ibid., p. 16.
31. Ibid., p. 16.
32. See Tarski 1930–1, in Tarski 1983, p. 162; Tarski 1944, in Linsky 1952, pp. 19–20.
33. Tarski 1944, in Linsky 1952, p. 20.
34. Tarski 1969, p. 89.
35. Tarski 1944, in Linsky 1952, p. 20.
36. Ibid.
37. Tarski writes: "It would be superfluous to stress here the consequences of rejecting the assumption II, that is, of changing our logic (supposing this were possible) even in its more elementary and fundamental parts. We thus consider only the possibility of rejecting the assumption I" (ibid., p. 21).
38. Ibid., pp. 22–3.
39. Ibid., p. 22.
40. Russell 1971, p. 371.
41. Church 1976, p. 756.
42. Tarski 1930–1, in Tarski 1983, p. 164.
43. Tarski 1969, p. 89.
44. Tarski 1930–1, in Tarski 1983, p. 164.
45. Ibid., pp. 164–5.
46. Ibid., p. 165 (Tarski's emphasis). See also p. 267.
47. Ibid., p. 267.
48. See Bar-On 1993.
49. Paul Ziff, for one, would reply to this question with an emphatic no; see Ziff 1988, p. 8.
50. Russell 1971, p. 371.

51. Russell 1908, in van Heijenoort 1967, p. 154.
52. Tarski considers the language of the calculus of classes; see Tarski 1930–1, in Tarski 1983, p. 247.

CHAPTER 2

1. Cantor (1890–1), in Zermelo 1932, pp. 278–81.

   Ivor Grattan-Guinness suggests that the first use of the diagonal argument was not Cantor's, citing an earlier use in du Bois-Reymond 1877; see Grattan-Guinness 1978, p. 134, n. 1. In a similar vein, Wang (1974, in Benacerraf and Putnam 1983, pp. 530–70) points to du Bois-Reymond's use of the diagonal method in his theory of growth "nearly twenty years before Cantor published in 1892 his famous diagonal proof of the theorem that every set has more subsets than elements" (p. 570). Wang cites the following papers: du Bois-Reymond 1869, 1873, 1875, 1877.

   But there are significant differences between the diagonal method employed by du Bois-Reymond and Cantor's later use in his 1890–1 paper. One major difference in particular deserves mention. In the terminology to be developed below in Section 2.3, Cantor's diagonal arguments of 1890–1 involve the formation of a *countervalue,* while du Bois-Reymond's diagonal argument does not. Du Bois-Reymond's argument is close to another kind of diagonal argument now familiar in mathematical analysis; for an example of this, see Rudin 1976, Theorem 7.23, pp. 156–7. This other type of diagonal argument, and its relation to Cantor's 1890–1 argument, is also worthy of study – though I shall not pursue its analysis here. As Wang 1974 points out, the theorem that du Bois-Reymond proves is analogous to Cantor's theorem that every fundamental sequence of ordinal numbers defines a greater ordinal. It may then be reasonable to conjecture that this second type of diagonal argument generates Burali-Forti's paradox. At any rate, given the differences between these two types of diagonal argument, I find Grattan-Guinness's and Wang's suggestions too strong.
2. Cantor's earlier proof appeared in Cantor 1874. The paper is reprinted in Zermelo 1932, pp. 115–18. This earlier proof was controversial because it relied on considerations about irrational numbers; for a discussion of this, see Dauben 1979, p. 165.
3. A "simply infinite" sequence is a denumerable sequence, one that can be put into 1–1 correspondence with the natural numbers.
4. Cantor 1890–1, in Zermelo 1932, p. 278. I follow the translation in Dauben 1979, p. 166.
5. Cantor 1890–1, in Zermelo 1932, p. 279.
6. By "linear continuum" here, Cantor means the reals between 0 and 1, rather than the entire real line.
7. Of course, Cantor's second proof does not establish what is generally called "Cantor's power set theorem." But Cantor's second proof is easily extended to a proof of the power set theorem.

Notice first that there is a natural association of a function f in M with a subset of L: We may associate with a function f the set of those elements of L for which f gives value 1. So there is a 1-1 correspondence between M and the power set of L. And since M is of greater power than L, so is the power set of L.

Clearly, Cantor's second proof can be applied to any set – given a set S, we show that the appropriate set of single-valued functions is of greater power than S. And then we use the simple extension of the previous paragraph to complete a proof of the power set theorem.

8. This definition is easily extended to proper classes.

9. There is another way in which we generalize the notion of a diagonal: We extend it to nondenumerable arrays. (This generalization is implicit in Cantor's use of the diagonal method to prove the power set theorem.) For an array in which one or both of side and top are finite, there is a clear sense to the intuitive notion of the diagonal. For an array in which the side or top is denumerably infinite, the diagonal is now understood as infinitely extendible. And even where the side or top is nondenumerable, we might think of the diagonal as a line at 45° to the axis.

10. It is usually Thomson who gets the credit for pointing out the connection between this theorem, various paradoxes, and the diagonal argument (1962, in Butler 1962). But Russell had, in effect, made the connection; see Russell 1903, pp. 366–8, esp. sec. 347. Herzberger 1970 uses (Ru) and variants to analyze a family of diagonal arguments. This theorem is also discussed in Martin 1977 and in Goddard and Johnston 1983.

11. The proof is largely in the style of Kalish, Montague, and Mar 1980.

12. Russell 1903, p. 366.

13. Ibid., pp. 366–8.

14. Ibid., p. 368.

15. Richard 1905, in van Heijenoort 1967, pp. 143–4.

16. I discuss this in my upcoming "On Richard's and Poincaré's Ways Out."

17. Van Heijenoort 1967, p. 136.

18. Russell himself wrote in 1908 that Richard's paradox "is solved . . . by remarking that 'all definitions' is an illegitimate notion. Thus the number [N] is *not* defined in a finite number of words, being in fact not defined at all" (see Russell 1908, in van Heijenoort 1967, p. 155). See also Russell 1906, p. 645.

19. As we will see later, a bad diagonal argument can take the form of a direct or reductio argument. (For an example of the latter, see the upcoming discussion of Cantor's paradox.) Either way, a bad diagonal argument will always contain some assumption that is *not* made toward a contradiction and that asserts the existence of a diagonal component that is not well-determined.

20. Gödel 1931; in van Heijenoort 1967, pp. 596–616.

21. Ibid., p. 598.

22. Ibid.

23. Following Gödel's terminology, let [c, n] be the result of substituting a name

of the number n for the free variable in the class sign c. Then c is true of n if [c, n] is a sentence that is true in the standard interpretation; and c is provable of a number n if [c, n] is a theorem of PM.

24. The bar over *'Bew'* denotes negation.

25. Gödel 1931, in van Heijenoort 1967, p. 598.

26. In implicitly assuming the soundness of PM here, I am following Gödel's sketch of the proof. ("Let us suppose that the proposition [R(q); q] were provable; then it would also be true," ibid.) The rest of the argument for the existence of an undecidable sentence follows Gödel's presentation closely.

27. Rogers 1967, p. 11.

28. The terminology here is taken from Kleene 1952, pp. 220, 221.

29. Here I have paraphrased Rogers 1967, pp. 10–11.

30. It may seem that the diagonal argument establishes the same result for any formally characterized class of algorithmic functions. The problem is avoided by allowing sets of instructions for nontotal partial functions as well as for total functions.

    Following Rogers (1967, p. 12), suppose now we have a list of sets of instructions for partial functions. Let the $(x+1)$st set of instructions be Q_x, and let ψ_x be the partial function determined by Q_x. Now define the partial function φ as follows: to compute $\varphi(x)$, find Q_x, compute $\psi_x(x)$, and if and when a value for $\psi_x(x)$ is obtained, give $\psi_x(x)+1$ as the value for $\varphi(x)$. We have instructions for computing the partial function φ, which we may suppose to be in our list. Suppose it is the (x_0+1)st set of instructions; then $\varphi = \psi_{x_0}$. But now, $\psi_{x_0}(x_0) = \varphi(x_0) = \psi_{x_0}(x_0)+1$ does not yield a contradiction because $\varphi(x_0)$ may not have a value.

31. As before, the mere conversion of this bad diagonal argument into a good one does not constitute a solution to paradox. For a solution to Russell's paradox, we would need a natural account of the notion of *set* that yields the consequence that there is no set M. Nowadays, of course, the received conception of set is the iterative conception, embodied in the cumulative hierarchy of ZF set theory.

32. By the definition of K, we have that $W_x \subset \bar{K} \rightarrow x \in \bar{K} - W_x$. This property of $\bar{K}$ is given a recursively invariant formulation in the definition of a *productive* set. Productiveness is closely linked to diagonalization: Theorems concerning productive sets provide further examples of diagonal arguments.

33. See, e.g., Tarski 1930–1, in Tarski 1983, p. 248.

34. Ibid., p. 248, n. 2.

35. For the usual systems of Gödel numbering, F is a diagonal that does not pass through every column.

36. It is possible to draw a close parallel between our presentation of Tarski's theorem and his own presentation (1930–1, in Tarski 1983, pp. 247–51). Tarski's function '$\psi(n)$' (introduced on p. 250) corresponds exactly to our countervalue H.

37. I have adapted Rogers's presentation of Kleene's theorem to our analysis of diagonal arguments; see Rogers 1967, p. 26.

38. For example, there are other ways of generating a new diagonal than that embodied in Theorem 2.3. Consider this variant:

    Theorem 2.4. Let R be an array, and F be a diagonal on D_1 and D_2. Let j be a 1–1 function from the range of F onto D_1, and let k be a 1–1 function from D_1 (the domain of F) into D_2. Then H does not occur as a row, where

    (i) $\forall x \forall y (\exists z Hj(y)k(x)z \leftrightarrow Fxy)$,

    and (ii), (iii), and (iv) are as in Theorem 2.3.

    Proof. Take F as in the proof of Theorem 2.3, and let

    $$F' = \{\langle j(y_1), k(x_1)\rangle, \langle j(y_2), k(x_2)\rangle, \langle j(y_3), k(x_3), \ldots\}.$$

    Then the proof is similar to the proof of Theorem 2.3.

39. For example, more cases of bad diagonal arguments are discussed in Russell 1903, sec. 348. One in particular is worthy of mention; we may call it the *paradox of propositions*. A simplified version of this paradox is generated through consideration of a proposition that is about exactly those propositions not about themselves. For further discussion of this paradox, see Simmons 1993.

CHAPTER 3

1. For example, Fitch is motivated by the intuition that philosophy can be formalized within a universal formal metalanguage, the construction of which is made possible by allowing truth-value gaps (see Fitch 1964). See also Martin 1976, discussed next.
2. Martin 1976, p. 288.
3. Ibid., p. 287.
4. Another kind of difficulty can be raised for particular truth gap approaches. Typically, truth gap theorists will motivate gaps in ways independent of semantic paradox – for example, by way of considerations of category or of vagueness. One can ask whether such considerations are appropriate where the Liar is concerned. One might argue that the application of 'true' or 'false' to the sentence ' "Heterological" is heterological' does not appear to be a category mistake: The sentence ' "Heterological" is heterological' seems to be the sort of thing to which 'true' and 'false' apply. And one might argue that 'true' and 'false' do not appear to be vague predicates. The problem raised in this section is more general and cuts across the different ways gap theorists motivate the gaps.
5. Paul's *Treatise*, p. 4.
6. We can ask a similar question about the view of Roger Swineshead, c. 1330–5. According to Swineshead, a true sentence, by definition, not only corresponds to reality, but also is not self-falsifying. A false sentence either fails to correspond to reality or is self-falsifying. Liar sentences like 'This sentence

is false' are self-falsifying; hence, they are false. (Paul Spade writes, "A sentence 'falsifies itself' just in case it is 'relevant' (*pertinens*) to inferring that it is false" and goes on to note that this notion of relevance is complicated and needs further study. See Spade 1982, in Kretzmann, Kenny, and Pinborg 1982, p. 250.) Swineshead's solution divides sentences into three groups: those that are true, those that are false and don't correspond to reality, and those that are false and yet *do* correspond to reality. Insolubles belong to this third group.

But now we can, using the terms of Swineshead's own resolution, divide sentences into two mutually exclusive and exhaustive groups: those that correspond to reality and those that do not. And now, the sentence 'This sentence does not correspond to reality' *does* generate a new paradox, despite Swineshead's tripartite division.

Interestingly enough, Swineshead considers such sentences and argues that they are neither true nor false (see Spade 1979). This would seem to escape one form of the Revenge Liar, expressed in the terms of Swineshead's solution, only to fall foul of another, expressed in terms adapted to truth gap approaches.

7.   Kripke 1975 is reprinted in Martin 1984.

8.   Kleene 1952, sec. 64, pp. 332–40.

9.   Note that, by "increase," we don't mean "strictly increase."

10.   Notice that it would be false to say that, for any ordinal, there is a sentence of $\mathcal{L}$ that is first declared true at that ordinal level. It is false for every limit ordinal.

11.   See Kripke 1975, in Martin 1984, p. 69.

12.   There are fixed points other than the minimal fixed points. For example, fixed points are constructible where we assign an arbitrary truth value to sentences that are ungrounded but not paradoxical, like the Truth Teller.

13.   Martin and Woodruff demonstrate the same degree of semantic universality by a *maximal* fixed point construction; in 1975, reprinted in Martin 1984.

14.   Elsewhere, I have presented Kripke's theory, and the result just mentioned, in a fully rigorous way; see Simmons 1987a, pp. 150–63. We use Y. N. Moschovakis's 1974 notion of an acceptable structure; see his chap. 5. We start with the first-order language L of an acceptable structure A. We extend L to $\mathcal{L}$ by adding a predicate T (intuitively, T is the truth predicate for $\mathcal{L}$), and we extend A to a structure A_T that provides the extension and the anti-extension of T. We show that the set of truths of $\mathcal{L}$ is *elementary* on A_T – that is to say, there is a predicate of $\mathcal{L}$ (in fact, T) whose extension is the set of truths of $\mathcal{L}$. We go on to show, by a diagonal argument, that the complement relative to the domain of A_T of the set of truths of $\mathcal{L}$ is *not* elementary on A_T.

15.   Kripke is aware of the necessity to ascend to a hierarchy but perhaps understates the problem when he writes, "The ghost of the Tarski hierarchy is still with us" (Kripke 1975, in Martin 1984, p. 80). It is a fully substantial Tarskian hierarchy that remains.

16. See ibid., p. 80, n. 34.
17. For an objection to Kripke along these lines, see Burge 1979, in Martin 1984.
18. Kripke 1975, in Martin 1984, p. 80, n. 34.
19. Perhaps we should be suspicious of this talk of a certain stage of natural language; see Burge 1979, in Martin 1984, p. 88, n. 9. But I shall not pursue such worries here.
20. Kripke contrasts two intuitions about how to adapt Tarski's Convention T to the three-valued approach. According to the first intuition, which Kripke endorses, if 'k' abbreviates the name of the sentence A, T(k) is to have the same truth conditions as A itself; so, in particular, T(k) suffers a truth gap if A does. Now, "an alternate intuition would assert that, if A is either false or undefined, then A is *not true* and T(k) should be *false* and its negation *true*" (1975, in Martin 1984, p. 80). Here, "not" is exclusion negation. In a footnote, Kripke says: "I think the primacy of the first intuition can be defended philosophically, and for this reason I have emphasized the approach based on this intuition. The alternate intuition arises only after we have reflected on the process embodying the first intuition" (ibid., p. 80, n. 35). So Kripke treats exclusion negation along with "grounded" and "paradoxical" – it is a derivative notion belonging to the metalanguage: "The sense in which we can say, in natural language, that a Liar sentence is not true must be thought of as associated with some later stage in the development of natural language, one in which speakers reflect on the generation process leading to the minimal fixed point" (ibid., p. 80).
21. T. Parsons 1984, p. 149.
22. For example, the concept corresponding to the countervalue

$$H(x,x) = \begin{cases} u, & \text{if } x \text{ is true of } x, \\ t, & \text{if } x \text{ is false of } x, \\ f, & \text{if } x \text{ is undefined of } x, \end{cases}$$

is expressed by *undefined of those expressions true of themselves, true of those expressions false of themselves, and false of those expressions undefined of themselves.*
23. T. Parsons 1984, p. 150.
24. Nicholas Asher has suggested to me that a Kripkean theory of truth can handle Strengthened Liar arguments by allowing metalinguistic ascent. The idea is that when in strengthened reasoning we move from

(1) (1) is not true

to

(2) (1) is not true,

we move from a statement about truth in (1) to a statement about grounded truth in (2). In uttering (2), we are no longer using truth, but a slightly different conception of truth like grounded truth. So we are to interpret (2) as a sentence of the language of the theory of truth and thereby capture something of the reflective capacity of agents who reason about the Strengthened Liar.

However, as we have just seen, the paradoxes that threaten Kripke's account are constructed from semantic notions that are available to the ordinary speaker, quite independently of reflection on the Liar or the Strengthened Liar. It would be quite implausible to represent these notions as technical notions expressible only in the language of the theory of truth.

And there is another related difficulty. As Asher points out, a new predicate like grounded truth must be treated analogously to the original truth predicate, on pain of paradox. We will need to form a new concept – say, *supergroundedness* – that reflects on the groundedness of sentences in the language augmented with the grounded truth predicate, and so on through a hierarchy of semantic predicates. Now consider the following stretch of reasoning. Suppose that someone unwittingly produces (an empirical version of) the Liar sentence (1). We go through some strengthened reasoning, and conclude by uttering (2). Now suppose we produce an anaphoric addition to (2), so as to obtain

(3) (1) is not true and neither is this sentence.

We can now argue that this conjunction is pathological, and so conclude

(4) (3) is not true.

Suppose that we accept the suggestion about the hierarchy. Then the notion of truth in (1) is ordinary truth. The notion of truth in (2) is grounded truth. With (3), we produce a paradox for this latter notion of grounded truth. Further strong reasoning yields (4). On the proposed hierarchical line, there is a shift between (3) and (4), from the notion of grounded truth to the notion of supergrounded truth. And a new anaphoric paradox incorporating (4) will in turn yield a new reflection and a new semantic notion (supersupergrounded truth?); and so on.

But this is surely implausible. The speaker is repeating the same kind of reasoning, and there is no indication that she is employing different and increasingly sophisticated semantic concepts at each new step in the sequence. I would find it far more plausible to retain the univocality of *true* and to take the speaker to be employing the same semantic notion throughout. This is possible on the nonhierarchical singularity proposal to be developed in this book.

25. Let me mention here three further objections to Kripke's theory.

(1) Kripke does not limit his attention to the minimal fixed point. He discusses other fixed points (e.g., maximal fixed points, intrinsic fixed points) and valuation schemes other than Kleene's strong scheme. Between these various valuation schemes and fixed points, Kripke maintains an official neutrality (see 1975, in Martin 1984, p. 77). But this professed neutrality is puzzling. For as we have seen, Kripke wishes to capture an intuition about truth, an intuition crystallized in the notion of groundedness (see the beginning of this section and ibid., pp. 57, 65–6). Now, of the various fixed points Kripke discusses, it is *only* the minimal fixed point that satisfies this intuition. The minimal fixed point provides a natural algorithm for determining

the truth value of a sentence itself involving the notion of truth. We could teach this procedure to a person who does not yet understand 'true' without saddling her with technical notions from set theory. Our subject needs only to understand how to evaluate quantifications and truth-functional compounds, and how to "keep going" in the appropriate way. The instructions for this procedure can be given quite intuitively, without mention of set-theoretic notions like *ordinal number*. Things are different with the other fixed points. To determine whether a sentence is true in an intrinsic fixed point, for example, our subject would need to find out if it has a conflicting truth value in any other fixed point – and this is a mathematical matter, not an intuitive one.

A parallel point can be made about certain other valuation schemes. Consider van Fraassen's valuation scheme, adapted to Kripke's monotonic construction. Suppose T is interpreted by the disjoint pair $\langle S_1, S_2 \rangle$. We want to know under what conditions a sentence A of $\mathcal{L}(S_1, S_2)$ is true. On the supervaluation scheme, A is a true (false) sentence of $\mathcal{L}(S_1, S_2)$ iff A is true (false) in every classical interpretation that extends $\langle S_1, S_2 \rangle$, i.e., iff for every pair $\langle S_1^*, S_2^* \rangle$ such that $\langle S_1, S_2 \rangle < \langle S_1^*, S_2^* \rangle$ and $S_1^* \cup S_2^* = D$, A is true (false) under the interpretation $\langle S_1^*, S_2^* \rangle$. Let S_1' and S_2' be respectively the set of true sentences and the set of false sentences of $\mathcal{L}(S_1, S_2)$. It is easy to show that the operation $\psi(\langle S_1, S_2 \rangle) = \langle S_1', S_2' \rangle$ is monotonic. Now we can go on to construct the minimal fixed point and others. But *these* monotonic constructions, using van Fraassen's operator ψ, cannot be explained intuitively. As is evident, we cannot explain the construction using supervaluations without bringing in technical notions. So this is not an account of the ordinary, intuitive account of truth.

If Kripke is concerned with 'true' in natural language and with providing a model of a stage of natural language, it is hard to see why he concerns himself with fixed points and valuation schemes that do not fit ordinary intuitions about 'true'. Kripke cannot maintain his neutrality *and* claim that his approach is in "agreement with intuitions about natural language in a large number of instances" (ibid., p. 81).

(2) As we have noted earlier, a *grounded* sentence is defined as having a truth value in the minimal fixed point. According to Kripke, it is a "principal virtue" of his theory that it provides a formal definition of groundedness: "What hitherto has been, as far as I know, an intuitive concept with no formal definition, becomes a precisely defined concept in the present theory" (ibid., p. 71; see also p. 57 and n. 8). But this claim is surely too strong. For there are sentences that are intuitively grounded but are not in the minimal fixed point, for example, the grounded sentences of the metalanguage in which Kripke's paper is written. Such sentences are not captured by Kripke's definition. And the definition does not deal with sentences in which 'grounded' itself appears. This is a critical shortcoming, since the intuitive notion of groundedness itself gives rise to paradox. We will treat paradoxes of grounding in Chapter 9.

(3) Our diagonal theorem has shown that Kripke cannot avoid the ascent to a Tarskian metalanguage; and this is just the first step up a Tarskian hierarchy. Given Kripke's awareness of the hierarchy, one might take the point of his paper to present an improved version of Tarski's theory. But if we take Kripke this way, then the criticisms that he levels against the Tarskian account carry over to his "improved" version. We can object to Kripke's theory that "our language contains just one word 'true', not a sequence of distinct phrases 'true$_n$', applying to sentences of higher and higher levels" (ibid., p. 58); and we can complain that no account of the transfinite levels of the Tarskian hierarchy has been offered (ibid., pp. 60–1).

26. Zadeh 1975.
27. Ibid., p. 415.
28. Ibid., p. 407.
29. Ibid., p. 416. For a presentation of Zadeh's theory that is a little more detailed than the one I have given here, see Haack 1978, pp. 162–9.
30. See Herzberger 1970 and 1981. Donald Davidson has also taken this view; see 1967, in Davidson 1985, pp. 17–36. Davidson seems to suggest that natural languages are not universal; for example, we as speakers of English have the concept of 'true-in-Urdu', which Urdu speakers do not have. (See ibid., pp. 28–9, where Davidson also says, "There may in the nature of the case always be something we grasp in understanding the language of another (the concept of truth) that we cannot communicate to him.") Though I shall not pursue the matter here, there seems to be some tension between what Davidson says here and claims that he makes elsewhere that imply there can be no untranslatability between languages (see, e.g., Davidson 1974, reprinted in Davidson 1985, pp. 183–98, where he seems to reject the possibility of total, and even partial, failures of translatability.)
31. This characterization of inexpressibility carries over to the variously enriched conceptual systems that Herzberger goes on to consider; see his 1970 and 1981.
32. Herzberger 1981, pp. 113–14.
33. Martin 1976 has also argued against Herzberger's inexpressibility claim, though not along the lines I suggest below.
34. As Martin 1976 points out, this raises an awkward question for Herzberger: if the expression 'is not true of itself' does not have the extension it seems to have, then what *is* its extension? (see p. 284).

CHAPTER 4

1. See Herzberger 1982 and Gupta 1982, in Martin 1984.
2. Herzberger 1982, in Martin 1984, p. 133.
3. Ibid., p. 142.
4. See Gupta 1982, in Martin 1984, pp. 215–16.
5. Ibid., p. 212.

6. Ibid., p. 216.
7. So on Herzberger's (but not Gupta's) treatment of limit stages, there are sentences such that neither they nor their negations are in the extension of T. That is, Herzberger admits truth-value gaps at limit stages (which are closed at the succeeding level). We can ask if truth gaps are really in the spirit of the "naive semantics" Herzberger takes himself to be articulating.
8. Gupta 1982, in Martin 1984, p. 233.
9. Ibid., p. 225.
10. Ibid., p. 225.
11. Ibid., p. 233. I have adjusted the terminology here – Gupta's use of 'L' is replaced by '£'.
12. Gupta has suggested (in correspondence) that we treat the notions of *truth* and *semantically unproblematic truth* in different ways: truth in the way proposed in Gupta 1982, and semantically unproblematic truth in the hierarchical way.
13. Perhaps I should emphasize that I am *not* endorsing a Tarskian resolution of these versions of the Strengthened Liar. My point is rather that any adequate resolution should treat these two versions in the same way: a "mixed" theory that treats them differently is unfaithful to our ordinary usage.
14. See Gupta 1982, in Martin 1984, pp. 203–5.
15. We will critically examine hierarchical approaches to the Liar more thoroughly in Chapter 6. See also Simmons 1991.
16. There are other reasons to think that the formal constructions of Herzberger and Gupta do not match up with our ordinary semantic concepts. We saw in Chapter 3 that Kripke's minimal fixed point construction captured certain intuitions about truth, without saddling the ordinary speaker with technical set-theoretic notions. But in contrast, the notion of stabilty makes essential reference to the mathematical notions of ordinal and level.

    Indeed, it may be argued that the formal constructions as a whole rest on *arbitrary* limit rules. As we have seen, both Herzberger and Gupta start out with an arbitrary extension for truth (U). At a limit stage, on Gupta's treatment, a locally unstable sentence gets into the extension of T iff it is in U. Herzberger, on the other hand, throws out locally unstable sentences from the extension of T at limit stages. Following Belnap 1982, let us call U a "Bootstrapper." Belnap argues that it is a defect of Gupta's account that the *same* Bootstrapper is used at every limit stage to arbitrarily decide the truth status of locally unstable sentences – and an even greater defect of Herzberger's account that, at limit stages, only locally stable truths get into the extension of T, so that the initial arbitrariness disappears for no reason. Both Herzberger and Gupta adopt a "Bootstrapping Policy" that is the *same* for each limit stage; Belnap argues that no such constancy is called for. Belnap suggests an alternative Bootstrapping Policy that incorporates, for each limit stage, the arbitrariness of decisions about the truth status of locally unstable sentences. Belnap proposes that we adopt schemes that define a separate Bootstrapper for each limit stage.

Belnap's discussion emphasizes the arbitrariness of Herzberger's and Gupta's choice of limit rule. If Belnap's suggestion is accepted, there will be *no* cycling phenomenon, in particular, no Grand Loop, and no alignment points. In trying to connect the formal constructions to ordinary language, we saw that we are led to the alignment points, as we are led to Kripke's fixed points. This connection cannot be made out if the alignment points turn out to be artifacts of an arbitrary choice of limit rule.

17. Feferman 1984, in Martin 1984. The classical modification of Kripke's construction is developed in sec. 13.

18. Feferman's axioms describe the notion of truth, but they do not pick out a unique intended model. The models of the axioms are all the Kripke fixed points.

19. Feferman 1984, in Martin 1984, p. 266.

20. McGee 1989 and 1990.

21. McGee 1989, p. 535.

22. McGee 1990, pp. 216–17. See also McGee 1989, p. 535.

23. When, of course, we talk McGee's way, in terms of definite truth. To obtain the Kripkean analogue of (DT), replace 'definitely true' throughout by 'true', and 'definitely not true' by 'false'.

24. See McGee 1989, p. 536, and 1990, pp. 160ff. See van Fraassen 1966 for his notion of supervaluation.

25. See Kripke 1975, in Martin 1984, p. 76.

26. Ibid., pp. 76–7.

27. McGee 1989, p. 536.

28. See McGee 1990, p. 7.

29. Ibid., p. 7. In the same vein, McGee 1989 writes:

> That our conventions do not insure a sentence's truth does not imply that there are conventions that forbid our making conventions that would insure its truth. So the fact that a sentence $[\varphi]$ is not definitely true does not entail that it is definitely true that $[\varphi]$ is not definitely true. This is important, since otherwise we could use the *Definite Liar* sentence
>
> > This sentence is not definitely true
>
> to reinstate the antinomy. As it is, it is perfectly possible for the definite liar to be unsettled without it being settled that the definite liar is unsettled. The theory propounded here leaves the status of the definite liar completely open. (p. 538)

30. Compare the move from 'φ is neither true nor false' to 'φ is not true'.

31. One explanation will be in terms of the distinction between object language and metalanguage; but McGee will strongly resist this way out, as we will see in a moment. So McGee must provide some other explanation.

32. Yablo 1989, p. 541. Notice, as Yablo goes on to point out, that the threat of contradiction would naturally lead us to adopt a convention according to which (1) is not to be determined as definitely true. According to this convention, then,

(3) (1) is not definitely true.

Again we seem forced to a metalanguage: such a convention cannot be stated in the object language.

33. McGee 1990, p. 92. See also McGee 1989, p. 532: "I would like to see how our naive theory of truth can be replaced by a scientifically reconstructed theory that accomplishes the same purposes without inconsistency. This new conception of truth should compare to the naive conception in much the same way that relativistic notions of space and time compare to prescientific notions." A danger of this methodology is that the reconstructed notion of truth will be so far removed from our notion of truth that no light will be shed on our semantic concepts or the paradoxes. Consider, in this connection, McGee's 1990 diagnosis of ordinary paradox-producing reasoning about the Liar sentence (pp. 218–21). We start with the Liar sentence:

(i) (i) is not true.

We observe that

(ii) (i) = '(i) is not true'.

We assume, for conditional proof,

(iii) (i) is true.

Substituting, we get

(iv) '(i) is not true' is true.

By a rule of inference – McGee's rule R1 – that allows us to infer $[\varphi]$ from $[[\varphi]$ is true], we obtain

(v) (i) is not true.

According to McGee, we have just committed a fallacy: We have applied the rule R1 within a conditional proof. That is, our "mistake" is to suppose that, if $[\varphi]$ is true, then φ. As Yablo 1989 points out, this is a mistake only relative to "an alien construal of 'true'," removed from our notion of truth (p. 540). Exactly parallel remarks can be made about McGee's 1990 diagnosis of our ordinary reasoning about the definite liar sentence (pp. 221–2). There our "mistake" is to suppose that, if $[\varphi]$ is definitely true, then φ.

34. Kripke 1975, in Martin 1984, pp. 79–80.
35. See McGee 1990, pp. 162–3.
36. Ibid., p. 147.
37. McGee 1989, p. 532.
38. McGee 1990, p. 104. He also says, "the Kripke–Feferman axioms have a great deal to recommend them as a theory of truth" (p. 105). McGee is not fully satisfied, however. He points out that, in the Kripke–Feferman theory, we can prove things that are untrue. For example, consider the sentence $\varphi \vee \neg\varphi$, where φ is a Liar sentence. We can prove $\varphi \vee \neg\varphi$ in the Kripke–Feferman theory, but we can also prove $\neg T(\varphi \vee \neg\varphi)$ (see p. 106).
39. McGee 1989, p. 537.
40. Ibid., p. 538; my emphasis.

41. I have followed ibid., p. 538. The consistency of Γ_∞ is easily demonstrated: "We can expand A to a model of Γ_∞ by letting the extension of D be Γ_∞ and the extension of T be a maximal consistent set that includes Γ_∞" (ibid.). For a full presentation, see McGee 1990, pp. 159–60, Theorem 8.1.

42. McGee 1990, pp. 162–3. See also McGee 1989, pp. 538–9.

43. McGee 1990, p. 163. See also McGee 1989, p. 539. For the mathematical details, see McGee 1990, chap. 8.

44. In Rescher and Brandom 1979.

45. See, e.g., Priest 1979. Since 1979, there have been many papers, by Priest and others, developing such an approach.

46. Rescher and Brandom 1979, p. 6.

47. Ibid.

48. Ibid., p. 34.

49. Ibid., sec. 26 and p. 4.

50. Ibid., p. 138.

51. See Priest 1979, 1984.

52. Priest 1984, p. 161. See also Priest 1987, chaps. 1 and 9.

53. Priest has informed me (in correspondence) that he now rejects the truth conditions for the truth predicate that he gave in Priest 1979 and endorses the account given in chap. 5 of Priest 1987. On the preferred account, it is possible that an assertion that a sentence is paradoxical is true but not false. Priest writes: "There seems to be no reason why, *in general,* if α is a dialetheia [i.e., a sentence that is both true and false], $T\alpha$ is too. If α is a dialetheia, $T\alpha$ is certainly true, but it might be simply true, and not also false" (ibid., p. 100). However, he admits that this is not a possibility for a Liar sentence like L: "The liar sentence seems to be a very special case however, just because it is equivalent to (the denial of) its own truth" (ibid.). So the truth predicate is only "a *partial* consistenciser" (ibid.). And since it is the Liar sentence with which we are concerned, the difficulties I have raised remain.

54. In correspondence.

CHAPTER 5

1. Diogenes Laertius 1950, II, p. 108.

2. Aristotle 1955, 180a27–b7.

3. See Bocheński 1961, p. 133.

4. Diogenes Laertius 1950, VII, 196–7.

5. An indispensable survey of medieval approaches to the Liar is provided by Spade 1975. Spade 1982, in Kretzmann, Kenny, and Pinborg 1982, is a very useful summary of medieval work on the Liar. Although I take issue with Spade at various points in this chapter, it should be clear that I am indebted to his extensive work on the medieval Liar.
   Paul of Venice 1499 provides another useful survey. Paul discusses and rejects fourteen previous opinions, before turning to his own. As in Chapter 1, all quotes from Paul's Treatise are taken from an unpublished manuscript

by Marilyn Adams. Again, a terminological note: "the first opinion" is to be understood as "the first opinion discussed by Paul of Venice", and so on.

6. Medieval authors invoked the following Aristotelian fallacies: the fallacy *figurae dictionis* (the first opinion, f.192RB); the fallacy *non causam ut causam* (the second opinion, f. 192RB); the fallacy of equivocation (the seventh opinion, f.192VA); the fallacy *accidentis* (the fourteenth opinion, f.194RAB); and the fallacy *secundum quid et simpliciter* (the tenth opinion, f.192VB).

7. One resolution labeled *transcasus* claims that the insoluble makes reference not to itself but to an utterance immediately preceding it (the third opinion, f.192VA). Another builds on Aristotle's fallacy of equivocation and distinguishes an utterance "in process" from a "conceived" utterance (the seventh opinion, f.192VA). According to Paul's brief description, a further view holds that "an insoluble is true or false, but is not true and not false" (the ninth opinion, f.192VB). The views of Bradwardine, Swineshead, Heytesbury, and d'Ailly were original and influential. The tenth opinion (f.192VB) may be Bradwardine's (see Spade 1975, p. 82); the eleventh opinion (f.192VB) is also close to Bradwardine's. Paul's own solution (the fifteenth opinion, f.194RB) is an elaboration of Swineshead's, as Spade 1975 points out (p. 83). The twelfth opinion (f.192VB–193RB) is Heytesbury's. The thirteenth opinion (f.193RB) is d'Ailly's.

8. According to the *cassantes,* he who utters an insoluble says nothing (the fifth opinion, f.192VA). According to a closely related view, "No one can say that he himself says what is false, and there can be no proposition from which an insoluble can be generated" (the fourth opinion, f.192VA). Spade 1982 points out a more sophisticated medieval version of *cassation* that better approximates its modern counterpart (see p. 247). This version of cassation is discussed in a tract by Pseudo-Sherwood, in Roure 1970. In 8.01–8.03, Pseudo-Sherwood presents three arguments providing semantic grounds for the claim that my utterance, 'a falsehood is said,' is not a proposition. Pseudo-Sherwood goes on to reject the arguments.

9. Paul writes: "The eighth opinion posits that no insoluble is true or false, since no insoluble is a proposition. For although any insoluble is an indicative expression, and its signification signifies as is [the case] or as is not [the case], nevertheless this is not enough to warrant its being called a proposition" (f.192VA).

10. Paul writes: "The sixth opinion posits that an insoluble is neither true nor false, but a mean indifferent to each" (f.192VA). According to Bradwardine, insolubles are neither true nor false, but have some intermediate value; see Spade 1975, p. 107.

11. This is anticipated in the claim of the *restringentes* that "in no proposition does a part supposit for the whole of which it is a part." The *restringentes'* claim is presented by Paul as a presupposition of the fourteenth opinion. I will argue that the rule of the *restringentes,* though it anticipates modern approaches that ban self-reference, does not itself constitute such an approach.

12. Moody 1953 raises this possibility (p. 109). As we shall see, Roure finds such an anticipation in the approach of the *restringentes,* Pseudo-Sherwood, and Burley, in Roure 1970. According to Bocheński 1961, d'Ailly accepts the distinction between language and metalanguage (p. 249 and 35.44). Here, Bocheński follows Paul's account of d'Ailly.

13. Again, we will see that Roure argues this way. Several authors take Ockham's solution to be an application of his doctrine of impositions and intentions, and thereby an anticipation of Russell or Tarski. The following are cited in Spade 1981: Boehner 1958, in Buytaert 1958, pp. 254–60; Ashworth 1974, p. 104; Bottin 1976, pp. 173–5.

14. Bocheński 1961 attributes the idea of the vicious circle principle to d'Ailly (see p. 395). See Spade 1980, par. 297, for the relevant passage from d'Ailly's treatise. For more on this, see Chapter 1, note 22.

15. The view that the Liar sentence is a true contradiction is attributed to d'Ailly by Goldstein 1985, p. 9. I find this claim dubious. D'Ailly places his solution within the context of the fallacy *secundum quid et simpliciter:* "Therefore, it does not follow that it [i.e., the insoluble] is absolutely false. . . . But it does correctly follow that it is false in a certain respect (*secundum quid*), that is, according to one signification" (in Spade 1980, par. 375, p. 92). And d'Ailly concludes, "Thus, according to Aristotle's intention, the sentence is true and false in a certain respect, and yet it is not absolutely true" (ibid., par. 383, p. 93). So according to d'Ailly, insolubles are true in a certain respect and false in a certain respect; they are *neither* absolutely true *nor* absolutely false. D'Ailly does not say that such sentences are true contradictions. For more on d'Ailly's account, see Simmons 1987a, pp. 28–42.

16. The relevant passages in Ockham are 1488, III, 3, chap. 45; before 1328, book II, chap. 10, sec. 4; and 1488, III, 1, chap. 4. The tracts by Pseudo-Sherwood and Burley are edited in Roure 1970. Martin Grabmann attributes Pseudo-Sherwood's tract to William of Sherwood. De Rijk argues that there is not sufficient evidence for the attribution. See Roure 1970, p. 205, and Spade 1975, p. 26. I mark this uncertainty by the label "Pseudo-Sherwood."

17. In Pseudo-Sherwood's example, 'Socrates' is replaced by 'I'. Both examples are found in Burley.

18. For a name, the medieval notion of *supposition* is roughly equivalent to the notion of reference; for a predicate, the notion is roughly equivalent to the converse of the satisfaction relation. In particular, then, to say that the term 'false' supposits for a given utterance is to say that the utterance is in the extension of 'false'.

19. As we shall see, Ockham and Burley qualify this rule; Pseudo-Sherwood does not.

20. Roure 1970, pp. 259–60, 11.01. As Pseudo-Sherwood presents it, this inference is the first of two steps leading from the assumption that Socrates says a falsehood to a contradiction. The second step is from 'That Socrates says a falsehood is false' to 'Socrates does not say a falsehood' (ibid., pp. 249–50, 1.05).

21. In 11.01–11.03, Pseudo-Sherwood equivocates on the use of *'secundum quid'* and *'simpliciter'*. The terms are applied not only to the term 'falsehood' as it occurs within the argument, but also to (i) the dictum 'that I say a falsehood', (ii) the term 'false' taken as a predicate of sentences, as in ' "Socrates says a falsehood" is false', and (iii) sayings, as in Socrates' saying 'Socrates says a falsehood'. This equivocation does not lead to any inconsistency, however. The application to the term 'falsehood' should be regarded as basic, and (i), (ii), and (iii) are derivative in obvious ways.

22. Ockham, before 1328, book II, chap. 10, sec. 4. The entire argument from the assumption that Socrates says a falsehood to a contradiction may be put this way: Suppose 'Socrates says a falsehood' is false. Socrates says this false-hood; therefore Socrates says a falsehood. So Socrates says what is true, and consequently Socrates says the truth. (Cf. Ockham 1488, III, 3, chap. 45.)

23. Ockham also takes insolubles to be fallacies *secundum quid et simpliciter* in 1488, III, 1, chap. 4. The fallacy is not central to Burley's treatment. It is only briefly mentioned, in Roure 1970, p. 275, n. 10, 4.04 and 4.05. In dis-cussing the inference 'Socrates says this falsehood; therefore, Socrates says a falsehood', Burley suggests that to say this falsehood is to say *secundum quid* a falsehood. Burley writes, "Thus the determination *'secundum quid'* should govern 'to say' and not 'falsehood' " (4.04). In 4.05, he argues that if Socrates says that he says a falsehood, then, since he says the word 'false-hood', he *secundum quid* says falsehood (taken in material supposition). Thus, Burley does not appeal to the fallacy in the same way as do Ockham and Pseudo-Sherwood.

24. But as we shall see in the next section, significant points arise from the details of their account of these arguments.

25. For example, Paul Spade and E. J. Ashworth encourage such a view. See Spade 1974; 1975, pp. 112, 119–20; 1982, p. 248, ns. 25, 26; 1976, pp. 337–8; 1981, pp. 54–5. And see Ashworth 1974, p. 104.

26. Roure 1970, p. 251, 3.02. In 3.02, Pseudo-Sherwood sets out the *restrin-gentes'* argument. In 3.03, he argues further along similar lines. In 4.05–4.08, he defends the *restringentes* against various attacks laid out in 4.01–4.04. In 4.10, he clearly endorses the *restringentes'* rule, *without qualification*. In 11.01 and 11.02, he makes use of the *restringentes'* rule, and in 11.02 he de-defends its use by the argument of 3.02.

    So Paul Spade is mistaken when he writes of Pseudo-Sherwood: "The opinion of the *restringentes* is also rejected (3.01–4.10). . . . The author re-plies (4.01–4.10) by setting out unproblematic instances of self-reference, and by distinguishing between an integral whole and a universal whole" (1975, p. 27). The objections to the *restringentes* that Spade cites occur in 4.02 and 4.04; Pseudo-Sherwood *replies to them* in 4.06 and 4.08, respectively. Pseudo-Sherwood objects not to the *restringentes'* rule, but to their treat-ment of the fallacious argument (for details, see 4.10).

27. In 2.05 and 2.06, Burley argues against the *restringentes'* rule and, in 3.03, states the restricted version. Ockham 1488, III, 3, chap. 45, qualifies the

restringentes' rule. Spade 1974 argues persuasively that Ockham rejects the *restringentes'* rule in all but exceptional cases, and that these would seem to be the insolubles.

28. Roure 1970, p. 273, 3.07.
29. There are further examples of this in Burley's work. In 4.05, he considers the following case: Socrates says only 'Socrates says a falsehood', and Plato says 'Socrates does not say a falsehood'. Burley argues that the following inference does not hold (where the reference of the demonstrative 'this' is Plato's utterance): 'A contradictory of *this* proposition is said by Socrates; therefore the contradictory of a proposition is said by Socrates'. Applying Burley's rule in the natural way, 'proposition' in the conclusion cannot supposit for *Plato's* utterance. In 4.08, in the course of discussing an inference presented in 1.08, Burley writes, "For the term 'antecedent' in 'Socrates draws an inference from an antecedent' cannot supposit for 'Socrates draws an inference from a falsehood'." The treatment of these cases suggests a way in which the Ockham–Burley–Pseudo-Sherwood line might deal with *loops* (e.g., Socrates says only 'Plato says a falsehood', and Plato says only 'Socrates says a falsehood') and *chains* (e.g., (1) (2) is false; (2) (3) is false; (3) (4) is false; ...).
30. In just one place (3.03), Burley treats his rule as limiting that of the *restringentes*. Elsewhere (3.02, 4.01, 4.03, 4.06, 4.09) he cites his rule and makes no mention of that of the *restringentes*. Burley does not provide a precise characterization of his rule: it is not clear exactly what counts as something self-reflexive with a privative determination. But what *is* clear is that Burley is operating with some general rule that does not coincide with that of the *restringentes*.
31. Roure 1970, p. 272, 3.02.
32. Ockham 1488, III, 3, chap. 45.
33. The point made in this paragraph can be extended to quantifiers. Suppose Socrates says only 'Everything Socrates says is a falsehood'. Again, the natural way to apply the Ockham–Burley–Pseudo-Sherwood solution to this case is to restrict the supposition of 'falsehood' so that what Socrates says is equivalent to 'Everything Socrates says is a falsehood that is A', which is a falsehood. *No* restriction is placed on the quantifier.
34. See Spade 1982, p. 247, and the introduction to Spade 1980, p. 4. Spade is surely right about many medieval solutions of this kind.
35. See Roure 1970, pp. 229–30. Roure writes, "La solution de Shyreswood qui s'insère, ou pretend s'insérer, dans le cadre de la solution *per secundum quid et simpliciter.* . ." (p. 229).
36. Broadly speaking, on the medieval view an integral whole is a composite entity, and an integral part is obtained by physical division of the whole. A stock example of an integral whole is a house, which has walls, a roof, and a foundation as its parts; another example of an integral whole is an individual man. For a discussion of this, see Kretzmann in Kretzmann, Kenny, and Pinborg 1982, p. 230, esp. n. 77.

37. And it seems that this is the example Spade and Roure have in mind. It is the only example they mention in discussing the fallacy and medieval solutions to the Liar. See Spade 1980, p. 4, and Roure 1970, p. 226.

38. The universal whole is taken as an aggregate, rather than an abstract object like a set. Part of the universal whole composed of all the men is all the Caucasians.

39. See Kretzmann, in William of Sherwood 1966, pp. 153–4, n. 124, where he distinguishes "four or more" kinds of determination in a certain respect (or "unstrict determination") that are to be found in de Rijk 1962. One example Kretzmann cites, the inference from 'a chimera is thinkable' to 'a chimera is', is particularly relevant to our considerations below. Some of these early authors discuss both the fallacy and ampliation (see, e.g., the anonymous tract *Dialectica Monacensis,* in de Rijk 1962, vol. 2, part 2, pp. 626–30, 670–1), but none connected the two.

40. The case of the Ethiopian is an example of this form of the fallacy.

41. Ockham 1970, 246. See also 1488, III, 4, chap. 13.

42. Albert of Saxony 1522, Treatise V, chap. ix, Article iii.

43. Aristotle 1955, 166b38–167a4.

44. Ockham 1488, III, 4, chap. 13. Ockham discusses the ampliating effect of verbs in the past and future tense in ibid., II, chap. 7, 269. For Albert of Saxony's theory, see 1522, Tract Two, Ch. X. Albert's seventh rule for ampliation says, "When a proposition has a present tense copula but a predicate that includes the verb 'can' – such as verbal nouns that end in 'able' – the subject is ampliated to supposit for what is or for what can be." Other rules cover verbs in the past and future tense.

    Theirs was a common medieval account. See also Paul of Venice 1499, pt. I, 'On the *Suppositio* of Terms', f.25VA, line 21–45, f.25VB, line 38–72 (ed.). This theory takes the range of the supposition of a term to be presently existing things, which may be ampliated by certain adjoining terms. According to an alternative account (see, e.g., Peter of Spain in de Rijk 1972, p. 209), a term by itself supposits for all things, past, present, or future, but its range of supposition may be restricted under special conditions. (For a discussion of this, see de Rijk in Kretzmann, Kenny, and Pinborg 1982, pp. 171–2.) On either view, there is a shift in supposition between a universal whole and a universal part.

45. Another fallacious inference that Ockham treats in the same way is 'Where no rose exists, a rose is understood; therefore, a rose exists'. The term 'rose' here has determinate personal supposition, and it is clear how this kind of supposition may be widened. Ockham and Albert do not explain how their theory of ampliation works for terms like 'the Antichrist' or 'Socrates'. These terms have discrete supposition, and it is unclear how this kind of supposition may be widened. Perhaps they would find the following line agreeable. The sentences 'A rose exists' and 'The Antichrist is' each are true iff there is a presently existing suppositum of the subject term. The sentences 'A rose is understood' and 'The Antichrist is conceivable' are each true iff there is a

presently existing suppositum of the subject term, or a thinkable that is a suppositum of the subject term; and here, in each case, there is a widening of the range of things from which supposita can be drawn. The only difference between the cases is the number of supposita. There are many supposita for 'rose' in both of its occurrences; there are no supposita for 'the Antichrist' in the first of its occurrences, and just one in the second.

46. See note 13, this chapter. In Spade 1981, it is pointed out that (i) Ockham nowhere appeals to this doctrine in his discussion of the Liar, and (ii) the plausibility of such an anticipation is undermined by Ockham's adoption of the *restringentes'* rule *only* in exceptional circumstances.

47. Roure 1970 links the *restringentes'* solution with Russell's theory of types (see pp. 224–5). Roure would presumably extend such links to Pseudo-Sherwood and Burley, since Roure finds no real difference between Pseudo-Sherwood and the *restringentes* (p. 230) and finds Burley to be the most authentic of the *restringentes* (p. 234). (See also the upcoming quote given in this note.) Roure ascribes to Burley implicit recognition of the distinction between levels of language as a way of resolving the paradox (p. 234). Roure also raises the question as to whether there are resemblances between medieval and modern solutions to the Liar (p. 244) and answers this question in the affirmative, arguing that the appeal to two levels of discourse as a way of solving the paradox "n'est pas absolument inconnu des logiciens médiévaux, encore qu'il ne soit pas toujours explicité. Nous l'avons recontré à diverses reprises au cours de notre étude; notamment chez certains 'restricteurs', ainsi que chez Burleigh et Shyreswood" (pp. 246–7). Roure links Burley's solution to Ockham's (p. 234, n. 2); there is every reason to suppose that Roure would carry over her analysis to Ockham.

48. See ibid., p. 222 (concerning the *restringentes*), p. 229 (concerning Pseudo-Sherwood), and p. 232 (concerning Burley).

49. According to Roure's interpretation, Burley claims that, at this second level, Socrates says *neither a truth nor a falsehood* (1970, p. 232). Roure takes this as evidence that Burley implicitly rests his solution on a distinction of language levels (p. 234). I suggest a different interpretation. It follows from Burley's analysis that Socrates does not say anything *about* his utterance. In saying what he does, Socrates does not say that what he says is true or false. If Socrates says that he says a falsehood, we cannot infer, just from what Socrates says, that he says a truth or that he says a falsehood. This, I think, is how to take Burley's discussion, which occurs in 3.04. There is nothing here that suggests a distinction of levels of language.

As Roure points out, Ockham makes an exactly similar claim (p. 234, n. 2). But with it comes an elaboration that clearly rules out Roure's interpretation: "For when Socrates begins to speak by saying 'Socrates says a falsehood', and one asks whether Socrates says the truth or a falsehood, it must be replied that Socrates says neither a truth or a falsehood, *just as it must be granted that he neither says a truth nor a falsehood other than this [proposition]*" (Ockham 1488, III, 3, chap. 45; my emphasis). For Ockham, the sense in which Socrates says neither a truth nor a falsehood is this: Socrates says neither a truth nor a falsehood that is A.

50. The *restringentes* proceed differently, diagnosing the argument either as a fallacy *figuram dictionis* (see Bradwardine, 5.01, and Pseudo-Sherwood, 3.01; it is this part of the *restringentes'* solution to which Pseudo-Sherwood is opposed), or as a fallacy *non causam ut causam* (see Bradwardine, 5.03).

51. Here we follow an example of the kind suggested by Ockham, Burley, and the *restringentes*. The remarks that follow apply equally well to Pseudo-Sherwood.

52. Where he argues that there is no problem in talking *about* propositions or falsehoods, Pseudo-Sherwood does not give any suggestion of a distinction of levels of language (10.08–10.11).

53. Such an account is "Tarskian" in the sense that it treats natural languages the way that Tarski treats formal languages. But as we saw in Chapter 1, Tarski himself does *not* endorse such accounts of natural language.

54. In the case of Burley, as we have seen, it is not only the semantic predicates that are so treated – see note 29 and the associated text, this chapter.

55. Roure 1970, p. 252, 4.03.

56. Ibid., 4.07.

57. Ockham, before 1328, bk. II, chap. 10, sec. 4.

58. As Laurence Goldstein has remarked (in correspondence), Pseudo-Sherwood, Ockham, and Burley do not offer here an *argument* for the context sensitivity of the truth predicate. Any full-fledged contextual account must give some reason for thinking that 'true' is a context-sensitive predicate. Contemporary contextual theories of truth are largely motivated by the Strengthened Liar, as we will see in Chapter 6.

59. Gödel 1944, in Schilpp 1944, p. 149.

60. Ibid.

61. Gödel raises two objections: "What makes the above principle particularly suspect, however, is that its very assumption makes its formulation as a meaningful proposition impossible, because x and y must then be confined to definite ranges of significance which are either the same or different, and in both cases the statement does not express the principle or even part of it. Another consequence is that the fact that an object x is (or is not) of a given type also cannot be expressed by a meaningful proposition" (ibid.).

62. Ibid., p. 150.

63. Gödel's idea is developed along these lines in Thomson 1962, in Butler 1962. See also Church 1932; Hintikka 1956 (esp. p. 241), and 1957; Herzberger 1981 (esp. pp. 115–18).

Gödel's suggestion may call to mind Frege's initial response to Russell's paradox. After reconstructing Russell's argument, Frege 1967 writes: "We see that the exceptional case is constituted by the extension itself, in that it falls under only one of two concepts whose extension it is; and we see that the occurrence of this exception can in no way be avoided. Accordingly the following suggests itself as the criterion for equality in extension: The extension of one concept coincides with that of another when every object that falls under the first concept, except the extension of the first concept, falls under the second concept likewise, and when every object that falls under the second concept, except the extension of the second concept, falls under the first concept likewise" (p. 139).

64. Gödel writes, "The obvious objection that every concept can be extended to all arguments, by defining another one which gives a false proposition whenever the original one was meaningless, can easily be dealt with by pointing out that the concept 'meaningfully applicable' need not itself always be meaningfully applicable" (in Schilpp 1944, p. 149).

But this response only encourages another version of the Strengthened Liar. If the sentence '"Is not meaningfully applicable to itself" is not meaningfully applicable to itself' is meaningless, then the term 'is not meaningfully applicable to itself' is not meaningfully applicable to itself. But now we have asserted what we just claimed was meaningless.

65. C. Parsons 1974; Burge 1979; Barwise and Etchemendy 1987; and Gaifman 1988 and 1992.

66. C. Parsons 1974, in Martin 1984, p. 38.

67. Ibid., p. 34.

68. Burge 1984 argues that the terms 'necessary', 'believes', 'knows', and all propositional attitude predicates are indexical.

69. Burge 1979, in Martin 1984, p. 107.

70. Ibid., pp. 37–8.

71. See, e.g., Burge 1982, p. 357.

72. See, e.g., Burge 1979, in Martin 1984, p. 96; and C. Parsons 1974, in Martin 1984, p. 40.

73. See Burge 1979, in Martin 1984, p. 107; C. Parsons 1974, in Martin 1984, p. 28, n. 13.

74. To deal with such global sentences, Burge distinguishes between *schematic* and *indexical* occurrences of 'true'. These global sentences are taken to be *schematic* generalizations (see Burge 1979, in Martin 1984, pp. 107–8, 116). The Ockham–Burley–Pseudo-Sherwood line does not seem to require any such distinction. However, in subsequent chapters, we will see difficulties for the claim that there are unrestricted occurrences of the truth predicate (see Chapter 6, note 23, and Section 9.4).

CHAPTER 6

1. Russell 1903, p. 528. This is how Russell characterizes a typed response to the paradox of all propositions (pp. 527–8). Later, of course, Russell 1908 adopted a doctrine of types for propositions.

2. Tarski 1983, p. 267.

3. Here is one place where we depart from the Ockham–Burley–Pseudo-Sherwood resolution. According to that resolution, Liar sentences are straight-

forwardly true or false. According to our resolution, they are pathological. As we will see, on our upcoming approach a pathological utterance is neither true nor false in its context of utterance. So we admit truth gaps where the medieval authors do not. Still, as we will also see, this admission is heavily qualified: There are other contexts in which the pathological utterance *is* true or false. Ultimately, bivalence is upheld on our account.

4. See C. Parsons 1974, in Martin 1984; Burge 1979, in Martin 1984; Barwise and Etchemendy 1987; and Gaifman 1988 and 1992.

5. Our reasoning involves a self-referential sentence and the notion of falsity. Neither feature is essential to strengthened reasoning. Burge gives the following example: "Suppose I conduct you into a room in which the open sentence type 'it is not true of itself' is written on a blackboard. Pointing at the expression, I present the following reasoning: Let us consider it as an argument for its own variable or pronoun. Suppose it is true of itself. Then since it is the negation of the self-predication of the notion of *being true of,* it is not true of itself. Now suppose it is not true of itself. Then since it is the negation of the self-predication of the notion of *being true of,* it is true of itself. In response you suggest that it is undefined for itself, from which we conclude that it is not true of itself. But then, I ask, why have we not made the same predication we were just criticizing? If we have, we seem committed to its being true of itself after all" (1979, in Martin 1984, pp. 90–1). Any adequate solution to the Liar must account for this version of the Strengthened Liar too. (See note 13, this chapter).

6. The strengthened reasoning about (S) goes like this:

> If (S) is true, then it's false; and if (S) is false, then it's true. So (S) is neither true nor false. So
>
> (P') (S) is not false.
>
> But (S) says that it is false. So, given (P'), and given what (S) says,
>
> (R') (S) is not true.

(P') is a partial explicit reflection; (R') is a complete explicit reflection.
Alternatively, the last line of our reasoning might be

> (R") (S) is false.

Here, (R") is a complete explicit reflection. (This last version of the strengthened reasoning about (S) is also presented in Yablo 1989, p. 541.)

We can also produce strengthened reasoning about the Truth Teller (introduced in Chapter 1). We start with the Truth Teller:

> (T) (T) is true.

We may reason as follows:

> (T) is pathological, so
>
> (P*) (T) is not true.
>
> But (T) says it is true, and so, given (P*), and given what (T) says,
>
> (R*) (T) is not true.

(P*) is a partial explicit reflection; (R*) is a complete explicit reflection. Alternatively, the last line of our reasoning might be:

(R**) (T) is false.

Like (R*), (R**) is a complete explicit reflection.

7. This has been emphasized by Ziff 1972 among others; see pp. 21–38.
8. A shift of relevant information may not always occur in Strengthened Liar reasoning: I may intentionally produce a pathological utterance, in order to reflect on it.
9. Even where the speaker intentionally produces a pathological utterance, there is a shift in intentions. At the first stage, the speaker intends to produce a pathological utterance and establish its pathology; at the second stage, the speaker intends to evaluate the utterance qua pathological.
10. Burge 1979, in Martin 1984, p. 95.
11. Given our evaluation (R), what (L) says is the case. So we may infer that (L) is not true. And given that (L) is not true, and given what (L) says, we may infer that (L) is true. On our account, both these inferences are valid. Consider an instance of the truth schema for 'true$_R$':

    '(L) is not true$_L$' is true$_R$ iff (L) is not true$_L$.

    The first inference moves from the left-hand side to the right-hand side of this biconditional, and the second from right to left.
12. Evaluations in this third category may be quite innocent, like an utterance of '"$2+2=4$" is true'; or they may be pathological, like (L). Also in this category are what I will call *nonexplicit reflections* (see later in this chapter).
13. A similar analysis may be given of the strengthened reasoning presented in note 5, this chapter. Let 'Or' denote the original context in which I present you with the open sentence on the board. Let 'Refl' denote the final reflective context in which we declare the open sentence to be true of itself after all. We represent the open sentence as 'is not true$_{Or}$ of itself'. Consider the schema associated with 'is true$_{Or}$ of'. (An instance of the schema is the biconditional: 'Even' is true$_{Or}$ of 'two' iff two is even.) When we plug the open sentence into its associated schema, we obtain:

    'is not true$_{Or}$ of itself' is true$_{Or}$ of 'is not true$_{Or}$ of itself' iff 'is not true$_{Or}$ of itself' is not true$_{Or}$ of itself.

    Since the left-hand side of this biconditional is equivalent to

    'is not true$_{Or}$ of itself' is true$_{Or}$ of itself,

    we obtain a contradiction. This is what is going on at the first stage of the strengthened reasoning. So we conclude that the open sentence is undefined for itself and cancel the implicature that the open sentence is to be evaluated via its associated schema. Since the open sentence is undefined for itself, we infer that it *isn't* true$_{Or}$ of itself. This is a partial explicit reflection. But now, since the open sentence isn't true$_{Or}$ of itself, and since that is what its self-predication says, we conclude that the open sentence *is* true of itself – i.e., true$_{Refl}$ of itself. This is a complete explicit reflection. The ordered pair of the open sentence with itself is not in the extension of 'is true$_{Or}$ of', but it *is* in the extension of 'is true$_{Refl}$ of'.

14. C. Parsons 1974, in Martin 1984, pp. 37–8.
15. See Burge 1982, p. 357.
16. Gaifman 1988, p. 52.
17. Ibid., p. 58.
18. Barwise and Etchemendy 1987, p. 135.
19. Ibid., p. 155.
20. Ibid., p. 174.
21. Of course, philosophical discussions of the Liar provide exceptions to this general rule.
22. Gödel 1944, in Schilpp 1944, p. 149.
23. Here is another place where we diverge from the Ockham–Burley–Pseudo-Sherwood account. The medieval account places (minimal) restrictions on occurrences of the semantic predicates within insolubles, but seems to place no restrictions on other occurrences of 'true' and 'false' (see Section 5.3). The medieval account seems to countenance global occurrences of 'true' and 'false'; our account does not. Notice that any account that allows a global truth predicate, call it 'true$_U$', immediately runs into trouble. We can form a new version of the Liar, via the sentence:

    This sentence is not true$_U$.

    For more on this, see Section 9.4.
24. As we saw in Chapter 1, such chains may be quite empirical in character.
25. Compare Burge's Principle of Justice (1979, in Martin 1984, p. 110).
26. Hughes 1982, p. 51.
27. Ibid., p. 51.
28. Our formal characterization of groundedness will be like that of Kripke. In particular, we will use Kleene's strong valuation scheme (see Section 3.2). A is ungrounded. Notice that if the first conjunct of A had been false, then A would also be false, in accordance with the strong Kleene scheme.
29. Gödel 1944, in Schilpp 1944, p. 150.
30. Ibid., p. 150.
31. There are some disanalogies, just like those between the medieval resolution and Gödel's suggestion (detailed in Section 5.3). According to my singularity proposal, pathological sentences are meaningful and ultimately true or false; according to Gödel's proposal, pathological sentences are meaningless. And according to my proposal, singularities of truth and falsity shift with the context; on the natural way of developing Gödel's suggestion, it is semantic predicate types *simpliciter* that have singularities: Semantic concepts have *standing* singularities.

CHAPTER 7

1. In Chapter 6, note 6, and associated text.

2. There are some similarities between our treatment of the evaluations we call nonexplicit reflections and that of Gaifman 1988 and 1992. But beyond this, there are very substantial differences between the theories (see note 7, this chapter). We can mention one here. Gaifman's account does not have the resources to distinguish (0) and (0′), or (1) and (1′), or (ii) and (iii), because the account does not accommodate the purely pragmatic differences between them. For Gaifman, a chain like (1), (2), ... yields a "black hole": Any attempt to evaluate (1) is itself sucked into the chain (see 1988, p. 58). Gaifman's account, then, does not provide room for explicit reflections like (0′).

3. Of course, this is an idealization: I do not mean to suggest that ascertaining the pragmatic features of an utterance is an easy matter in practice. It is clearly a very substantial and worthwhile project to develop a formal pragmatics for stretches of discourse like Strengthened Liar reasoning. I am not attempting this project in the present work. However, I am claiming that, where explicit reflections are concerned, one may treat the pragmatic component independently of the semantic component. And I am supposing that our pragmatic characterization of explicit reflections, in terms of the relevant contextual parameters identified in the previous chapter, is sufficiently well-developed for present purposes.

4. See Section 3.2.

5. Later we will also characterize reflections as grounded, but grounded in semantic facts.

6. These correspond to Kripke's grounded sentences, using the strong Kleene valuation scheme. There are two main differences. First, ours is a theory of sentence types in a context, while Kripke's is a theory of sentence types. Second, we will also admit reflections as another kind of grounded sentence.

7. The hierarchy, and the role of Symmetry in its construction, bear some resemblance to Gaifman's 1988 and 1992 operational pointer semantics. Gaifman's work developed for the first time a rigorous account of what I have called symmetrical networks in terms of a logic of pointers. (The present work was developed independently of Gaifman's). But there is a fundamental difference. For Gaifman, the hierarchy embodies a Tarskian resolution of the Liar (see Section 6.1). The hierarchy plays no such role in the singularity theory, as the remarks here in the text make clear.

   Let me mention here a number of other significant differences. (i) Gaifman does not distinguish explicit and nonexplicit reflections. (ii) Gaifman's treatment of Strengthened Liar reasoning extends only to what I call partial explicit reflections like (P), and not to complete explicit reflections like (R) – Gaifman's semantics does not provide for the evaluation of a complete explicit reflection like (R). (iii) There is a difference in the evaluation of trees. For example, we will see that, on my account, the Liar sentence (L) receives the value T on its evaluated tree: This evaluation is the result of excluding the key singularity from the extension of 'true' in (L) and corresponds to the reflective evaluation of (L) as true. In contrast, (L) receives a gap in Gaifman's semantics.

   For more on Gaifman's account, see note 2 in this chapter.

8. So we define the key singularities of an occurrence O of 'true' in terms of the prime container of O. An example will illustrate the need to consider prime containers. Consider these sentences:

   (1) (3) is true.
   (2) (3) is not true.
   (3) (1) is true and (2) is not true.

   Let O be the first occurrence of 'true' in (3). Suppose we were to define the key singularities of O in terms of the entire sentence (3), and not the prime container of O. That is, we say, "The key singularities of O are the first evaluated sentences occurring in the infinite branches of (3)'s pruned tree." Then (2) would be a key singularity of O. Intuitively, this is not what we want. We will see later that (2) is a singularity of O, but not a key singularity: Its exclusion from the extension of O does not determine a truth value for the first conjunct of (3), or for (3).

   Notice the qualification 'largest' in the characterization of a prime container. An example will illustrate the need for this qualification. Suppose I write just one sentence on the board:

   (A) Any sentence on the board is such that both it and 'snow is white' is true.

   We may represent my utterance as

   $$[\forall x(B(x) \rightarrow T(x) \ \& \ T(\text{'snow is white'}))]_A.$$

   The final part of my utterance (A) may be represented by $[T(\text{'snow is white'})]_A$. Both this part of my utterance, and my entire utterance (A), contain the same occurrence of 'true'. The types of each of these utterances are prime for the propositional calculus. But by our definition, only the entire utterance (A) is the prime container. Notice that (A) is ungrounded, while $[T(\text{'snow is white'})]_A$ is not. By taking the largest sentence, we capture any relevant pathology.

   Notice that the expression 'the largest sentence that contains O and is prime for the propositional calculus' has a perfectly clear referent in the imagined circumstances: In the case we have given, (A) is not part of any larger sentence, and so (A) is the referent in question.

9. The singularities of an occurrence of 'true' (and 'false') fall into two groups. In the first group are those sentences that are singularities through common membership of a symmetrical network. In the second group are those sentences that are singularities through anaphoric back reference. A more precise account of singularities other than key singularities is given in Section 8.2.

10. The clauses for & and $\rightarrow$ are obtained in the usual way from the clauses for $\neg$ and $\vee$; and the clause for $\forall$ is obtained in the usual way from the clause for $\exists$.

11. The proof is just like the corresponding proof at the base level, in Section 7.2.6.

CHAPTER 8

1. Kripke 1975, in Martin 1984, pp. 59–60.
2. There are singularities of these occurrences of 'true' other than the key singularities: For example, (1) is a singularity of 'true' in (1). We will take up the topic of further singularities in Section 8.2.
3. This case was introduced in Cohen 1957. It is discussed in Prior 1961, p. 20, and Burge 1982, pp. 361–3.
4. For example, consider this variant on our loop:

   (C^+) What Joanne is saying now is true and snow is white.

   (J) What Claire is saying now is true.

   The node $[C]_C$ does not appear as a second node of the pruned$_0$ tree for C^+; $[C]_{C^+}$ appears instead.

CHAPTER 9

1. Herzberger 1970, pp. 151–2.
2. Notice the importance of the ordering of Steps 2 and 3. There are nodes of the form $G(\rho)$ that belong to both finite and infinite branches. For example, consider this pair of sentences:

   (i) (ii) is grounded.

   (ii) (ii) is not true and snow is white.

   It's easy to check that the node $[G([ii]_{ii})]_i$ belongs to (one) infinite and (infinitely many) finite branches of the pruned$_0$ tree for (i). Intuitively, we want to count (i) as false, because (ii) is ungrounded, as the presence of the infinite branch indicates. We capture this intuition by considering infinite branches first, in Step 2, and finite branches second, in Step 3. In this example, Step 2 yields the evaluated$_0$ tree for (i). It is simply

   $$\langle [G([ii]_{ii})]_i, F \rangle.$$

3. We might also use the term 'singularity' in a context-sensitive way. For example, I might try to generate a new paradox from the sentence

   This sentence is a singularity,

   where by 'singularity' I mean 'neither in the extension of "true" nor in the extension of "false" in the present context of utterance'. Here, the term 'singularity' is sensitive to the context of utterance. This kind of usage of the term 'singularity' will be discussed in the next section.
4. The Superliar presents a problem for any contextual approach. Burge denies that we can quantify over all contexts here; the generalization found in (X) must be represented schematically (see Burge 1979, in Martin 1984, pp. 107–8, 115–17). This denial strikes me as unpersuasive: Why *can't* we use 'true in some context' or 'true in every context' non-schematically?

5. The proof of this is just like the proof of the corresponding claims in Section 7.2.6.
6. The definition of the ungrounded ancestors of a given sentence (presented in Section 8.2) applies quite straightforwardly to a key singularity of Proposition 9.1.
7. Notice also that the grounded predicate of this expanded object language will be more comprehensive than that of the original object language. The former will include sentences of the singularity theory and evaluations of them; the latter will not.
8. Of course, the proper treatment of quantification over the levels of the hierarchy, as exhibited in (Sup), is no easy matter. Charles Parsons 1974 suggests that the kind of generality found in a discourse about the Liar must lie in "a sort of systematic ambiguity": There is no "absolute" interpretation (in Martin 1984, p. 28, n. 13). Burge resists the idea that we can quantify over all levels, so as to produce paradox-producing sentences like (X) or (Sup): Such generalizations can be had only schematically (Burge 1979, in Martin 1984; see esp. pp. 107–8, 115–17). In a different direction, one might accommodate quantification over all levels by the introduction of proper classes. There are difficulties with each of these approaches, but I shall not pursue them here.
9. Barwise and Etchemendy 1987, p. 135. In the same vein, Barwise and Etchemendy write, "Of course the Liar shows us that we cannot have full closure, since the falsity of the Liar proposition f_s automatically diagonalizes out of any actual situation s" (p. 159).
10. Ibid., p. 155.
11. The example of the formal language of chemistry is mentioned in Tarski 1969, p. 90.
12. Throughout, we have simplified our discussion by limiting its scope to one natural language, English. We think of 'true' as applying to sentences of English; and when we speak of the singularities of a context-sensitive occurrence of 'true', we speak only of those singularities that are sentences of English. And we think of the singularity theory as a theory of a portion of English, and 'true$_{obj}$' as the truth predicate for that portion of English.

    Now there are versions of the Liar that involve sentences of two or more languages. Claire may say 'What Pierre is saying now is true', while Pierre is saying 'C'est-que Claire dit maintenant est faux'. So, in a more general account, we will admit singularities of an occurrence of 'true' that are sentences of languages other than English. Similarly, in a more general account, a context-independent use of 'true' will include in its extension non-English sentences that involve context-sensitive uses of non-English semantic predicates.

    The introduction of languages other than English would no doubt greatly complicate the formal theory. But it does not appear to threaten the spirit of the singularity account. The intuitive sketch of the two perspectives, just presented in the text, may be broadened to include other natural languages.
13. Tarski 1983, p. 164.

14. See, e.g., Kripke 1975, in Martin 1984, p. 79, and note 34.

15. It is natural to ask whether we can somehow combine context-sensitive uses of 'true' so as to produce a universal truth predicate. The answer is in the negative.

Suppose that c_1 and c_2 are distinct contexts. We know that each of 'true$_{c_1}$' and 'true$_{c_2}$' have singularities (one need only consider appropriate anaphoric versions of the Liar). But given that there is overlap between the extensions of these predicates (see, e.g., the fourth paragraph of 7.2.2), we might wonder if their joint extension comprises all the truths; is 'true$_{c_1}$ or true$_{c_2}$' a universal truth predicate? No, because this predicate too has singularities. Consider the sentence

(L$_2$) This sentence is neither true$_{c_1}$ nor true$_{c_2}$.

The sentence (L$_2$) is a singularity of 'true$_{c_1}$ or true$_{c_2}$'. Clearly, the situation is similar for a disjunction of truth predicates of any length – there are singularities of the predicate 'is true$_{c_1}$ or true$_{c_2}$ or ... or true$_{c_n}$', like

(L$_n$) This sentence is not true$_{c_1}$ nor true$_{c_2}$ nor ... nor true$_{c_n}$.

And as we have seen, even the predicate 'true in some context' has singularities. Compounding truth predicates in this way, even compounding all of them, does not generate a universal truth predicate; all such compounds have singularities.

Bibliography

Adams, Marilyn McCord. "Paul's Treatise," a translation of Paul of Venice's *Logica Magna* II, 15 (Treatise on Insolubles). Unpublished.

Albert of Saxony (1316–90). *Perutilis Logica.* Venice, 1522.

Anonymous. *Dialectica Monacensis,* in de Rijk (1962), vol. 2, part 2, pp. 453–638.

Aristotle, *Metaphysics.* (Works, vol. 8). English translation by W. D. Ross. Oxford 1908.

    Sophistical Refutations, translated by R. D. Hicks. Cambridge, Mass., Harvard University Press 1955.

Ashworth, E. J. *Language and Logic in the Post-Medieval Period.* Dordrecht, Reidel 1974.

Bar-On, Dorit. "Indeterminacy of Translation: Theory and Practice." *Philosophy and Phenomenological Research,* 1993.

Bar-Hillel, Y. "New Light on the Liar," *Analysis* 18 (1957), pp. 1–6.

Barwise, Jon, and Etchemendy, John. *The Liar.* Oxford University Press 1987.

Belnap, Nuel. "Gupta's Rule of Revision Theory of Truth," *Journal of Philosophical Logic* 11 (1982), pp. 103–16.

Benacerraf, Paul, and Putnam, Hilary (eds.). *Philosophy of Mathematics: Selected Readings,* 2d edition. Cambridge University Press 1983.

Bocheński, I. M. *Ancient Formal Logic.* Amsterdam, North Holland 1957.

    A History of Formal Logic. Notre Dame, Ind., University of Notre Dame Press 1961.

Bochvar, D. A. "On a Three-Valued Logical Calculus and Its Application to the Analysis of Contradictions," *Matematiceskij Sbornik* 4 (1939), pp. 287–308.

Boehner, Philotheus. "Ockham's Theory of Supposition and the Notion of Truth," in Buytaert (1958), pp. 232–67.

Boolos, George, and Jeffrey, Richard. *Computability and Logic,* 3d edition. Cambridge University Press 1989.

Bottin, Francesco. *Le Antinomie semantiche nella logica medievale.* Antenore, Padua 1976.

Braakhuis, H. A. G. "The Second Tract on Insolubilia Found in Paris, B.N. Lat. 16.617: An Edition of the Text with an Analysis of its Contents," *Vivarium* 5 (1967), pp. 111–45.

Burge, Tyler. "Semantical Paradox," *Journal of Philosophy* 76 (1979), pp. 169–98; reprinted in Martin (1984), pp. 83–117.

Bibliography

"The Liar Paradox: Tangles and Chains," *Philosophical Studies* 41 (1982), pp. 353–66.

"Epistemic Paradox," *Journal of Philosophy* 81 (1984), pp. 5–29.

Burley, Walter (c. 1275–after 1344), *Insolubilia* (probably before 1320), in Roure (1970), pp. 205–326.

Butler, R. J. (ed.). *Analytical Philosophy*. Oxford 1962.

Buytaert, Eligius M. *Collected Articles on Ockham*. New York, St. Bonaventure 1958.

Cantor, Georg. "Ueber eine Eigenschaft des Inbegriffes aller reellen algebraischen Zahlen," *Journal für die reine und angewandte Mathematik* 77 (1874), pp. 258–62; reprinted in Zermelo (1932), pp. 115–18.

"Ueber eine elementare Frage der Mannigfaltigkeitslehre," first published in *Jahresbericht der Deutschen Mathematiker-Vereinigung* 1, pp. 75–8 (1890–1); reprinted in Zermelo (1932), pp. 278–81.

Church, Alonzo. "A Set of Postulates for the Foundation of Logic," *Annals of Mathematics,* 33 (1932), pp. 346–66, and 34 (1933), pp. 839–64.

"Comparison of Russell's Resolution of the Semantical Antinomies with That of Tarski," *Journal of Symbolic Logic* 41, no. 4 (1976), pp. 747–60.

Cohen, L. Jonathan. "Can the Logic of Indirect Discourse be Formalized?" *Journal of Symbolic Logic* 22 (1957), pp. 225–32.

Curry, Haskell B. "The Paradox of Kleene and Rosser," *Transactions of the American Mathematical Society* 50 (1941), pp. 454–516.

"The Inconsistency of Certain Formal Logics," *Journal of Symbolic Logic* 7 (1942), pp. 115–17.

Dauben, J. W. *Georg Cantor*. Cambridge, Mass., Harvard University Press 1979.

Davidson, Donald. "Truth and Meaning," *Synthese* 17 (1967), pp. 304–23.

"On the Very Idea of a Conceptual Scheme," *Proceedings and Addresses of the American Philosophical Association* 47 (1974), pp. 5–20.

Inquiries into Meaning and Interpretation. Oxford University Press 1985.

de Rijk, L. M. *Logica Modernorum: A Contribution to the History of Early Terminist Logic*. Assen, Van Gorcum: vol. 1, *On the Twelfth Century Theories of Fallacy* (1962); and vol. 2, *The Origins and Early Development of the Theory of Supposition* (1967).

"The Origins of the Theory of the Properties of Terms," (1982), chap. 7 of Kretzmann, Kenny, and Pinborg (1982), pp. 161–73.

Diogenes Laertius, *Lives of Eminent Philosophers,* translated by R. D. Hicks. Cambridge, Mass., Harvard University Press 1950.

Du Bois-Reymond, Paul. "Bemerkungen über die verschiedenen Werthe, welche eine Function zweier reellen Variabeln erhält, wenn man diese Variabeln entweder nach einander oder gewissen Beziehungen gemäss gleichzeitig verschwinden lässt," *Journal für die reine und angewandte Mathematik* 70 (1869), pp. 10–45.

"Eine neue Theorie der Convergenz und Divergenz von Reihen mit positiven Gliedern," *Journal für die reine und angewandte Mathematik* 76 (1873), pp. 61–91.

Bibliography

"Ueber asymptotische Werte, infinitäre Approximationen und infinitäre Auflösung von Gleichungen," *Mathematische Annalen* 8 (1875), pp. 363–414.

"Ueber die Paradoxen des Infinitarcalcüls," *Mathematische Annalen* 11 (1877), pp. 146–67.

Dumbleton, John (d. probably 1349). *Summa Logicae et philosophia naturalis* I, 1 (1335–40). For a list of the known MSS, see Spade (1975), p. 63.

Feferman, Solomon. "Towards Useful Type-Free Theories, I," *Journal of Symbolic Logic* 49 (1984), pp. 75–111; also in Martin (1984), pp. 237–87.

Fine, Kit. "Vagueness, Truth, and Logic," *Synthese* 30 (1974), pp. 265–300.

Fitch, Frederic B. "Self-Reference in Philosophy," *Mind* 55 (1946), pp. 64–73.

"Universal Metalanguages for Philosophy," *Review of Metaphysics* 17 (1964), pp. 396–402.

"Comments and a Suggestion," in Martin (1970), pp. 75–7.

Frege, Gottlob. *The Basic Laws of Arithmetic.* Berkeley and Los Angeles, University of California Press 1967.

Gaifman, Haim. "Operational Pointer Semantics: Solution to Self-referential Puzzles I," in *Proceedings of the Second Conference on Theoretical Aspects of Reasoning about Knowledge,* ed. M. Vardi. Los Altos, Calif., Morgan Kaufman 1988, pp. 43–60.

"Pointers to Truth," *Journal of Philosophy* 89 (1992), pp. 223–61.

Garver, Newton. "The Range of Truth and Falsity," in Martin (1970), pp. 121–6.

Goddard, Leonard, and Johnston, Mark. "The Nature of Reflexive Paradoxes: Part 1," *Notre Dame Journal of Formal Logic* 24 (1983), pp. 491–508.

Gödel, Kurt. "Ueber formal unentscheidbare Sätze der Principia mathematica und verwandter Systeme I," *Monatshefte für Mathematik und Physik* 38 (1931), pp. 173–98. Gödel's paper is translated in van Heijenoort (1967), pp. 596–616.

"Russell's Mathematical Logic," 1944, in Schilpp (1944), pp. 123–53.

Goldstein, Laurence. "The Paradox of the Liar – A Case of Mistaken Identity," *Analysis* 45 (1985), pp. 9–13.

Grattan-Guiness, Ivor. "How Bertrand Russell Discovered His Paradox," *Historia Mathematica* 5 (1978), pp. 127–37.

Gupta, Anil. "Truth and Paradox," *Journal of Philosophical Logic* 11 (1982), pp. 1–60; reprinted in Martin (1984), pp. 175–235.

Haack, Susan. *Philosophy of Logics.* Cambridge University Press 1978.

Hart, W. D. "On Self-Reference," *Philosophical Review* 79 (1970), pp. 523–8.

Herzberger, Hans G. "Paradoxes of Grounding in Semantics," *Journal of Philosophy* 67 (1970), pp. 145–67.

"New Paradoxes for Old," *Proceedings of the Aristotelian Society* 81 (1981), pp. 109–23.

"Notes on Naive Semantics," *Journal of Philosophical Logic* 11 (1982), pp. 61–102; reprinted in Martin (1984), pp. 133–74.

Heytesbury, William. *Regulae solvendi sophismata,* ca 1: *De insolubilibus* (1335) (Venice, Bonetus Locatellus, for Octavianus Scotus, 1494 (Hain 8477)), ff. 4va–7rb.

219

Bibliography

Hintikka, Jaakko. "Identity, Variables and Impredicative Definitions," *Journal of Symbolic Logic* 21 (1956), pp. 225–45.

"The Vicious Circle Principle and the Paradoxes," *Journal of Symbolic Logic* 22 (1957), pp. 245–9.

Hughes, G. E. (trans). *John Buridan on Self-reference* (chap. 8 of Buridan's *Sophismata*). Cambridge University Press 1982.

Kalish, Donald; Montague, Richard; and Mar, Gary. *Techniques of Formal Reasoning,* 2d edition. San Diego, Calif., Harcourt Brace Jovanovich 1980.

Kleene, S. C. *Introduction to Metamathematics.* New York: Van Nostrand 1952.

Kneale, W. C. "Russell's Paradox and Some Others," *British Journal for the Philosophy of Science* 22 (1971), pp. 321–38.

Kretzmann, Norman; Kenny, Anthony; and Pinborg, Jan (eds.). *The Cambridge History of Later Medieval Philosophy.* Cambridge University Press 1982.

Kripke, Saul. "Outline of a Theory of Truth," *Journal of Philosophy* 72 (1975), pp. 690–716; reprinted in Martin (1984), pp. 53–81.

Linsky, Leonard (ed.). *Semantics and the Philosophy of Language.* Urbana, University of Illinois Press 1952.

Lukasiewicz, J. "O logice trojwartosciowej" (On three-valued logic), *Ruch Filozoficzny* 5 (1920), pp. 170–1; translated in McCall (1967), pp. 16–18.

"Philosophische Bemerkungen zu mehrwertigen Systemen des Aussagenkalkuls" (Many-valued systems of propositional logic), *Comptes rendus des séances de la Societé des Sciences et des Lettres de Varsovie* Cl iii, 23 (1930), pp. 51–77; translated in McCall (1967), pp. 40–65.

Martin, Robert L. "Toward a Solution to the Liar Paradox," *Philosophical Review* 76 (1967), pp. 279–311.

"On Grelling's Paradox," *Philosophical Review* 77 (1968), pp. 321–31.

(ed.). *The Paradox of the Liar.* New Haven, Conn., Yale University Press 1970.

"Are Natural Languages Universal?" *Synthese* 32 (1976), pp. 271–91.

"On a Puzzling Classical Validity," *Philosophical Review* 86 (1977), pp. 454–73.

(ed.). *Recent Essays on Truth and the Liar Paradox.* Oxford University Press 1984.

Martin, Robert L., and Woodruff, Peter. "On Representing 'True-in-L' in L," *Philosophia* 5 (1975), pp. 213–17; reprinted in Martin (1984), pp. 47–51.

McCall, S. *Polish Logic.* Oxford University Press 1967.

McGee, Vann. "Applying Kripke's Theory of Truth," *Journal of Philosophy* 86 (1989), pp. 530–9.

Truth, Vagueness, and Paradox. Indianapolis, Hackett 1990.

Mendelson, Elliott. *Introduction to Mathematical Logic.* New York, Van Nostrand 1964.

Moody, Ernest A. *Truth and Consequences in Medieval Logic.* Amsterdam, North Holland 1953.

Moschovakis, Y. N. *Elementary Induction on Abstract Structures.* Amsterdam, North Holland 1974.

Parsons, Charles. "The Liar Paradox," *Journal of Philosophical Logic* 3 (1974), pp. 381–412; reprinted in Martin (1984), pp. 9–45.

Bibliography

Parsons, Terence. "Assertion, Denial, and the Liar Paradox," *Journal of Philosophical Logic* 13 (1984), pp. 137–52.

Paul of Venice. *Logica Magna.* Venice: Albertinus (Rubeus) Vercellensis, for Octavianus Scotus, 1499 (Hain 12505).

Peter of Spain. *Tractatus called afterwards Summulae Logicales,* ed. L. M. De Rijk. Assen, Van Gorcum 1972.

Popper, Karl. "Self-reference and Meaning in Ordinary Language," *Mind* 63 (1954), pp. 162–9.

Priest, Graham. "The Logic of Paradox," *Journal of Philosophical Logic* 8 (1979), pp. 219–41.

"Logic of Paradox Revisited," *Journal of Philosophical Logic* 13 (1984), pp. 153–79.

In Contradiction: A Study of the Transconsistent. The Hague, Nijhoff 1987.

Prior, A. N. "Epimenides the Cretan," *Journal of Symbolic Logic* 23 (1958), pp. 261–6.

"On a Family of Paradoxes," *Notre Dame Journal of Formal Logic* 2, no. 1 (1961), pp. 16–32.

Rescher, Nicholas, and Brandom, Robert. *The Logic of Inconsistency.* Totowa, N.J., Rowman and Littlefield 1979.

Richard, Jules. "Les principes des mathématiques et le problème des ensembles," *Revue générale des sciences pures et appliquées* 16 (1905), p. 541; translated in van Heijenoort (1967), pp. 143–4.

Rogers, Hartley. *Theory of Recursive Functions and Effective Computability.* New York, McGraw-Hill 1967.

Roseth, Roger (fl. 2d quarter, 14th c.), *Quaestiones super sententias* (before 1337). For a list of the known MSS, see Spade (1975), p. 101.

Roure, Marie-Louise. "La problématique des propositions insolubles au xiiie siècle et au début du xive, suivie de l'édition des traités de W. Shyreswood, W. Burleigh et Th. Bradwardine," *Archives d'histoire doctrinale et littéraire du moyen âge* 37 (1970), pp. 205–326.

Rudin, Walter. *Principles of Mathematical Analysis,* 3d edition. New York, McGraw-Hill 1976.

Russell, Bertrand. *The Principles of Mathematics.* Cambridge University Press 1903.

"Les Paradoxes de la Logique," *Revue de Metaphysique et de Morale,* t. 14 (May 1906), pp. 294–317.

My Philosophical Development. New York, Simon and Schuster 1959.

"Mathematical Logic as Based on the Theory of Types," *American Journal of Mathematics* 30 (1908), pp. 222–62; reprinted in van Heijenoort (1967), pp. 150–82.

Logic and Knowledge. New York, Capricorn Books 1971.

Schilpp, P. A. (ed.). *The Philosophy of Bertrand Russell.* La Salle, Open Court 1944.

Sexgrave, Walter (d. by June 1349). *Insolubilia* (before 1333). For a list of the known MSS, see Spade (1975), p. 113.

Bibliography

Simmons, Keith. *The Liar Paradox*. Ph.D. dissertation, University of California, Los Angeles 1987a; University Microfilms International, Ann Arbor, Michigan.

"On a Medieval Solution to the Liar Paradox," *History and Philosophy of Logic* 8 (1987b), pp. 121–40.

"The Diagonal Argument and the Liar," *Journal of Philosophical Logic* 19 (1990), pp. 277–303.

"Outline of a Contextual Theory of Truth," *Proceedings of Logica 1991, an International Conference in Logic,* pp. 43–57.

"On an Argument Against Omniscience," *Noûs,* 1993.

Skyrms, Brian. "Return of the Liar: 3-Valued Logic and the Concept of Truth," *American Philosophical Quarterly* 7 (1970a), pp. 153–61.

"Notes on Quantification and Self-Reference" (1970b), in Martin (1970), pp. 67–74.

Spade, Paul Vincent. "Anonymous 14th Century Treatise on 'Insolubles': Text and Study," M.S.L. dissertation, Pontifical Institute of Medieval Studies, Toronto 1969.

The Medieval Liar: A Catalogue of the Insolubilia-Literature. Pontifical Institute of Medieval Studies, Toronto 1975.

Review of Ashworth, *Dialogue* 15 (1976), pp. 333–40.

"Roger Swyneshed's *Insolubilia:* Edition and Comments," *Archives d'histoire doctrinale et littéraire du moyen âge* 46 (1979), pp. 177–220.

(trans.). *Peter of Ailly: Concepts and Insolubles* (annotated). Dordrecht, Reidel 1980.

"Ockham on Terms of First and Second Imposition and Intention, with Remarks on the Liar Paradox," *Vivarium* 19 (1981), pp. 47–55.

"Insolubilia," in Kretzmann, Kenny, and Pinborg (1982), pp. 246–53.

Swineshead, Roger (d. before May 12, 1365). *De insolubilibus* (c. 1330–5). For a list of the known MSS see Spade (1975), p. 102. See also Spade 1979.

Tarski, Alfred. "O pojeciu prawdy w odniesieniu do sformalizowanych nauk dedukcyjnych" (On the notion of truth in reference to formalized deductive sciences), *Ruch Filozoficzny* 12 (1930-1). A German translation was published under the title "Der Wahrheitsbegriff in den formalisierten Sprachen," *Studia Philosophica* 1 (1936). An English version, under the title "The Concept of Truth in Formalized Languages," appears in Tarski (1983), pp. 152–278.

"The Semantic Conception of Truth," *Philosophy and Phenomenological Research* 4 (1944), pp. 341–76; reprinted in Linsky (1952), pp. 13–47.

"Truth and Proof," *Scientific American* 220 (1969), pp. 63–77.

Logic, Semantics, Metamathematics, 2d edition. Indianapolis, Hackett 1983.

Thomson, J. F. "On Some Paradoxes," in Butler (1962), series 1, pp. 104–19.

van Fraassen, Bas. "Singular Terms, Truth-Value Gaps, and Free Logic," *Journal of Philosophy* 63 (1966), pp. 464–95.

"Presupposition, Implication and Self-Reference," *Journal of Philosophy* 65 (1968), pp. 136–52.

"Truth and Paradoxical Consequences," in Martin (1970), pp. 13–23.

Bibliography

van Heijenoort, Jean (ed.). *From Frege to Gödel.* Cambridge, Mass., Harvard University Press 1967.

Wang, Hao. "The Concept of Set," in Wang (1974), pp. 181–223; reprinted in Putnam and Benacerraf (1983), pp. 530–70.

From Mathematics to Philosophy. New York, Routledge and Kegan Paul 1974.

William of Ockham. *Tractatus super libros elenchorum* (before 1328), MS. Paris, Bib. Nat. 14721.

Summa Logicae, Paris (Johannes Higman) 1488 (Hain 11948).

Opera theologica [OT] II: Scriptum in librum primum Sententiarum, Ordinatio; Distinctiones II–III, ed. S. Brown and G. Gál. St. Bonaventure, The Franciscan Institute 1970.

William of Sherwood. *Introduction to Logic* (Norman Kretzmann, ed.). University of Minnesota Press 1966.

Yablo, Stephen. "Truth, Definite Truth, and Paradox," *Journal of Philosophy* 86 (1989), pp. 539–41.

Zadeh, L. A. "Fuzzy Logic and Approximate Reasoning," *Synthese* 32 (1975), pp. 407–28.

Zermelo, E. (ed.). *Gesammelte Abhandlungen mathematischen und philosophischen Inhalts.* Berlin, J. Springer 1932.

Ziff, Paul. *Understanding Understanding.* Ithaca, N.Y., Cornell University Press 1972.

"Linguistic and Communication Systems," *Philosophia* 18 (1988), pp. 3–18.

Index

Adams, Marilyn McCord, xi, 183 *n*6, 199–200 *n*5
affirmative insoluble, *see* insoluble
Albert of Saxony, 90, 204 *n*44
algorithmic function, 31-2, 189 *n*30
ampliation, 90-1, 204 *ns*39&44, 204-5 *n*45
anaphoric Liar, 108, 109, 124, 133, 177, 178, 181, 193 *n*24; *see also* singularity
anaphoric singularity, *see* singularity
Aristotelian conception of truth, 11
Aristotle, 83, 89, 90
Asher, Nicholas, 192-3 *n*24
Ashworth, E. J., 201 *n*13, 202 *n*25
asymmetrical network, 112, 120; *see also* nonexplicit reflection

Bain, David, xii
Bar-Hillel, Y., 183 *n*6
Bar-On, Dorit, xii, 186 *n*48
Barwise, Jon, x, 96, 101, 106, 179, 183 *n*1, 214 *n*9
basic tree, 113, 115, 119, 125-6; extended definitions of, 161, 167, 176, 178
Belnap, Nuel, 196-7 *n*16
β-level reflection, 134
β-reflective sentence, 135
bivalence, *see* principle of bivalence
Bocheński, I. M., 185-6 *n*22, 199 *n*3, 201 *n*12, 201 *ns*12&14
Bochvar, D. A., *see* three-valued logic
Boehner, Philotheus, 201 *n*13
Boolos, George, 183 *n*1
Bottin, Francesco, 201 *n*13
Bradwardine, Thomas, 183 *n*8, 184 *n*11, 200 *ns*7&10
Brandom, Robert, x, 9, 78–80
Burali–Forti's paradox, 187 *n*1
Burge, Tyler, x, xi, 96–8, 101, 104, 106, 179, 192 *ns*17&19, 207 *ns*68&74, 208 *n*5, 210 *n*25, 213 *ns*3(Ch8)&4(Ch9), 214 *n*8

Buridan, John, 4, 110, 111, 183 *n*3
Burley, Walter, x, 84–98, 184 *n*9, 186 *n*22, 201 *ns*12&19, 202 *n*23, 202-3 *n*27, 203 *ns*29&30, 205 *ns*47&49, 206 *ns*54&58; *see also* Ockham–Burley–Pseudo-Sherwood solution

Cantor, Georg, 187 *ns*1&2
Cantor's diagonal argument, *see* diagonal argument
Cantor's paradox, 35; as a diagonal argument, 35, 188 *n*19
Cantor's power set theorem, 20, 21, 27, 35, 39, 187 *n*1, 187-8 *n*7, 188 *n*9
Cantor's theorem, 16-17, 19, 20-1, 22-5, 26, 27, 29, 32, 187 *n*1
cassantes, see cassation
cassation, 183 *n*8, 200 *n*8
category mistake, 9, 55
chains, 4–6, 8, 100, 109–12, 119, 127, 128-9, 138, 150-1, 151-2, 155, 156, 183 *n*4, 203 *n*29, 211 *n*2; *see also* heads a chain
choice negation, 53; *see also* exclusion negation
Chrysippus, 83
Church, Alonzo, 13, 206 *n*63
Church's thesis, 44
Cohen, L. Jonathan, 213 *n*3(Ch8)
complete explicit reflection, *see* explicit reflection
context-independent uses of 'true', 173-5, 177, 180, 181, 182
contextual approaches to the Liar, 93–4, 96–8, 101–6
Curry's paradox, 3–4, 148-9
cycling paradoxes: semantic, 27, 37; set-theoretic, 27, 34-5

d'Ailly, Pierre, 184 *n*10, 185-6 *n*22, 200 *n*7, 201 *ns*12,14,&15

Index

Dauben, J. W., 187 $n4$
Davidson, Donald, 195 $n30$
Definite Liar, 74–6, 78; as a diagonal argument, 73–4
definite truth, 72–8
de Rijk, L. M., 201 $n16$, 204 $ns39\&44$
diagonal argument, Cantor's use of, 16–7, 20–2, 26, 27, 187 $n1$
diagonal argument, general analysis, 22–6, 37–9; array of, 22, 37–8; cells of an array, 23; countervalue of a diagonal, 24–5, 38; diagonal, 23–4, 38, 188 $n9$; occurrence as a row, 25, 38; side of an array, 22; top of an array, 22; value of a diagonal, 24, 38; values of an array, 22, 37
diagonal arguments, direct and indirect: direct, 26, 29–33, 35, 36, 37; indirect, 26, 29, 33, 35, 37
diagonal arguments, good and bad: good, 20, 27, 29–37, 45, 52–3, 56–8, 61, 62, 66–7, 68, 71, 73–4, 75, 76, 78, 189 $n31$; bad, 20, 27, 28–9, 31–7, 45, 60–1, 188 $n19$, 189 $n31$, 190 $n39$
diagonal theorems: basic, 25; generalized, 38, 43, 190 $n38$
Diogenes Laertius, 83
Du Bois-Reymond, Paul, 187 $n1$
Dumbleton, John, 183 $n6$

Etchemendy, John, x, 96, 101, 106, 179, 183 $n1$, 214 $n9$
Eubulides, 83
evaluated sentence, 102; *see also* evaluation
evaluated tree, 114–15, 115–16, 119
evaluated$_0$ tree, 132; extended definition of, 161
evaluated$_\beta$ tree, 137; extended definitions of, 161, 167, 176, 178
evaluation, 102; *see also* explicit reflection; nonexplicit reflection
exclusion negation, 53–5, 192 $n20$; *see also* choice negation
explicit reflection, 102, 118–20, 123, 127–8, 211 $n2$; complete explicit reflection, 103, 118–21, 128, 208–9 $n6$, 209 $n13$, 211 $n7$; partial explicit reflection, 102–3, 118–21, 128, 208–9 $n6$, 209 $n13$, 211 $n7$; *see also* nonexplicit reflections
expressive incompleteness, 18–19, 36, 45–7, 58–61, 66–7, 73, 78, 98

fallacy *secundum quid et simpliciter,* 83, 85–6, 89–91, 94, 202 $ns21\&23$, 203 $n35$, 204 $ns37\&40$
false$_0$ sentence, 123

false$_1$ sentence, 132
false$_\alpha$ sentence, 139
Feferman, Solomon, x, 70–2, 77, 197 $ns17\&18$
Fine, Kit, 185 $n17$
Fitch, Frederic B., 183 $n8$, 184 $ns9\&10$, 190 $n1$
Frege, Gottlob, 55, 206–7 $n63$
further singularities, *see* singularity
fuzzy logic, 56–8; Zadeh's fuzzy logic, 57–8, 185 $n17$
fuzzy truth values, 57–8, 59

Gaifman, Haim, x, 96, 101, 106, 211 $ns2\&7$
Garver, Newton, 183 $n6$
global sentences, 97, 182, 207 $n74$
global truth predicate, *see* universal truth predicate
Goddard, Leonard, 188 $n10$
Gödel, Kurt, 94–6, 107, 116, 188–9 $n23$, 189 $n26$, 206 $n61$, 206–7 $n63$, 207 $n64$, 210 $n31$
Gödel's first incompleteness theorem, x, 20, 27, 29–31, 32; as a diagonal theorem, 30–1
Goldstein, Laurence, 201 $n15$, 206 $n58$
Grabmann, Martin, 201 $n16$
Grattan-Guinness, Ivor, 187 $n1$
Grelling's paradox, *see* heterological paradox
grounded sentence, 15, 100, 121–3, 129, 136, 139, 159–63, 176, 181, 210 $n28$, 211 $ns5\&6$; grounded β-reflective sentence, 136; grounded reflection-free sentence, 129; grounded sentence of level α, 139, 160; *see also* Kripke's theory of truth; paradoxes of grounding
Gupta, Anil, x, 62–9, 70, 72, 196 $ns7\&12$, 196–7 $n16$
g-witness, 122–3; extended definitions of, 167, 176, 178

Haack, Susan, 195 $n29$
halting problem, 33–4
Hart, W. D., xi, 184 $n10$
heads a chain, 127
Herzberger, Hans G., x, 58–61, 62–9, 70, 72, 188 $n10$, 195 $n31$, 196 $n7$, 196–7 $n16$, 206 $n63$
heterological paradox, 1, 2, 9, 19, 27, 45–6, 52, 95, 96; as a diagonal argument, 17–18, 35–6, 41, 42, 59–61; three-dimensional version, 40–1; n-dimensional version, 42; *see also* superheterological paradox
Heytesbury, William, 183 $n6$, 200 $n7$

226

Index

hierarchy of languages, *see* Tarskian hierarchy of languages
Hintikka, Jaakko, 206 *n*63

inconsistent worlds, 78–80
insoluble: affirmative, 86, 88, 89, 96; negative, 86, 87, 88

Jeffrey, Richard, 183 *n*1
Johnston, Mark, 188 *n*10

Kalish, Donald, 188 *n*11
Kaplan, David, xi
key singularity, *see* singularity
Kleene, S. C., 43, 189 *n*28, *see also* three-valued logic
Kneale, W. C., 183 *n*6
Kretzmann, Norman, 203 *n*36, 204 *n*39
Kripke, Saul, 6
Kripke's theory of truth, x, 47–55, 62, 63, 66, 70, 72, 73, 76, 77–8, 184 *n*12, 185 *n*13, 191 *n*15, 192 *n*20, 192–3 *n*24, 193–5 *n*25, 215 *n*14; grounded sentences, 47–8, 66, 192–3 *n*24, 193–4 *n*25; minimal fixed point, 49–52, 53, 66, 73, 75, 76, 193–4 *n*25, 196–7 *n*16; paradoxical sentences, 48

Liar paradox, 1–7; empirical versions of, 5–6, 7–8, 11–12, 13; *see also* anaphoric Liar; Definite Liar; Revenge Liar; Strengthened Liar; Superliar paradox
Löb's theorem, 183 *n*1
looped sentence, 4–6, 100, 110–12, 127, 151–2, 156, 203 *n*29; Nixon/Dean loop, 142–5; policeman/prisoner loop, 145–8
Łukasiewicz, J., *see* three-valued logic
Lycan, William, xi

Mar, Gary, 188 *n*11
Martin, D. A., xi
Martin, Robert L., 9, 45, 46, 55, 184 *n*s10&12, 188 *n*10, 191 *n*13, 195 *n*s33&34
McGee, Vann, x, 9, 72–8, 197 *n*s29&31, 198 *n*s33&38, 199 *n*41
metalanguage, 12–13, 18, 99; and Feferman, 71–2; and Herzberger and Gupta, 67–9; and Kripke, 52–3, 62, 76, 192 *n*20; and McGee, 75, 76–8; and Ockham-Burley-Pseudo-Sherwood, 92–3; and Priest, 80–2; and Rescher and Brandom, 80; and singularity approach, 117, 140–1, 159, 174–5, 181; *see also* object language; Tarskian hierarchy of languages; theoretical language
Minimality, *see* principle of Minimality

Montague, Richard, 188 *n*11
Moody, Ernest A., 201 *n*12
Moschovakis, Y. N., 191 *n*14

negative insoluble, *see* insoluble
nonexplicit reflection, 112, 115, 120, 127, 129, 135, 209 *n*12, 211 *n*2; *see also* explicit reflections
Normore, Calvin, xi

object language, 12–13; and Feferman, 71; and Herzberger and Gupta, 67–8, 71; and Kripke, 62, 76; and McGee, 76; and Ockham-Burley-Pseudo-Sherwood, 92–3; and Priest, 80–2; and Rescher and Brandom, 80; and singularity approach, 117, 140–1, 159, 160, 164, 168, 173–81; *see also* metalanguage; Tarskian hierarchy of languages; theoretical language
Ockham, *see* William of Ockham
Ockham-Burley-Pseudo-Sherwood solution, 83–98, 100, 203 *n*29&33, 207 *n*74, 207–8 *n*3, 210 *n*23

paraconsistent approach to the Liar, *see* Brandom, Robert; Priest, Graham; Rescher, Nicholas
paradox of propositions, 190 *n*39, 207 *n*1
paradox of stable truth, 66–9; as a diagonal argument, 66–7; *see also* stable truth
paradoxes of grounding, 159–60, 162–3
Parsons, Charles, x, 96–8, 101, 106, 179, 214 *n*8
Parsons, Terence, 54, 55
part-whole distinction: integral part, 89, 203 *n*36; integral whole, 89, 203 *n*36; universal part, 89–90, 204 *n*38; universal whole, 89–90, 204 *n*38
partial explicit reflection, *see* explicit reflection
Paul of Venice, 7, 46, 183 *n*s6&8, 184 *n*s10&12, 199–200 *n*5, 200 *n*s9&10, 201 *n*12, 204 *n*44
Peter of Spain, 204 *n*44
PM, 29–31, 188–9 *n*23, 189 *n*26
power set theorem, *see* Cantor's power set theorem
Priest, Graham, 9, 80–2, 199 *n*s45&53
prime container, 130, 212 *n*8
prime for the propositional calculus, 130, 212 *n*8
primitive recursive derivation, 32
primitive recursive function, 31–2
principle of bivalence, 8, 96, 116, 117

principle of Minimality, 107–9, 112, 114, 118, 120, 125, 140, 141, 145, 157, 175, 178
principle of Symmetry, 110, 112, 118, 119, 120, 129, 131, 136, 153–4, 155, 157
Prior, A. N., 183 n6, 213 n3
productive set, 189 n32
proper classes, 188 n8, 214 n8
propositions, 7–8, 10–11, 83, 94–5, 106, 179, 200 ns8&9; *see also* paradox of propositions
pruned tree, 113–14, 115, 119
pruned$_0$ tree, 126
pruned$_0^R$ tree, 128
pruned$_\beta$ tree, 133
pruned$_\beta^R$ tree, 134
Pseudo-Sherwood, x, 84–98, 184 n10, 200 n8, 201 ns12,16,19,&20, 202 ns21,23,&26, 205 n47, 206 ns52&58; *see also* Ockham–Burley–Pseudo-Sherwood solution

quantification over contexts, 165–74, 176, 182, 213 n4(Ch9)

range of significance, 95, 96
redundant contextual subscript, 166; clause for, 166
reflection-free sentences, 124, 129; *see also* β-level reflection; β-reflective sentence
reflective hierarchy, 124–41; and English, 124–5, 139–41
Rescher, Nicholas, x, 9, 78–80
Resnik, Michael, xi
restringentes, 87, 89, 92, 93, 184 n9, 201 n12, 202 n26, 205 n47, 206 n50; *see also restringentes'* rule; self-reference
restringentes' rule, 84, 86–9, 94, 184 n9, 185–6 n22, 200 n11, 202 n26, 202–3 n27, 203 n30, 205 n46; *see also restringentes;* self-reference
Revenge Liar, 7, 191 n6
Richard's paradox, 27–9, 31, 33; as a diagonal argument, 28
Rogers, Hartley, 31, 189 ns29,30,&37
Roseth, Roger, 184 n9
Roure, Marie-Louise, 89, 92, 201 ns12,13,&16, 203 n35, 204 n37, 205 n47, 205–6 n49
Rudin, Walter, 187 n1
Russell, Bertrand, x, 10, 15–16, 20, 25, 27, 29, 99, 185 n19, 188 n10, 190 n39, 207 n1
Russell's paradox, x, 33, 34, 37, 189 n31, 206 n63; as a diagonal argument, 33
Russell's theory of types, 8, 10–11, 13, 28, 83, 92, 94–5, 107, 186 ns25&26, 201 n13, 205 n47, 206 n61, 207 n1

Russell's vicious circle principle, 10, 18, 28, 83, 185 n19, 185–6 n22, 188 n18

schematic worlds, 78–9
secundum quid et simpliciter, see fallacy *secundum quid et simpliciter*
self-reference, 8, 83, 86–9, 94, 184 ns9&10, 200 n11; *see also restringentes; restringentes'* rule
semantic closure, *see* semantic universality
semantic universality, 12–13, 15–16, 18–19, 46–7, 52–3, 58, 62, 98, 117, 174, 179–82; *see also* universality
sentence (as sentence type in a context), 113, 120
Sexgrave, Walter, 184 n9
Simmons, Keith, 188 n16, 190 n39, 191 n14, 201 n15
singularity, 95–6, 108, 114, 212 n9; actual vs. possible, 108, 158; anaphoric, 157, 177–8, 181, 182, *see also* anaphoric Liar; as notion in the object language, 163, 171, 213 n3; further singularities, 114, 153–8, 168–9, 213 n2; key singularity, 130, 136, 139, 168
singularity approach to the Liar: antihierarchical nature of, 108–9, 116–17, 125, 139–41, 174–80; as a contextual solution, 101–6; informal presentation of, 100–12; pragmatic and semantic components of, 118–21
Skyrms, Brian, 184 n11
Spade, Paul Vincent, 89, 183 n6, 184 ns9&11, 191 n6, 199 n5, 200 ns8&10, 201 ns13&16, 202 ns25&26, 203 n34, 204 n37, 205 n46
stable truth, 15, 64–9; *see also* paradox of stable truth
Strawson's theory of presuppositions, 9, 55
Strengthened Liar, 6–7, 68–9, 72, 96, 97, 101–6, 116, 118, 192–3 n24, 196 n13, 206 n58, 207 n64, 208 n5, 209 n8, 209–10 n13, 211 ns3&7; *see also* strengthened reasoning
strengthened reasoning, 119–20, 208–9 n6, 209 n13; *see also* Strengthened Liar
superheterological paradox, 46–7, 52, 54–5; as a diagonal argument, 54
Superliar paradox, 164, 171–4, 181, 182, 213 n4
supervaluations, 73, 194 n25, 197 n24
supposition, 84, 201 n18
Swineshead, Roger, 190–1 n6, 200 n7
symmetrical network, 110–12; β-level symmetrical network, 135; reflection-

Index

free symmetrical network, 129; *see also* asymmetrical network
Symmetry, *see* principle of Symmetry

Tarski, Alfred, ix, xi, 11–13, 14–15, 47, 99, 186 *ns*27&37, 187 *n*52, 201 *n*13, 206 *n*53, 214 *n*11
Tarskian hierarchy of languages, x, 8, 12–13, 18, 28, 36, 83, 92, 107; and Herzberger and Gupta, 67–9; and Kripke, 52–3, 191 *n*15, 192–3 *n*24, 195 *n*25; and Ockham–Burley–Pseudo-Sherwood, 97, 201 *n*13, 205 *ns*47&49, 206 *ns*52&53; and Parsons and Burge, 97; and Priest, 80–2; and Rescher and Brandom, 80; and singularity approach, 99–100, 106, 108–9, 116–17, 174–80; *see also* metalanguage; object language; theoretical language
Tarski's schema T, 11–12, 13, 192 *n*20
Tarski's undefinability theorem, ix, x, 18, 19, 20, 27, 36, 52, 66, 179, 189 *n*36; as a diagonal theorem, 18, 36–7
theoretical language, 140–1, 159, 173–181; *see also* metalanguage; object language; Tarskian hierarchy of languages
theory of types, *see* Russell's theory of types
Thomson, J. F., 188 *n*10, 206 *n*63
three-valued logic: Bochvar, 184 *n*11; Kleene, 48, 73, 123, 184 *n*11, 193 *n*25, 210 *n*28; Łukasiewicz, 56, 184 *n*11
tokens and types, 96, 100–1, 113, 120, 164–7, 169, 177
transcasus, 200 *n*7
true$_0$ sentence, 123
true$_1$ sentence, 132
true$_\alpha$ sentence, 138
true$_{obj}$ sentence, 174
true$_{obj+}$ sentence, 177
truth in a context, 15, 163–74
Truth Teller, 3, 67, 103, 120, 132, 191 *n*12, 208–9 *n*6

truth-value gaps, 7, 8–9, 15, 36, 45–7, 58, 59, 83, 97, 184 *n*12, 190 *n*4; and category mistakes, 9, 55; and Kripke 47–8, 52–5, 61, 62; and presuppositions, 9, 55; and vagueness, 9, 56, 72–8
truth-value gluts, 9, 78–82, 83
types, *see* tokens and types

ungrounded ancestor, 155, 156, 169, 214 *n*6
universal truth predicate, 97, 179, 181, 207 *n*74, 210 *n*23, 215 *n*15
universality, 13–15, 19, 46–7, 53, 56, 71, 76, 98, 117, 140, 179–82; *see also* semantic universality
unsettled sentences, 72–5, 78
utterance, *see* sentence

vagueness, *see* truth-value gaps
van Fraassen, Bas, 9, 55, 184 *n*12; *see also* supervaluations
vicious circle principle, *see* Russell's vicious circle principle

Wang, Hao, 187 *n*1
Whitehead, Alfred North, 29
William of Ockham, x, 84–98, 184 *n*9, 186 *n*22, 201 *ns*13&19, 202 *ns*22&23, 202–3 *n*27, 204 *n*44, 204–5 *n*45, 205 *ns*46&47, 205–6 *n*49, 206 *n*58; *see also* Ockham–Burley–Pseudo-Sherwood solution
William of Sherwood, 201 *n*16
Woodruff, Peter, 184 *n*12, 191 *n*13

Yablo, Stephen, 75, 197–8 *n*32, 198 *n*33, 208 *n*6

Zadeh, L. A., *see* fuzzy logic
ZF set theory, 15, 29, 189 *n*31
Ziff, Paul, 186 *n*49, 209 *n*7